The Daily Grind

The Daily Grind

How Workers Navigate the Employment Relationship

Marquita R. Walker

LEXINGTON BOOKS
Lanham • Boulder • New York • London

Published by Lexington Books
An imprint of The Rowman & Littlefield Publishing Group, Inc.
4501 Forbes Boulevard, Suite 200, Lanham, Maryland 20706
www.rowman.com

Unit A, Whitacre Mews, 26-34 Stannary Street, London SE11 4AB, United Kingdom

British Library Cataloguing in Publication Information Available

Library of Congress Cataloging-in-Publication Data Available

ISBN 978-0-7391-9333-4 (cloth: alk. paper)
ISBN 978-0-7391-9334-1 (electronic)

♾ ™ The paper used in this publication meets the minimum requirements of American National Standard for Information Sciences Permanence of Paper for Printed Library Materials, ANSI/NISO Z39.48-1992.

Printed in the United States of America

Contents

Acknowledgments

This book is the result of many years of thinking about, engaging in, and writing about work. I began my working career right out of high school by applying for a position with a large paper cup manufacturing facility in Springfield, Missouri. Three days after filling out the application for the position, the firm hired me, and I went to work packing into boxes paper cups which were glued together on one side of the plant and then forced by air through overhead tubes at the rate of hundreds per minute to the waiting boxes. I worked one of four women's shifts which were six hours long. The plant manager didn't believe women should work eight-hour shifts because they had "other" work to do at home. So, I worked from 1 am to 7 am, went home to care for my one-year old son, and napped periodically throughout the day as he napped in order to get enough sleep to go back to work the next night. My career with this firm lasted twenty-nine years and four months. Two years into my career, the firm was unionized by the International Brotherhood of Electrical Workers (IBEW), and I began my journey into the realm of organized labor.

Over the course of my manufacturing career and my eventual segue into academia, I have been fascinated by the tensions existing between management and workers and the policies which inform and often dictate the roles workers must play in the labor management relationship. I have watched workers adjust and accommodate to management's and administrators' demands in order to maintain jobs and provide for their families and have seen firsthand how poorly the majority of workers are treated in the firm's quest to make profits. This profound and lasting impression of a worker's disadvantaged place within the employment relationship should be a concern for all interested in issues of social justice and workers' rights.

I owe debts of gratitude to many people for making this book a reality: my colleagues in the Department of Labor Studies, Drs. Michael Patchner, Irene Queiro-Tajalli, Joe Varga, Lynn Duggan, Paul Mishler, Gerrie Casey, Thandabantu Iverson, Bill Mello, Rae Sovereign, and Mark Crouch; my union associations in the IBEW, UAW, USW, UNITE-HERE, and AFSC-ME; and my most precious family—my children, Craig Jones, Dana Walker, Matthew Walker, and Jeremy Walker, and my grandchildren, Jason Walker, Abigale Ross, and Adam Walker.

The biggest debt of gratitude though goes to those who are no longer with us—my husband, Gary Brown, who passed away while I was finishing this manuscript and my parents—Clyde and Cloie McNabb, who managed through the Great Depression to raise six children on the family farm in southwest Missouri, instill in each of us the virtue of hard work and the idea that one never gives up, and who still serve as my role models. It is to them I dedicate this book.

Introduction

Workers are continually buffeted about by forces within the workplace: demanding supervisors, 24/7 work schedules, continued harassment to produce more with less, and constant human or electronic surveillance. Is it any wonder that at the end of a work day, workers then feel tired, disgruntled, unappreciated, and devalued? The current state of employment relationships in the United States places workers at an extreme disadvantage by stripping away workers' powers and rights and disadvantaging workers' ability to respond and resist in the wake of increased efforts to produce. The control and resistance dichotomy of labor and management is a central theme of this book because it highlights the tensions workers experience in the daily tug-of-war with management. In the following chapters, the text explores the historical evolution of labor's power as it is buffeted about by the money, influence, and polity of the owners of production, the constant reaffirmation of capitalist economic power by the courts and government, and the toll the dismantling of workers' rights has on the worker, the collective, and the broader community. This then is a story of employee power versus employer power, worker rights versus property rights, and the collective versus privatization.

The employment system in the United States has its roots in a European system which involved forms of contractual or indentured servitude in which a worker agreed to work for a specific period of time in exchange for passage to the United States, or slavery, a form of involuntary servitude eventually outlawed by the Thirteenth amendment (Hogler, 2004, p. 251). From these beginnings, the employment relationship from the 1700s to the 1930s is altered by external forces such as the rise of industrialization, wars, and the Great Depression, and by internal forces such as worker collectivities organizing in response to managerial control, experiments in participatory de-

1

mocracy, and the emergence of New Deal legislation protecting workers' rights. This era saw managerial power grow and with that growth the emerging law of the labor market featuring employment at will, a relationship between the employer and the employee reflecting the ability of the employer to hire and fire at will and the ability of the employee to quit at will. Using the tools at their command such as court decisions, legislation, and public opinion, employers successfully took control of labor processes previously under the purview of craft workers and made employment at will a bedrock institutional practice still in effect today.

In a capitalist economy which depends on competition and consumerism to drive the market, industrial strife, the antagonism and distrust between employers and employees, curtails production through employee work stoppages and employer lockouts. Families, communities, and the larger economy are affected when goods and services are not produced and available for purchase. Strikes and lockouts cause employees to lose wages which they may never recover, weaken firms' finances, and "reduce stockholders' dividends" (Shreve, 1948, p. 431). Government, capital, and labor strive to secure industrial peace, a necessity in a capitalist economy, in order to promote a strong economy through reduced unemployment, a sound social order, and stable government policies which attract domestic and foreign investment. The Commerce Clause of the U.S. Constitution is interpreted as a mandate for industrial peace through the prohibition of interference with interstate commerce. The Constitutional framers believed Congress had the power to make rules governing the manner in which the exchange or trade of goods occurred and the ability to regulate that exchange and trade. "In sum, according to the original meaning of the Commerce Clause, Congress has power to specify rules to govern the manner by which people may exchange or trade goods from one state to another, to remove obstructions to domestic trade erected by states, and to both regulate and restrict the flow of goods to and from other nations (and the Indian tribes) for the purpose of promoting the domestic economy and foreign trade" (Barnett, 2001). The economic success of a capitalist system depends on the free movement of goods and services between state boundaries; because that free movement of goods cannot occur unless goods and services are produced, there results a tension between the owners of production and the workers who produce the products. Based on an efficiency framework which extolls the virtue of the wisest use of resources, owners of production seek to contain costs in the production of goods and services in order to maintain a profit. Without profit retention, the firm exits the market. No one seriously defends a position that a firm should not make a profit. Everyone benefits when firms are profitable, workers make money, and government coffers, filled via taxation, provide public services to citizens. The consternation within the labor-management tension arises when firms extract from workers excess effort for which they are not compensated. Workers, pushed to produce more goods for less compensation, have few options in the labor-management dyad. They can continue working for low wages or exit the firm.

Capitalists defend low compensation to workers by relying on an employment contract; in an employment contract, a worker enters into an agreement with an employer for a stipulated wage. The logic is that if the worker did not wish to work for that wage, the worker would not have entered into the contract. That logic is problematic because it assumes workers actually have a choice in determining for whom they will work. For millions of workers, choice is simply an illusion for many reasons: location of the firm and distance they must travel to work, educational, skill, and/or ability requirements of the job, time restraints involved with family, faith, or civic duties, and so on. Consequently, many workers have no choice but to fill available positions in which they are exploited, devalued, and abused. The lack of legal redress and workplace protections spurred workers to counter managerial power by forming their own collectives in the form of labor unions and worker organizations. Organizing around class-based interests, the Noble and Holy Order of the Knights of Labor gained popularity during the early 1880s by allowing skilled and unskilled workers, women, and blacks into their secret society and demanding an end to child and convict labor, equal pay for women, a progressive income tax, and cooperative employer-employee ownership of the mines and factories. A lack of leadership, unsuccessful strike activity, disorganization, dissention between skilled and unskilled workers, and public negativity against labor unions led to the Knights' demise by the end of the decade. Some of the Knights' members gravitated toward the newly formed American Federation of Labor (AFL) organized in 1896 to represent craft unions. Later broadened to include unskilled workers represented by the Congress of Industrial Organization (CIO), the principles of the AFL are still considered foundational in representing workers. The Industrial Workers of the World (IWW), better known as the Wobblies, promoted industrial unionism for all workers and distanced themselves from the AFL which they thought divided the working classes. Led by Big Bill Haywood and Eugene Debs, this radical labor organization proposed the abolition of the wage system and capitalism, encouraged workers to organize as a class and take possession of the means of production, and promoted strike activity as the mechanism for change. Their influence waned as public opinion turned against them with the onset of World War I.

Conflicts between labor and management continued to escalate with continued strike activity in retaliation for any encroachment by employer authority. The Haymarket Riot in 1881, the Homestead Strike in 1892, the Pullman Strike in 1894, and the Ludlow Massacre in 1914 serve as examples of crushing defeats for labor and workingmen trying to resist employer exploitation. The extremely important concept of industrial peace became very apparent during WWI when the federal government needed to ramp up war-time production in order to produce enough munitions, uniforms, and food rations for the military. The cooperation between labor and firms during this period was birthed out of the necessity to protect the strategic position of the U.S. military as a world power; negotiations between the government, labor, and management resulted in cooperation, increased unionization, and the first major piece of U.S. labor law legislation to recognize collective bargaining, the 1926 Railway Labor Act. This act, the result of the federal government collectively bargaining with railroad unions on a national basis, jump-started the labor movement's increase in membership to around five million and served as an example that negotiations and collective bargaining agreements could successfully ensure industrial peace (Shreve, 1948).

After WWI, the beginning of an era of economic depression emerged, unemployment increased, and union membership declined. Employers thwarted unionization through hiring practices involving "yellow dog" contracts, a signed statement by a potential employee that he would not join the union, and the American Plan, a strategy which encouraged union-free open shops as well as company unions. The American Plan materialized through the efforts of the National Association of Manufacturers (NAM), a group of manufacturers formed in Ohio in 1895 to promote export trade and launch a public relations campaign about the necessity of privatization and the free market. NAM is the forerunner of the Chamber of Commerce.

By 1930, managerial power reached a peak by engaging in extreme anti-unionism and moved toward the creation of welfare capitalism in efforts to encourage industrial peace through workforce stability and the eradication of unions. Through welfare capitalism employers offered to employees a buffet of benefits or non-cash payments such as use of company libraries, social clubs, and company-owned housing. Noted examples of welfare capitalism are Henry Ford's five-dollar-a-day program which offered to workers a salary of $2.50 per day plus another $2.50 per day for clean living, sobriety, and church attendance as noted by inspectors from Ford's Sociology Department. Much like the auxiliary benefits offered to employees of the Pullman Palace Car Company, George Pullman built Pullman's Village which housed a theater and recreational facilities and was noted for its lack of saloons. Pullman inspectors issued fines to workers appearing in public in disheveled clothing or for disorderly housekeeping. These capitalist entrepreneurs were the epitome of a patriarchal and Protestant interpretation of a social order which valued property rights and male dominance. They were attempting to develop model communities which encouraged employee loyalty, controlled alcohol consumption, and reduced labor turnover in the interest of maintaining industrial peace which contributed to company profits. These employer efforts to stabilize their workforces through controlling the social environment of their workers backfired and ended in bitter strikes.

The attempts by owners of production to consolidate their power and ensure industrial peace which led to welfare capitalism are the forerunners of modern human resource management and many of the techniques for dealing with employees are notable in current employment relationships. For instance, the ability to take control of work processes away from workers and place that control under management's purview has long been an employer's goal. Under the old system of skilled crafts, workers retained the knowledge and skill to design and create products. Though management "rented" the skilled craftsman's labor, the production of the product lay with the skilled craftsman. With the introduction of technology into the production process, the standardization of interchangeable parts, the assembly line which controlled workers' speeds, and the contributions of Taylor's principles of scientific management through time and motion studies, the osmosis of craftsmen's knowledge and skills to management became complete. Management now has complete control of the work process, leaving workers will little recourse and fewer options.

Growing discontent between employers and workers was exacerbated under the Hoover administration as the Stock Market Crash of 1929 signaled the beginning of a ten-year economic depression which had far-reaching results worldwide. Unemployment soared, suicide rates increased, and poverty was at an all-time high during this period. Under the new administration of Roosevelt, New Deal legislation was proposed to shore up the devastated economy. Government intervention in the free market was a new concept for a nation touting capitalism as the most beneficial economic system. The passage of the National Industrial Recovery Act of 1933 infused money back into the economy and provided jobs through programs designed to put Americans back to work. This legislation led to the National Labor Relations Act (NLRA) of 1935 which defined terms such as employee and employer and gave to workers the right to collectively bargain, to choose a representative bargaining agent of their choice, to form collectives, and to refrain from any of those activities. The effects of the NLRA were immediate and sustained, and the NLRA remains the cornerstone for collective bargaining today. As a result of New Deal legislation, social safety nets in the form of Social Security, fair labor standards, and unemployment insurance were also passed and remain in effect.

Labor law legislation in the form of the NLRA and public opinion favoring unions led to a twelve-year period of heightened union membership known as the Golden Age of Unionism in which one in every four workers was unionized. As the population exploded and exports increased, the need for more manufactured goods required greater numbers of less-skilled workers to man factories, mills, and mines. Since the semi-skilled and unskilled workers were not welcome in the craft unions belonging to the AFL, a new and different type of union was required to organize the unskilled into the union family. The Congress of Industrial Unionism (CIO), formed and headed by John Lewis, leader of the United Mine Workers of America, welcomed unskilled labor into its fold. Lewis built the CIO into an economic and political powerhouse which rivaled and eventually merged with the AFL. Industrial union membership soared in the first few years to three million (Hogler, 2004), and labor agreements with industries in steel and automobiles were reached, breaking historic gridlocks between labor and management.

As the United States entered World War II in December, 1941, new problems between labor and management appeared which precipitated more strikes than at any other time in U.S. history. Business responded with initiatives to restrict labor's power. Roosevelt called employers and employees together in an attempt to settle their differences to no avail, so Roosevelt, through executive order, established the National War Labor Board as an agency to settle labor disputes through compulsory arbitration. After WWII ended in 1945, unions sought to establish wartime labor wages as permanent wages, and employers resisted, citing market uncertainty. The result was the passage of the Labor-Management Relations Act also known as the Taft-Hartley Act of 1947 which gave rights and protections to employers as well as employees through the employers' right to file unfair labor practices against unions and the states' legislative right to open shops.

The quest for industrial peace by employers was somewhat mediated by the passage of the NLRA and the Taft-Hartley Act because the legislations provided a mechanism for management and labor to work out their differences through a grievance and arbitration system rather than a strike or lockout system. Reducing the labor-management conflict to paper rather than to picket lines, strikes, and boycotts, moved the settlement of problems into the business realm in a more sophisticated and nuanced approach. As a result of the passage of the NLRA, labor and management for the next thirty years operated in a more controlled environment which limited militancy and encouraged discussion. Though tensions between labor and management were no less antagonistic or adversarial, the expression of those tensions was less overt and combative; during this period workers' real earning power increased, and they received benefits in the form of vacation and holiday pay, retirement, and health insurance.

Beginning in the early 1970s a marked economic change occurred which affected workers' ability to gain any economic power in the employment relationship. Declining wages accompanied an increase in worker productivity, so workers actually saw their real earning power significantly decline over the next thirty years. Workers were working harder for less money. The catalyst for this phenomenon was attributed to neoliberal policies adopted by the United States in efforts to open trade with nations with whom trade had previously been restricted because of tariffs or regulatory rules. Neoliberal polices reflect the push toward globalization, a concept suggesting the removal of all barriers to trade and the opening of world markets through tariff reduction as a benefit to all people. Proponents of the neoliberal policies of privatization, deregulation, and deunionization believe a free market economy unfettered by government regulation will encourage economic growth through which private investors can thrive, invest their earnings back into the economy, create jobs, and solve the problems of unemployment and poverty. Opponents of neoliberal policies cite the devaluation and dehumanization of all workers in a competitive world market which has long-term consequences for the economic stability of the United States.

The quest for industrial peace had significant implications for the employment relationship between labor and management. Because the U.S. employment relationship is governed by man-made rules, "norms, conventions, networks, social groups, and formal organizations" which comprise an "institutional order" within which economic activity does or does not take place (Kaufman, 2012, p. 440), there is an assumption that labor and management could somehow mediate their differences within existing institutional structures and peacefully coexist. The idea that an institutional economy could confront the "labor problem," a term used to denote "various behaviors and outcomes growing out of the employer-employee relationship that adversely affected economic efficiency and human well-being" such as "poverty-level wages, low work effort, workplace accidents, excessive work hours, strikes and other forms of conflict, high employee turnover, and child labor" (Kaufman, 2003, p. 4) took root in the Wisconsin School and was fomented by Commons who wanted to improve labor's condition by "saving capitalism and making it good" (Commons, 1934, p. 143). Commons wished to introduce a "more progressive and humanized system of industrial relations" (Kaufman, 2003, p. 4) by stabilizing the labor markets, equalizing the economic bargaining power between employees and employers, and codifying industrial democracy through written agreements between owners of production and workers. Common's justification for these reforms was that an efficient economic system coupled with humanistic goals would in the long run result in economic efficiency, equity and justice in the workplace, and "personal growth and self-actualization" (Kaufman, 2003, p. 5). Working within the confines of an institutional system which promoted a laissez-faire market approach, an employer-autocratic model, and a commodity concept of labor, Commons (1934) sought to identify the causes of and develop solutions to the labor problem.

According to Kaufman (2003, 2012), Commons's efforts to reform and improve industrial relations developed in four stages. During phase one, Commons promoted collective bargaining, trade unionism, and trade agreements as tools to stabilize the employment relationship between employers and workers. Citing examples in coal (Commons, 1905) and shoemaking

(Commons, 1909), Commons suggested industry-wide bargains in which wages were taken out of competition by placing a floor under wages which ensured "reasonable labor conditions" (Kaufman, 2003, p. 6), encouraged voluntarism in collective bargaining by giving labor the same governmental and court-ordered rights as those given to employers, believed trade agreements stabilized wages and prices and thus contributed to the redistribution of profits to wages, ensuring purchasing power and a more stable economy, which he "called the 'profit-share' theory of business cycles" (Kaufman, 2003, p. 7), advocated for industrial unionism which covered more workers than did craft unionism, and argued the benefits of unions outweighed their defects by promoting the public interest and offsetting employers' power (Commons, 1913). Commons later changed his mind about industrial unionism and determined that craft unionism was a better fit for the current American conditions (Kaufman, 2003).

In phase two, Commons turned his attention to protective labor and employment law in an attempt to "expand governmental regulation of employment standards, improve the operation of labor markets, and protect workers' security through social insurance programs" (Kaufman, 2003, p. 8). Commons argued the freedom of contract, better known currently as the employment at will contract, favored employers and should take into consideration that economic forces which deprive workers of decent wages promote oppression. By codifying freedom of contract, the government then promoted worker oppression. Modifying labor law to extend protections already enjoyed by employers to workers would promote the public welfare by treating workers as humans and not commodities. Commons believed that by shifting the onus of worker protections to federal and state laws in the form of workers' compensation, health and disability insurance, and safety provisions, more workers would be covered than the few workers protected under industry trade agreements. Some employers pushed back and countered by offering retirement, unemployment, and accident insurance programs to workers, but their efforts were limited to small numbers of employees.

By 1920 Commons moved from championing unions as saviors of industrial relations to championing employers who pursued a goodwill or citizenship model of industrial relations. Phase 3 of Commons's "good will" strategy to improve industrial relations resulted from interactions with employers who adopted components of welfare capitalism and were gaining a competitive advantage in the market by "establishing a harmony of interest through mutual gain and fair dealing" (Kaufman, 2003, p. 16). Long a proponent of humanizing workers, Commons accepted the premise that there were some employers who depended on "good faith and good will" (Commons, 1919, p. 113) in dealing with workers because it increased efficiency, replaced adversarial relations with cooperative relations, elicited employee commitment and participation, ensured labor and management a voice in the workplace, and followed some form of administrative justice (Kaufman, 2003). Commons' shift in thinking was triggered by visits to industrial firms and talks with employers who managed programs of welfare capitalism through personnel departments, designed work systems which took "into account the human factor" (Kaufman, 2003, p. 13), introduced employee benefits, and instituted some form of non-union employee representation (Jacoby, 1985, 1997; Kaufman, 2001, 2003). Though Commons admitted the majority of employers did not embrace the goodwill model, he believed all employers could benefit from adopting the model (Commons, 1921). Kaufman (2003) posits this as the forerunner of the current "high performance or high commitment work system" (p. 14) administered through a firm's human resources or personnel department.

The second element of phase 3 was Commons's insistence on the Federal Reserve System as the overseer and stabilizer of credit. Commons believed the issue of monetary stabilization was necessary to secure industrialized peace and steady the economy. During this phase, Commons replaced the idea that corporations and labor unions could successfully tackle the unemployment problem, which he considered premier in an unstable market, through unemployment insurance. Unemployment insurance, a new idea in the early 1920s, would make it economically profitable for employers to keep workers instead of laying them off because the employer would pay part of the unemployment payment to workers. Employers then began adopting internal policies of using workers for maintenance during seasonal production swings, work-sharing programs, and "company-financed dismissal pay" (Kaufman, 2003, p. 15). He believed the Federal Reserve System to be the macro-foundational piece in equalizing the short and long cycles of economic expansion and depression and would contribute to a stable workforce.

By now Commons (1921) encouraged a two-pronged approach to industrial stabilization. Realizing that about 15 percent of industry would adopt a high-road or goodwill strategy which would preclude union involvement, he advocated a low-road strategy for 85 percent of industry who "fail to provide reasonable wages and working conditions" (Kaufman, 2003, p. 17). To this sector, Commons prescribed a need for trade unionism because employers used company unions as "avoidance devices" (Commons, 1919, p. 121) to pay lip service to equalizing employment relations.

After the Stock Market Crash of 1929 and the subsequent Great Depression, the "goodwill" approach to industrial peace was once again abandoned in favor of government intervention to shore up a devastated economy. Commons's idea of employer volunteerism and welfare capitalism to equalize the employment relationship as espoused in phase three was replaced with wide-scale industrial relations reform under Roosevelt's New Deal policies. This discernible change in industrial policy marked phase 4 in Commons's evolution of industrial strategy and solidified his place in history as the father of industrial relations. The extent of poverty and degradation experienced by workers during this period shifted the tide of public opinion against employers who valued shareholder dividends over workers' pay, proclaimed a love for American democracy while preventing workers from unionizing, and advocated dismantling anti-trust laws while resisting minimum wage laws and trade unionism (Kaufman, 2003; Slichter, 1931). The hypocrisy exhibited by employers led the way for a shift in national labor policy beginning with the passage of legislation to outlaw court injunctions and yellow-dog contracts ("Issuance of restraining orders and injunctions; limitation; public policy," 1932), the passage of prevailing wage legislation in the construction industry (Congress, 1931), and unemployment compensation. Roosevelt's signature legislations were the National Labor Relations Act (1935), the National Industrial Recovery Act (NIRA), the Social Security Act (SSA), and the Fair Labor Standards Act (FLSA). Commons's notions that the potential for a competitive consumer-based economic system unregulated by government interventions could encourage employers to undercut wages and prices in order to remain competitive was widely assumed to be one of the root causes of the Great Depression. Commons termed this notion *destructive competition* because employers competed to see who could offer the lowest prices for goods and services which necessitated lowering workers' wages to reduce input costs. This created a glut of product in the market accompanied by weakened consumer purchasing power as well as excess worker supply. Another root cause of the Great Depression shared by Roosevelt and Commons's Wisconsin School was the trend toward income inequality as a result of shifting workers' wages to increase firms' profits. It appears that Commons, who had earlier abandoned the idea that firms' greater profits created an oversupply in the market, did not buy into this second root cause.

The legislation passed under the New Deal redistributed wealth from capital to labor through the mechanism of trade unionism. The effect of wealth redistribution was to provide a balanced industrial relations strategy which would provide economic bargaining power to employers and workers in order to contribute to and sustain the free flow of goods and services in commerce. Important to maintaining the free flow of goods and services is a functional industrial relations strategy which requires employers and collectives to subscribe to working rules established by a sovereign power, the government. These working rules include labor laws which protect workers' rights, social programs which provide a safety net for workers experiencing downturns in the labor market, adequate protection for property rights of employers, and the establishment of fiscal and monetary policies in order to maintain economic stability and full employment (Kaufman, 2003). These laws and protections have a stabilizing effect on the economy by sustaining consumer purchasing power.

The Wisconsin School and Commons provide a backdrop for the current U.S. employment relationship. This book explores the historical and current tensions between labor and management in the quest to control the employment relationship in a representative form of democracy in which the people determine how their society should be structured, what institutions, laws, and policies should govern individual and collective actions, and how those laws and policies should be enforced. The onus of control between labor and management over the course of U.S. history reflects shifting power dynamics resulting from changing market forces, demographics, institutions, public opinion, and legislation. This narrative is situated in a control and resistance framework known as Labor Process Theory which explores the ultimate deskilling of workers in order to extract more effort from the worker, resulting in increased profits for owners of production. It is a story of the ebb and flow of worker power, management power, and the continued battle over the economic power relationship. The first four chapters discuss the employment relationship's position within the field of Labor Studies, the historical evolution of the employment process, the theoretical models through which we look at labor and management, and the current state of the U.S. employment relationship; the last five chapters explore the employment relationship as it relates to job security, wage compensation, globalization, race and ethnicity, and gender.

Chapter 1 introduces readers to the field of Labor Studies as a multidisciplinary educational field dealing with work, workers, society, and social justice and traces the field's evolution from educating the working class during the early 1900s in order to change the U.S. social structure from one of capitalism to socialism, to its involvement in 1935 with labor education which emphasized the practical needs of the trade union movement, to its current form which expanded educational opportunities necessitated by the changing nature of the globalized economy, multinational corporations, the changing nature of the employment relationship, and the workers' place in an economic, social, and cultural structure dictated by market forces, capital mobility, and a bent toward property rights. The chapter explains how the influences of America's beginning set the stage for the rivalry between workers and the owners of production through a religious and political system which elevated hard work and Godliness to precursors of success and explores the concept of social class as it pertains to workers, and workers' and organized labor's place in the social structure.

Chapter 2 looks at employment relations in historical perspective and traces the evolution of American labor from 1870 to the present by outlining the five major pieces of labor law legislation, articulating how public sentiment and public opinion affected the legislation, and defines how industrial unionism came to be the premier form of unionism in the twentieth century. Labor unions are almost conspicuous by their absence in most American history textbooks. Except for scant synopses of major strikes, usually portrayed in a negative way, or tirades about a few organized labor leaders who absconded with union funds, our history books remain silent about the benefits publicly organized labor facilitated throughout the last couple of centuries. The employment relationship is dictated by power relationships between labor and management, between property rights and worker rights, and between control-resistance dichotomies. From 1870–1930, the employment relationship shifted in favor of management through statutory law, court decisions, and public opinion.

Chapter 3 explores the historical evolution of American labor from 1935 to the present. For a brief period from 1935–1947, the power shifted to workers protected by new legislation in the form of the National Labor Relations Act of 1935, but once again shifted in 1947 to management with the passage of the Taft-Hartley Act. Public opinion and legislation necessary to facilitate this shifting power depend on a political process which allows citizens to put into legislative offices those who will favor labor or management and an economic system which allows those citizens to support candidates and issues of their choice. The tension between powerful corporations and labor exacerbates as government policies favoring privatization and deunionization gain strength. The text situates labor's transition within the impending crisis and emphasizes labor's response to the evisceration of workers' rights. Exploring the changing dynamics of public opinion and legislation necessary to swing the pendulum of power between labor and management during the industrial and post-industrial periods from 1870 to the present provides the reader insight into how powerful moneyed interests can control and manipulate legislation and shape public opinion.

Chapter 4 addresses the theoretical models associated with the labor movement and traces the irregular evolution of American labor resulting in the unequal terrain upon which labor and management currently function. Viewing the labor-management relationship through a different theoretical lens helps us conceptualize the shifting economic and political power struggles, understand how varied class relationships are determined, how they relate to the means of production, how they shape the environment, and how they drive historical change. Theoretical models also provide a way to envision the institutional and cultural structures which are continually reproduced from generation to generation which maintain and strengthen the unequal power relationship between labor and management. This chapter defines four theoretical lenses through which the collective is viewed and then explores social movement unionism as the convergence of collective action which engages a critical mass of individuals with shared backgrounds and experiences who fervently and intimately are involved in an issue and express despair through some conduit such as militancy, protests, or civil disobedience. Social movements as collective actions result from collective forces joining to change some objectionable wrong, fight oppression, or challenge the status quo. The shelf life of social movements lasts only as long as the stamina from the collective exists or the anticipated change occurs. This section explores how social movements take root and survive and the value of social movements to the renewal of the labor movement as a viable collective representing workers.

Chapter 5 looks at the current state of U.S. employment relationships as analyzed through the lens of institutional economic theory and how the employment relationship changes when the collective is introduced. This chapter covers the concepts of economic inequality, social mobility, the new economy, poverty in the United States, equity or fairness, minimum wage, and the Earned Income Tax Credit.

Chapter 6 shifts the focus of the text from the historical and present state of the employment relationship to ways in which the employment relationship influences workers' lives. In this chapter, readers learn how the nature of the unemployment relationship is determined by the social relationships people have to the means of production. Throughout history ways of producing goods and services from raw materials into salable products have been governed by the relationship people have with the production processes. Power in the employment relationship then involves ways individuals are regulated and controlled by other people and the laws, rules, and policies those people make concerning how resources are owned and allocated. When unequal distributions of power over productive resources exist then unequal appropriation of productive outputs exists. This chapter traces the changing nature of the employment relationship from feudalism to capitalism and its effects on owners of production and workers, the resulting standard of living for workers, the ability of workers to respond in a meaningful way to the relationship, and the security/insecurity of workers within their positions. The chapter concludes with a review of globalization's effect on workers, the logic used to promote globalization, and globalization's implications for job loss and free-trade policies. The logic used to promote globalization was to tear down all trade barriers between nations in an effort to promote a world market, provide production opportunities for underdeveloped and developing countries, and offer fiscal and investment opportunities to developed nations in order to raise the living standards of all people. World institutions such as the World Bank and the International Monetary Fund were established to carry out the mission.

Chapter 7 explores the fairness, adequacy, and reality of wage compensation for American workers and the mismatch between workers' perceptions of what they should receive in compensation and what they actually receive in compensation. Readers learn how human, social, and cultural capitals enhance/detract wages, how work and leisure differ, and how wage theft occurs and is combated. This mismatch between workers' perceptions of what they should receive in compensation and what they actually receive in compensation occurs for many reasons: different assessments of human, social, and cultural capital, the work/leisure debate, and the wage theft which occurs from workers' paychecks. As firms introduce technology into the workplace and eliminate human labor, workers are asked to work harder, faster, and smarter. These technological and organizational advances may increase short-term production outputs for the firm but place an increasing burden on the worker who often suffers physical, mental, and emotional distress as a result. This text explores the evolution of American worker agency, the ability of a worker to change his or her work circumstances under changing economic conditions, institutions, and structures. The text explores whether the intensity with which workers are expected to produce has diminished or increased since the Industrial Revolution as well as how American workers perceive whether a job is good or bad.

Chapter 8 surveys race and ethnicity as social constructs in the employment relationship and how the ideology of difference is used as a rationale to justify and prejudge others and validate the rationale of difference for economic, social, and immigration governmental policies which exclude rather than include various groups. These social constructs grew from eighteenth-century social mechanisms which referred to populations in colonial America and embody an inequality of status to rationalize the way Europeans thought about and treated conquered peoples. The ideology emphasized differences and is used as a rationale for colonialism of those with physical traits different than white European males. The ideology spread worldwide and was used to justify slavery and the eradication of Jews in Nazi Germany. Race then prejudges the difference of human groups, and ethnicity internalizes those perceptions of difference individuals have within their culture or group. The social construction of ethnicity also validates the extension of those differences as a rationale for economic, social, and immigration governmental policies which exclude rather than include various groups. Consequently, racial and ethnic attitudes and perceptions influence the employment relationship. This text then defines race and ethnicity, explores the relationship between race, ethnicity, and immigration, and discusses the causes and continuation of racial and ethnic disparities.

Chapter 9, the final chapter, focuses on gender as a social construct used to describe the behaviors, attributes, roles, and activities appropriate for males and females within a society and how gender historically influenced the way men and women were treated within the workplace and consequently has implications for policies governing the employment relationship. As women's placement in American society and social hierarchy results from the many cultural influences and values having to do with egalitarianism, individualism, patriarchy, marriage and family values, the Protestant work ethic, and the American ideal, women have consistently been given a secondary placement within U.S. society and culture and therefore have been relegated to subordinate positions within the workplace structure. This chapter explores the devalued status of women's roles as a result of historical notions of property rights, sexuality, care giving, and the notion of the idealized woman and how those historically societal, cultural, and economic influences lead to workplace discrimination within the employment relationship.

My rationale for writing this book is to provide readers with an overview of how the U.S. employment relationship, its history, and current status, have been shaped by external and internal forces skewed against workers. It is my hope that focusing on the economic power relationship between employers and employees within a control/resistance framework informs the argument between labor and management and contributes to a better understanding of the property rights versus workers' rights dichotomy. Understanding workers' devalued status in an employment relationship skewed toward employers helps readers acknowledge and proactively engage with the challenges workers face in the daily grind of navigating that employment relationship.

Chapter One

An Overview of the Field
of Labor Studies

WHAT IS LABOR STUDIES?

Work. Workers. Social Justice. Collectives. Labor Unions. Labor-management relations. Employment relationships. Advocacy. All these terms describe some facet one might study in the field of Labor Studies, a multidisciplinary approach to the study of cultural, societal, structural, economic, and power relationships involving labor and capital. Students engaged in Labor Studies seek to understand how workers historically and contemporaneously interact with powerful economic forces which restrict and constrain their ability to maintain living standards, become upwardly mobile in a class-based society, and influence policy which dictates local and global opportunities. The field of Labor Studies strives to provide knowledge, understanding, and competency-based skills to current and future workers within a globalized context and seeks to broaden access to education for working-class, equity-seeking, and underserved constituencies in order to provide opportunities for life-long learning and college degrees.

WORKERS' EDUCATION: 1900–1935

The historical evolution of Labor Studies had its roots in workers' education which was brought to the United States from Great Britain in the early 1900s. The basic idea was to create an educational program which would educate the working class in order to change the social structure of the United States from one of capitalism to one of socialism. Toward that end, the Rand School of Social Science in New York City, created by the Socialist Party, and the

17

Workers School of the Communist Party, also known as the Jefferson School, provided educational services for the International Ladies Garment Workers Union (ILGWU) and the Amalgamated Clothing Workers Association (ACWA). These unions, along with the Women's Trade Union League, began their own education programs shortly thereafter and focused on educating working women about "their rights as citizens and the need for trade unions on the job" (Dwyer, 1977, pp. 180–181). Even though education efforts to train working people were ignored by the American Federation of Labor (AFL), by the end of WWI, over 300 labor colleges existed.

This expansion of labor colleges from 1900–1935 was tremendous; much of the curriculum was delivered through extension programs which offered courses in social sciences and vocational training particularly geared toward workers. Trade unions coordinated workers' educational services with labor colleges. "The Workers Education Bureau of America (WEB) was formed for the purpose of coordinating workers' educational services conducted under trade union auspices" (Dwyer, 1977, p. 181). The basic goal of these educational endeavors was "the reordering of the social system" (Dwyer, 1977, p. 182) by creating "intelligent conscious union men and women . . . [who] strive for the reconstruction of society" (Lorwin, 1924 in Dwyer, 1977, 182). Women's programs, largely held during the summer on college campuses, continued to be popular such as the Bryn Mawr Summer School for Women Workers in Industry. Summer schools for working women emerged though they distanced themselves from any direct connection between the Labor Colleges and collective action. The goal of the women's schools was to prepare women to "contribute . . . in a democratic way [based on] new facts discovered in classes [and believed women] should assume responsibility leading to various forms of social action (Smith, 1932, p. 83 in Dwyer, 1977, p. 182). The purpose of the women's schools was stated as "primarily to offer to women of limited opportunity a chance for further study adapted to their needs. Any impetus to social reform which may come out of the school will be secondary and largely individual" (Dwyer, 1977, p. 182). The ultimate goal then of worker's education during this period was to "play an important and creative role in replacing rugged individualism by some sort of democratic collectivism" (Starr, 1941, 90 in Dwyer, 1977, p. 183) which would eventually "enable the workers to accomplish their special job which is to change economic and social conditions so that those who produce shall own the product of their labor" (Cohn, 1923, p. 10 in Dwyer, 1977, p. 183).

The curriculum in worker's education during this period was primarily in the social sciences with economics and English as the most prevalent courses. These courses were mostly delivered to trade unionists and non-trade unionists who were recruited as individuals interested in working-class issues. The programs were one to two years long, and the summer programs were eight weeks long.

LABOR EDUCATION: 1935–1960

Although labor colleges and summer schools during the workers' education period functioned primarily outside the auspices of the American Federation of Labor (AFL), the Workers' Education Bureau of America, formed in 1921, by unionists and educators interested in assisting labor colleges and training centers involved with the American labor movement, had a financial relationship with the AFL through funding mechanisms. The AFL eventually packed the WEB board with conservative influences that had a sobering effect on the progressive and left-wing activities of labor colleges and summer schools which included tamping down their curriculum to better reflect the AFL's political agenda of craft unionism. This move successfully began the transition from an era of workers' education which supported the move toward a new social order to that of labor education which emphasized the practical needs of the trade union movement. The WEB was formally integrated into the AFL as the Education Department, and after the merger of the AFL with the CIO, the Education Department was handed off to the George Meany National Labor College.

By 1930 several phenomenon were taking place which made shifting the focus of worker's education away from introducing a new social order a necessity. The Stock Market Crash of 1929 and the subsequent Depression forced the labor movement into survival mode. Monies provided by liberals and reformers with bank rolls to fund labor colleges and summer schools dried up and forced many labor colleges to close. In 1935, the National Labor Relations Act (NLRA) was passed which ushered in a legitimized American labor movement complete with laws which governed the labor-management relationship and a new mass industrialized work structure. The complex system of rules and regulations jacketing organized labor required a shift in educational programs and training to one which informed workers of the new rules under which they must operate. The formation of the Congress of Industrial Organization (CIO) in 1935 brought millions of new semi-skilled and unskilled workers under the umbrella of this new system and increased the need for utilitarian education in order for this new group of workers to navigate the system. Labor education's objective then focused on the maintenance of the union which included loyalty to organized labor, the mechanics of collective bargaining, and leadership training. Articulating this shift, John R. Commons, Professor at the Wisconsin School for Workers, believed that "collective bargaining was essential to harmonious industrial relations, [and] that the School for Workers should meet the practical needs of organized workers" (Dwyer, 1977, p. 190). The overarching philosophy was to enable workers to have the best possible life regardless of the economic or social system under which they lived. Large unions in rubber, textiles, automobiles, and steel established their own internal educational programs. The government also began publically funding worker's education programs in state universities through the Works Progress Administration (WPA), a New Deal program created by Roosevelt's Executive Order as a work-relief program. The program existed from 1935–1943 and employed 8.5 million workers. Subsequent passage of labor bills such as the Norris-LaGuardia Act, the Social Security Act, and the Fair Labor Standards Act required union leadership to be knowledgeable about the legal implications of labor law on union members.

Curriculum changes morphed into "bread and butter" courses which preserved the structure of the union and included courses in public speaking, contract negotiations, contract interpretation, leadership training, parliamentary law, current events, American labor history, and grievance procedures. The recipients of labor education were organized union members recruited through their unions instead of the general population. The training of stewards, union staff representatives, and business agents was paramount. Programs shrank in length to accommodate worker's schedules and were primarily financed through the WPA, extension programs in state universities via state government funding, or trade unions.

LABOR STUDIES: 1960–PRESENT

The need for labor union members to expand their educational opportunities was necessitated by the changing nature of a globalized economy which dealt with multinational corporations, the changing nature of the employment relationship, and the worker's place in an economic, social, and cultural structure dictated by market forces, capital mobility, and a bent toward property rights. As early as the 1950s, the idea took root that worker's education should encompass a broader spectrum of courses designed to educate the entire person by improving a worker's competencies so she or he can make informed choices in the work environment and the broader community, and that union workers should have the same opportunities as did businessmen to gain some sort of credentials in their educational endeavors. "Workers began to look to education as the road to a better more effective union, greater on-the-job satisfaction, and a richer community life" (Levine, 1966, 99 in Dwyer, 1977, 199). By the late 1960s, the emergence of international forces influencing U.S. trade and production policies moved the concern for worker's jobs into a more competitive arena which required workers to become more attuned to influences such as trade agreements, oil embargos, outsourcing, and issues of diversity.

Universities and unions responded by offering a liberal arts curriculum which offered non-credit courses dealing with "bread and butter" issues either through extension programs or embedded within the curriculum of a degree-granting program, and credit-bearing courses which focused on work, workers, and their education. Most Labor Studies programs are designed to help students become better individuals, who contribute to the broader society by making informed choices, and provide a broader understanding of the economic, social, and political problems faced by current society and how best to rectify those problems.

The curriculum offered in current traditional and online labor studies programs looks at the world through a lens of social justice and attracts students from union and non-union environments. The curriculum offers workshops, training courses of various lengths, and degrees in labor studies from the Associates to the Ph.D. The design of workers' education and the response of universities and organized labor to educational provisions continue to develop as work organizations change, the employment relationship evolves, and the policies governing worker's rights erode. Workers increasingly faced with challenges in their workplaces, communities, and a globalized world, seek the best and most affordable educational opportunities to help them deal with these challenges. Workers need to understand the role their decisions make in the broader context of their economic, social, and political environment. Educating workers then is an important step toward creating an informed citizenry which makes choices beneficial to themselves, their families, and the broader community.

WORKERS, CULTURE, AND SOCIAL CLASS

To begin a discussion about workers, culture, and social class, understanding how workers situate themselves within the broader social, cultural, economic, or political context is important. That context is known as the social structure and is defined as the patterned arrangement of socioeconomic institutions within a society. The social structure of a society houses such institutions as economic, political, governmental, social, cultural, educational, and religious systems. Organizations and individuals within each of these institutions interact in order to provide sustenance for themselves, participate in and influence their governance, remain safe and protected, engage in human interactions, support traditions, study and learn, and value and promote their belief system. Our discussion primarily centers on workers and their placement within the socioeconomic system, but other institutions in the social structure impact the decisions workers make. For instance, workers may make decisions which impact their economic life because they vote for certain politicians with whom they share political beliefs, or they may make cultural choices which impact their economic life because they hold a certain faith and value system. The social structure then acts as a framework within which individual and organizational decisions directly impact a worker's ability to function within the economic environment.

Toward Social Justice

Workers, individuals who sell their labor in the marketplace in return for compensation, must have the ability to earn enough money to maintain some standard of living to be successful in their personal and economic lives. As wage earners, workers are hired by an owner of production who compensates the worker for his or her labor; this relationship constitutes a contract (sometimes written, sometimes implied) which establishes an employment relationship. In the employment relationship, in which workers need owners of production and owners of production need workers, an economic exchange of labor for wages takes place. Under capitalism, workers supply labor to employers in order to earn wages with which to buy goods and services to satisfy their needs. Owners of production extract from workers excess labor beyond the point which satisfies workers' needs; that excess labor contributes excess value in the production of goods and service which then becomes excess value or profit. Owners of production use that excess value or profit for future investments, savings, or consumption. Because owners of production own the capital necessary to create goods and services and workers have only their labor to sell, workers are placed in a less powerful position in the employment relationship than the owners of production. Their only recourse in balancing this economic power relationship is to withhold their labor. Depending upon the pool of available workers which constitutes the labor supply, this may or may not be successful. As powerful interests continue to push for anti-worker legislation, privatization, and free-trade agreements, workers seek ways to create equity in the employment relationship through avenues of social justice. *Social justice* is the idea that all humans have the right to equitable treatment, opportunity, and resource allocation. That doesn't mean all opportunities for workers will result in equal outcomes, but it does suggest that all individuals should be treated fairly in the process of accessing and engaging with those opportunities. Social justice would once again move the construct of work from an economic activity in which the worker engages for survival to one in which workers have purpose, satisfaction, pleasure, dignity and self-worth.

Remember, we are looking at these issues from the perspective of the worker through the lens of social justice. Simply put, social justice is the ability of individuals to achieve their potential in a responsible society which provides opportunities in a fair and equitable manner. When society does not provide equitable opportunities for individuals to succeed, a tension grows between individuals and societal power structures which seek to control resources and their distribution. This perspective suggests that oppressed segments of society must find ways to counter the "shifting and dynamic and complex social processes"(Adams, 2007, p. 1) which constantly assault and oppress them. The term oppression compresses "the pervasive nature of social inequality woven throughout social institutions as well as embedded within individual consciousness" (Adams, 2007, p. 3). Oppression, sometimes subtle and sometimes overt, limits individual life chances and aspirations. Oppression is the result of privileged complex power relationships which confer on some groups special advantages and limit possibilities for other groups. For instance, a young black or Latino female currently seeking work in today's marketplace may have distinct difficulties over a young white male seeking the same work because of cultural, ethnic, racial, gender, educational, sexually oriented, or socio-economic disadvantages. These difficulties disadvantage certain segments of the population when society does not recognize the short- and long-term implications for the personal and economic well-being of its citizens and intervene with appropriate fixes. The role of society then is to provide a more equitable system of opportunities in which all individuals can achieve their full potential, contribute to the good of all society, and make the world a better place in which to live.

The move toward social justice seeks to remedy that inequity by providing social and educational opportunities for those disadvantaged in the marketplace This social and educational approach to social justice provides a framework through which workers who struggle can evaluate, examine, and counter the forces used against them to find effective ways to deal with their oppressors. Adopting this social justice perspective emphasizes access to and the distribution of resources as a way to achieve equity (Rawls, 1971). Individuals can explore and understand how their actions can have a sustained impact on the policies governing the redistribution of wealth, the power structures which limit their opportunities, and their engagement in their own exploitation.

Workers, as an integral part of society, make products or provide services which all humans need. Workers build the infrastructure, produce our food, and service our technological needs. Workers, for their efforts, receive compensation, usually in the form of wages or salaries, which they in turn spend on other goods and services. This cycle continues as workers make daily decisions about work: where to work, how long to work, what kind of work to do, whether to work or engage in leisure, or how hard to work. The millions of decisions workers make about work each day drive local and global production chains, trade forces, and, by extension, the economy. The compensation workers receive in exchange for their labor allows workers to consume goods and services. Without consumption, the purchasing of goods and services, our economic system would grind to halt, factories would close, unemployment would rise, and poverty would increase. The Great Recession of 2007 is a good example of what happens to an economy when workers are not working and purchasing goods and services. The decision-making power of the worker to work and to spend has great consequences for the economy.

Social Class

Since workers are such an important part of society, it makes sense to understand their placement in society. We know the individual worker's role is to produce goods or provide services, but we need to also understand workers as a whole or in the aggregate. To help us sort out workers' collective roles, we turn to a discussion on class, or aggregate groupings of individuals in our society. The term *social class* originally differentiated groups of individuals holding similar roles in the economic processes of production and exchange: landowner and tenant, employer and employee, lord and serf. These societal positions generally referred to various positions within an economic system in which power, politics, and status carried some heft. Eventually the term became more generalized and referred to any aspect of an individual's place in the social hierarchy. Each group of workers is now known as a class. Sweet and Meiksins (2013) write the contemporary divisions of class are more complicated than those described by Marx ([1867], 1970) who placed workers into the proletariat (workers) and the bourgeois (owners of production). Blurred work roles elevate some service workers to managerial status because they deal with the public and receive higher salaries while some professionals in white-collar positions may be given little authority and paid lower wages. Blurred work roles are often the result of employers attempting to circumvent laws requiring certain compensation for certain work roles or hours worked. Examples include avoiding paying overtime to hourly workers by moving them into a salaried management status in title only yet maintaining their hourly duties, thus eliminating the need to comply with laws requiring overtime after a certain number of hours worked, or employers subcontracting work to independent contractors, relieving the employer from the obligation to provide benefits. These contradictions in work roles make more difficult the specific placement of workers into rigid classifications. The placement of workers within these classifications has implications for access to opportunities within society such as education and training, job markets, skills, and social mobility. Sweet and Meiksins (2013) write, "Social class remains one of the most powerful forces shaping employment opportunities and access to resources in the new economy" (p. 14).

Within the United States there are different classes of workers. Dividing workers into classes helps us sort out our own placement in the American class structure, society, and labor movement. There is much discussion in the academy, in the news, and on the Internet about how the middle class is being squeezed and eliminated, how the upper class is becoming increasingly wealthier, and how the lower class with its increasing numbers, lives in poverty. Classes, or aggregate groupings of individuals, allow us to sort out and compare various groupings of individuals. Defining just what class is or how one's class is measured is difficult. Economic, social, or educational status or some hybrid mixture of income, social stature, and so forth have all been used to determine a worker's class.

Class is untidy, disorganized, and messy! Because the American class structure doesn't have a series of titles to bestow upon its citizenry as does the British class system, Americans have to figure out their own placement in the class structure. Class is not a neat and orderly system as in India where one is born into a certain social class or caste for life. Most of us like to think we have a relatively normal or average existence, so we generally place ourselves somewhere in the center of the class continuum. For example, individuals making modest incomes probably live in the same type of neighborhood, shop at the same stores, and expend similar monies on entertainment and education as do others making modest incomes. This existence is their predominant environment, so this environment becomes their norm. They have no reference point to those with lesser or greater incomes for purposes of comparison. That's not to say that individuals making modest incomes are unaware of others who make more or less money, but it is to say that individuals making modest incomes, for the most part, haven't lived an existence in which they made more or less money. For individuals, then, the environment in which they live becomes their average or norm. Their estimation of where they fall on the class continuum then is tempered by their own environment, and any comparisons they make are based on that environment. This hypothesis holds true for most individuals no matter what their income.

Individuals place themselves in this continuum for several reasons. One reason is human desire to be like most others in society. We don't like to be different from our neighbors, our families, or our friends. Our desire is to fit in with our peers, to not stand out in the crowd, and to blend into our environment in an effort to be accepted as part of the group. We could say we identify with our class. Though this is not a book about sociology, I will, from time to time, refer to social groups and their organization because individuals acting in concert exhibit certain behaviors under certain conditions. Workers and labor organizations are no different. They want to be an accepted part of society because society confers benefits upon those groups who conform (rewards) and disciplines those groups who do not conform (punishments).

Class is a complicated concept and is not universal. Not all societies have classes or social groupings. The hunter-gatherer society in prehistoric times did not have social classes, permanent leaders, or power structures. The main goal of the hunter-gatherer society was to survive, so they spent 80 percent of their time foraging for food. Only after the society gravitated toward agricultural methods for food production did leaders and social classes begin to emerge. But many societies have moved toward a hierarchical system of social classes, and the factors determining those classes vary widely. There may even exist different ideas about social divisions within the various groups in a single society.

Social class generally refers to some type of hierarchical distinction or stratification between individuals or societal groups or cultures. Some divisions are based on economic groupings such as wealth or income, political groupings, prestige or occupation, education or qualifications, or family background. The most basic class distinction is between those who have power and those who do not have power. The powerful attempt to control society through the use of money, restraint/intimidation (military), laws and policies, or fear/coercion. The powerful may adopt distinctive lifestyles emphasizing their power and prestige. This is sometime referred to as *cultural capital*. For instance, individuals having great amounts of wealth may be able to send their children to private schools, engage in elite entertainment (operas, theatres, etc.), live in fashionable neighborhoods, wear expensive clothing and jewelry, belong to elitist clubs, speak a language distinctively different from those who are less wealthy, and exhibit different tastes, sensitivities, and manners from those less powerful than themselves. These are visible signs of class differentiation which allow others to denote class.

WORKER'S PLACE IN THE SOCIAL STRUCTURE

During the years of the Industrial Revolution in America, which most scholars agree is from 1820–1870, work moved from the home to the factory. This advance was notable for many reasons: the biggest advance in per capita earnings ever, the movement away from craft production and the advent of mass goods production, the logistic movement of workers from the farm into urban areas, and opening of regional and national markets. But there were also aspects of this period which were detrimental to work and workers: control of work processes was wrested away from workers and put in management's hands; workers became deskilled and interchangeable much like the parts with which they worked; the absence of labor and safety laws encouraged child labor; dangerous, unsafe, and unsanitary work conditions abounded; unlimited work hours and schedules harmed and inflicted physical and mental anguish on workers; and the absence of environmental regulations increased pollutions and health hazards inside and outside the factories. Though many of those atrocities were, over the course of the next hundred years, ameliorated with the passage of fairer and safer labor standards and laws, workers continued to face challenges in their work environments. This necessitates a comparison of how "good" workers had it during the industrial economy as compared to the new knowledge-based or global economy.

The makeup of today's labor force has undergone dramatic changes since the mid-to-late twentieth century. There are more women, minorities, undocumented, and older workers and fewer union workers now than ever before. This changing demography has important implications for work opportunities and challenges available to all workers, for social structures which deal with retirement, health care, immigration, education, and housing, and the culture in general. These changes necessitate the exploration of agency, an individual's or collective's efficacy or power to effect change, and structure, the influence and/or power an existing institution has over an individual or collective. How has moving from an industrial economy to a knowledge-based economy affected workers? What specific changes have workers had to make in adjusting to new challenges and opportunities?

It is important to define the term *economy*. An economy is an organized system for managing resources. Economic systems are based on who owns the means of production and who allocates the goods and services. The United States has a free-market economic system called *capitalism*. In a capitalist system, the private sector owns and allocates production. That means private individuals own all the means of production, and private individuals decide who receives the goods and services produced. A free-market economic system is based on *markets*, places where buyers and sellers come together to exchange goods. These markets can be local, regional, national, or global. Free-market economies are grounded in the theory that competition between owners in the production of those goods and services is the best way to keep the costs of goods and services down. So capitalism is established on a theory of competition. Individuals in the private market compete with one another to produce and sell goods and services at the lowest cost in order to entice consumers to purchase their products. Without consumption, capitalism cannot survive.

The industrial economy was defined as an organized system for managing resources which reflects mass production in manufacturing goods, hierarchal workflows, scientific and bureaucratic management systems, interchangeable parts, local or regional markets, and rigid job definitions. The industrial economy generally centered on the manufacturing of durable goods such as automobiles, appliances, and steel products and was a system under which workers lost autonomy in the workplace because management gradually seized control of the work processes. Beginning with *Fordism*, a system of mass production which controlled workers' speed via the assembly line, workers' skill through the introduction of interchangeable parts, and workers' access to management through shop floor bosses, and workers became merely inputs in a production system which cranked out products for consumption. Devalued and dehumanized, workers sometimes fought back through forming bonds of solidarity via the collective or organized labor. Sometimes successful and sometimes not, these workers struggled against pro-corporate interests in government and manufacturing. Though some strides were made during the 1930s and 1940s in the form of labor laws which protected workers' rights, ultimately the property rights of the owners' of production trumped workers' rights, and by the 1970s and 1980s, we see organized labor losing membership. In 1983, the first year for which union data are available, membership was 20.1 percent or 17.1 million union members; by 2010, union membership had dropped to 11.8 percent or 14.8 million (Statistics, 2012).

As technology continually replaced workers in the manufacturing process, the industrial landscape began to change. The greatest technological advance since the steam engine, the cotton gin, and electricity involved the invention of the transistor, a small silicon-based unit which revolutionized the way humans and work interacted. Based on the discovery of the electron in 1897 by J. J. Thomson, a "new understanding of the properties of the electron that created the field of electronics, and that combined with our developing capability in the electrical, magnetic, and mechanical arts, enabled a rich array of new products and services" (Ross, 1998, p. 7). This new understanding of the electron kick-started the electronics' discipline, and the electronics industry quickly witnessed the invention of vacuum-tube technology and allowed the production of radios, televisions, fax machines, calculators, video tape recorders, and microwave ovens which became commonplace in American households and offices. But vacuum-tube technology was limited because it used considerable power, and tube life was short. The first computers based on vacuum-tube technology were slow and bulky in order to accommodate the excessive number of vacuum tubes needed to power a computer for short time periods (Ross, 1998). The transistor, a semi-conductor device which allowed electrons to flow more quickly through solid matter rather than through a vacuum tube, provided a more reliable, cheaper, and faster method of amplifying and switching electronic signals and power. The development of the transistor, brought about through scientific study, private and government funding, and some luck, catapulted work and workers into a digital age in which information and knowledge replaced manufactured goods as the new product. Most industries currently rely on some form of highly technical computerized systems to manufacture goods, increase productivity, handle financial transactions, and administratively deal with and monitor workers.

This move toward electronic technology birthed by the transistor revolutionized an entire economy to one in which an organized system for managing resources reflects digitized technologies, upgraded skill levels, flexible work arrangements, globalized markets, new managerial controls, lateral workflows, and an emphasis on service work rather than manufacturing work. The digital revolution has huge implications for the employment relationship in which workers must now compete in a worldwide job market. Since any service or good which is digitized can be sent offshore and serviced, read, interpreted, computed, analyzed, or managed for less cost, workers must constantly upgrade their digital and interpersonal skills to become and remain technologically savvy in order to maintain a competitive edge in the marketplace.

The digital revolution also requires firms to adjust to technological changes within a global context. Globalized markets have increased the power of consumption by opening up markets through trade agreements and eliminating trade barriers, so firms seek efficient ways of attracting and retaining the brightest, most productive, and most innovative workers to acquire and maintain their piece of the market pie. New models of managerial control such as teamwork (Vallas, 2003), participatory decision making (Bolman, 2013), and lateral workflows theoretically give greater decision-making power to low-level workers in the production chain but actually require fewer workers and more managerial staff, thus reducing the number of workers employed. This hegemonic concept may actually give workers a false sense of control and align workers with managers who undermine workers' collective ability to resist managerial ideology (Graham, 1995; Grenier, 1988). All these tenets allow for corporations to gain greater market shares, intensify productivity, and increase profits. These changes represent additional challenges and burdens for workers whose jobs have been outsourced or offshored, have to work two or three part-time jobs to make ends meet, have lost significant wages and benefits because of manufacturing declines, suffer when flexible work arrangements mean they lose scheduled working hours or have to increase working hours because of consumer demand, have to upgrade their skills to compete in the current job market, and are pushed to take service jobs which pay little and have no benefits. For many workers, the move toward a digitized economy is difficult, frustrating, and disheartening.

The transition from an industrial economy to a knowledge-based economy has significant implications for workers as they adjust to different job requirements, innovative approaches to acquiring knowledge, skills, and abilities (KSA), and new ways of thinking about work in a globalized context. Because the streamlined mass production of goods and services is now driven by technological changes in the production process and more manufacturing jobs require greater technological skills in science, technology, engineering, and math (STEM), millions of workers find themselves undereducated, underperforming, and unprepared for the high-tech and green jobs of the future. Many older workers who had industry-specific skills and long tenures with one firm must seek training and education to upgrade their knowledge, skills, and abilities to compete not only with younger workers who are more technologically attuned but with workers in other countries who work for lower wages. This training is time consuming and costly and may involve even more technology as training courses move into an online environment to reduce costs, carbon footprints, and increase access.

Coupling the technological deficit with the lack of soft or interpersonal skills in relationship building and communication which employers currently demand for all jobs, workers are faced with challenges and opportunities for which they are ill prepared to deal. Soft or interpersonal skills represent an individual's ability to understand "behaviors, cognitions, and attitudes of individuals (including oneself) and to translate that understanding into appropriate behavior in any given social situation" (Marlowe, 1986, p. 6). Interpersonal skills rank as one of the most important requirements for personal and organizational success. Much of the research in interpersonal skills occurs in the healthcare industry because administrators and educators believe healthcare providers should have an "excellent bedside manner" (Bedwell, 2011, p. 4), but local, state, national, and international firms are becoming more interested in their workers' abilities to develop and maintain relationships, collaborate within and across global boundaries, and communicate verbally and nonverbally with all interested parties. As workers seek to tackle the training and educational challenges they face, workers must also recognize their place within the social structure as a result of technology.

Workers hold a strategic place in the social structure as a result of their ability to affect change through collective bargaining and withhold their labor (strike). Goods and services are produced through some process. All industries such as manufacturing, service, construction, mining, health care, or education introduce some raw input into a production system which alters the raw input by adding value and producing some useable output available for consumption. The technological process for producing and distributing goods and services which requires workers to turn some raw input into some finished product which a consumer will buy is called adding value to the product. For instance, a manufacturing process may turn raw steel into tools or a university may instill in a student knowledge or competencies which produces an educated student. Karl Marx believed that workers who added value to a product should share in the wealth created when that product was sold. He reasoned that workers, who possessed the knowledge to produce the product, should be compensated for their knowledge as well as their ability to make the good or service. These workers would be in a very strategic position to keep the work flowing or disrupt the work process if necessary, so workers find their power diminished or strengthened based on their position with the production system.

A disruption of that process means decreased production, less available product for sale, and consequently less profit for the firm. Workers, through individual agency, have the ability to disrupt the work process at various production points in order to extract something like better wages, benefits, working conditions, and so forth, from the owners of production as a legitimate way to change the labor-management relationship in favor of the workers. Workers, who have certain skills and expertise, could withhold that skill and expertise in order to better their conditions in life (technological position). The ability of a worker to withhold his or her labor is one of the most valuable strengths a worker has. Workers have no other way in which to shift the balance of economic power within the employment relationship in their favor. Individually workers' power is weak, but collectively, workers' power is strong. Throughout history, policies have primarily been constructed to favor employer power over worker power, so the issue of withholding workers' labor is paramount in shifting the balance of power toward workers.

LABOR'S PLACE IN THE SOCIAL STRUCTURE

Another important concept is the position of labor as an organized collective within the social structure. Labor collectives, more commonly known as labor unions or labor organizations, have been able to survive and sometimes even grow because they occupy a strategic place in the social structure of our country. Labor organizations are primarily economic organizations formed to gain higher wages, better working conditions, and better benefits for those who join the union. The position of organized labor within the social structure is very much like that of the worker in the production process and depends upon strategic positioning to affect change for some equity-seeking group. Labor organizations have greater or lesser strength depending upon their ability to leverage their economic strength against management in the employment relationship. Successful labor organizations effectively gain for their members economic power which translates into higher wages, more and better benefits, and dignity, voice, and self-respect in the workplace.

To understand labor organizations and the importance of the collective in the social structure, it is necessary to define the terms *organization* and *collective action*. An *organization* is a group of individuals who band together for some purpose, for some period of time, and have some set of resources. This definition will work whether we're talking about hunter/gatherer groups thousands of years ago who banded together to forage for food and had as their ultimate purpose survival or a newly minted group of computer geeks who band together to create software to earn a living. Organizations are made up of individuals or more specifically groups of individuals who have something in common. There would be no reason for individuals to join groups if each individual could accomplish everything on his or her own. If one could function on one's own (provide food, clothing, education, protection, social culture, etc.), there would be no reason to join a group (work organization, university, society, etc.). Since individuals in isolation usually function poorly, individuals find other individuals who share with them common interests such as protection from crime, food availability, educational resources, and so forth. Therefore, groups of individuals join organizations because the organization functions with the common interests of the group in mind.

First and foremost, we must understand that labor unions are organizations made up of complex people and their ideas that now function in a global marketplace. Labor unions cannot be separated from other firms or businesses in that respect. Although labor unions offer a different product to the world (representation for workers' rights), labor unions are subject to the same economic forces as are firms that produce automobiles or textiles. Just as many firms are now experiencing difficult financial times in a depressed economy, so too labor unions. And just as many firms are restructuring, downsizing, off-shoring, and outsourcing for economic survival, so too labor unions must respond to the economic forces pummeling them. Being able to reframe or modify organizations to meet the challenges of globalization within a competitive market is a necessary tool with which to maintain organizations comprised of complex people and ideas; so every activity then becomes a collective action.

The function of an organization to further the common interests of its members is known as *collective action*. The ability of the labor union to provide representation, also known as a *collective good*, to their members rests in compulsory union membership. Compulsory union membership means union members must pay periodic dues to their representative bargaining unit in order to remain members in good standing with their union. This is known as a *closed shop* because workers must join the union as a condition of employment to be employed by the firm. The closed shop was in existence until 1947 with the passage of the Taft-Hartley Act which weakened the National Labor Relations Act (NLRA) of 1935 by allowing an *open shop*. Open shops do not require union membership but do require that workers pay an *agency fee* because they are protected by the NLRA, and the union is required to represent them in grievance and arbitration cases. These non-paying dues employees are known as *free riders*.

Compulsory membership in unions is necessary for the survival of the labor organization. Factory workers began forming labor organizations during the Industrial Revolution for protection from employer's oppressive tactics. Attempts to peacefully negotiate with employers fell on deaf ears so this formation was accompanied by strikes, pickets, and violence. Employers, functioning under a market system of *laissez-faire* capitalism, were primarily concerned with making profits, and, therefore, discounted any efforts by workers to better their own lot. The mindset of employers and the general public was that workers were responsible for their own situations and should be content to live and work for low wages. The idea that poverty was divinely ordained and certain classes of workers were poor because a divine plan dictated their poverty was known as the *Theory of Social Traditionalism*; this theory remains relevant even today in many political circles. Compulsory union membership was a mechanism by which labor organizations could remain viable in order to provide collective goods for their members. Withholding one's labor by striking was a way to force an employer to accept worker demands. A striking worker received no wages for the duration of the strike so the interests of the group were not furthered if the worker returned to work without the labor union's demands being met. The only way to ensure that all workers remain on strike thus forcing an employer to meet their demands is through compulsory union membership.

Compulsory union membership is based on the same premise as another type of compulsory membership—citizenship in the United States government. Citizens are required to pay income, sales, property, and other taxes in order for the government to function. The government uses taxpayer money for such things as military defense, infrastructure building, public education, pensions for the elderly, and so forth. It goes without saying that if there were no taxation system in the United States, very few, if any, of these programs would be provided. It is most unlikely that citizens would voluntarily pay taxes out of the goodness of their hearts. Therefore, the U.S. government requires and compels its citizens to pay taxes in order to provide the goods and services necessary to remain a viable and strong nation. These goods and services are known as public goods. It is in the best interest of all citizens that taxes are paid in order to ensure the public good. For instance, it is in the best interest of all citizens that free public education be provided to every child in the United States. This way all children, not just those who could afford to pay for private education, are educated, thus making the United States a better place for everyone. It is in the best interest of all citizens for the government to provide protection from foreign attack, not just for citizens who could afford to pay for private protection. Taxes are compulsory in order to ensure the public good. Olsen calls this type of public good a non-collective good. Non-collective goods are those which are provided by a government and for which no one makes a profit. Collective goods are those which are usually provided by the private sector and generally make a profit.

Compulsory union membership had its roots in the early British trade unions in which "the trade clubs of handicraftsmen in the eighteenth century would have scouted the idea of allowing any man to work at his trade who is not a member of the club" (Webb, 1902, pp. 214–215). Compulsory unionism also existed in early American trade unions such as the "carters, predecessors of the teamsters" (Olson, 1971, p. 69), the Cordwainers or shoemakers (Toner, 1942), and the printers (Stockton, 1911). These early unions enforced a closed shop as a condition of employment. The benefit of compulsory union membership was in the interests of union members because it furthered the goals of the group. These closed shops were the forerunners of the modern-day larger unions in which the actions of one member who does not attend union meetings, participate in the grievance procedure, or engage with the union in any way, are inconsequential and do not significantly affect the work of the entire group or organization. The compulsory dues workers remit require the labor union to represent all workers when bargaining for better wages and working conditions.

The growth of permanent labor organizations is affected by workers' strategic positions within the technological and market frameworks. During the early growth of labor unions, cutters, textile workers who cut the fabric, were the first to organize and became the nucleus of the organizing drive. In the coal industry, the miners, who owned their own tools and worked unsupervised, expanded the organization to include the entire group of miners. In the cotton textile industry, the loom fixer's skill was very important because a breakdown of the loom shut down the entire weaving process (Larson, 1987). These examples of workers holding strategic positions within the technological structure of the production system point out that workers have the ability to change their working environment and conditions through collective action.

The power of collective action allows workers to join together in groups and organizations and form bonds of solidarity. Sometimes, these strategic points are called points of infection because they can grow and spread. How far these points of infection can spread depends upon other factors. For example, some workers in a production process making widgets are working in cramped and dirty conditions for low pay. They band together in an effort to unionize. Their success is dependent on factors such as their firm's policy on talking about organizing in the workplace, their state's rules governing collective bargaining, their fortitude in extending the union fight over a prolonged period of time, the hostility of management to organizing efforts, their ability to build coalitions within the community sympathetic to labor unions, their ability to convince fellow workers of the benefits of unionizing, and their ability to collect authorization cards from employees, and so forth. The barriers to organizing are endless, so workers in today's corporate structure already know they have an uphill fight on their hands if they attempt to unionize their workplace. There exist other examples in which workers failed to expand their organizing efforts. One prime example is the failure of the craft unions to expand further than their own crafts by excluding unskilled and semi-skilled workers from their union which was ultimately the demise of the AFL.

Labor union growth by strategic placement in the technological and market structures has been replaced by labor union growth at the ballot box. Polices put into place via the Taft-Hartley Act have sufficiently ham-strung organized labor's ability to make strides in organizing through strategic placement of workers. Though there exist some examples of workers who disrupt the work process through strikes, it is much more common for workers to attempt change by such methods as *working to rule* or work slowdowns. Working to rule means employees refuse to perform tasks outside of their job description, follow the rules and procedures to the letter, and refuse voluntary overtime unless scheduled. Employees "working to rule" are not outside the boundaries of their contract and company policies, so they seldom are disciplined. Work slowdowns occur when employees simply slow down the pace of their routine as the result of some problem, real or manufactured, with the technology or the process. For instance, a worker on an assembly line might be given some defective parts with which to work. The worker obviously has to slow down his speed in order to get different parts or make the defective parts work. Though workers still maintain some leverage in disrupting the work process or flow, it is more likely that changes will be orchestrated by ballot at contract time or through the grievance and arbitration process.

The ability of organized labor to effect change for its members is predicated on the notion of compulsory membership which acts as a control mechanism to maintain membership, provide funding for the organization, and move toward a more equitable balance of economic power in the employment relationship through collective bargaining agreements. But organized labor is more than simply a mechanism for increasing its members' standard of living. Labor organizations are a part of the community just as are other organizations like civic clubs, church groups, arts clubs, or sports clubs. Labor organizations are made up of people who have roles in their communities. Union members are also PTA members, and city/county board members, and laymen in churches. They live in neighborhoods, shop at the local convenience store, are members of the local softball team, contribute to the community through recycling efforts, raise money for charitable causes, and participate in community-led efforts for the arts and sciences. Labor has always had strong ties to the community, so it is natural that other organizations in the community such as churches, civic organizations, and others would be sympathetic to union workers' struggles. After all, these workers are their neighbors.

Communities support labor organizations because the members of the community and the members of the labor unions are the same people. They are the fathers, mothers, brothers, sisters, aunts, and uncles of the families in the community. These bonds, built over time, are sustainable and a source of strength to unionists when employers cut their wages, ship jobs overseas, and close their plants. The support provided by communities in the form of friendship, offers of money, and other tangible items is invaluable to union members during union struggles. Union members reciprocate to other organizations in their times of need as well. This give and take atmosphere solidifies the bonds of community within all organizations.

The idea of community is particularly important today when the "bread and butter" issues of unionism, such as higher wages and better benefits, have been somewhat mediated by the workers' desires for better working conditions and a voice in the decision-making process. When employers attempt to cut costs by lowering wages or outsourcing/off-shoring work, the entire community suffers. The cost to a community when a manufacturing job that pays $20 per hour leaves town is four or five lower-paying jobs which can no longer be supported. For instance, when a General Motors plant lays off hundreds of workers who make around $20 per hour, other firms in the community follow suit because there is less money infused into the community via the wages of the auto workers. Therefore, layoffs at the drycleaners, the local fast-food restaurant, and the local service station may well follow. This is a particularly important facet in smaller communities in which a single manufacturing firm may be the largest and only employer in town.

An interesting aspect of community is the ability of the community to come together in hard times. Historically, union workers reside in working-class communities, so when a strike is called by the local union, many in the community will support the strike. During the late nineteenth century, for example, the militant strikes that erupted along the railroads in 1877, in the mines of the Rocky Mountains, or in the steel mills in the East and mid-West, and among black washerwomen in the urban South, were essentially community struggles (Kelley, 1999). We have lots of examples of employers calling in Pinkerton Guards or governments calling the state or national militias to squelch union struggles because employers feared union and community retaliation. Kelley (1999) writes that the workplace and the community were not divided as clearly in the 1800s as they are today. There are countless examples of communities who banded together to support striking workers in Flint, Michigan, in 1937 or the United Postal Workers (UPS) strike in 1997. When protest emerges in a democracy from representative groups such as organized labor and that protest is taken up by other aggrieved social groups, new structures for change often come to fruition. Examples of new structures emerging from social protest are 1) the creation of the CIO as a result of disgruntled semi-skilled and unskilled workers' inability to join craft unions, or 2) the passage of the Civil Rights Act of 1964 and the Voting Rights Act of 1965 as a result of the civil rights movement in the 1960s. These examples give hope to workers trying to effect change in the future through the avenue of mass protest.

Groups of individuals forming labor organizations are not the only type of collective action that takes place. Sometimes organizations join together and form coalitions for the purpose of achieving some collective action. Organized labor is continually exploring ways in which to build coalitions within the community in order to effect change. The stakes are high for labor unions and their existence; union's diminished power under corporate ownership suggests that reaching out to other community organizations might be an appropriate strategy to undertake. A larger discussion about social movement unionism occurs in chapter 4. As external and internal forces exert pressures on organized labor, the labor movement must respond by building bridges with other organizations via community coalitions.

Chapter Two

Employment Relations in Historical Perspective

THE EVOLUTION OF AMERICAN LABOR: 1870–1935

Labor unions are almost conspicuous by their absence in most American history textbooks. Except for scant synopses of major strikes, usually portrayed in a negative way, or tirades about a few organized labor leaders who absconded with union funds, our history books remain silent about the benefits and public good done by organized labor throughout the last couple of centuries. There is scarce mention about labor unions' drive to provide public education during the 1830s in the form of "common schools," free public education equally provided to all children in order to advance the United States morally, socially, and economically. This was an uphill battle because the general mindset at the time was that responsible parents could educate their own children through the avenues of the family, church, or voluntary efforts of like-minded citizens.

There also is little written in our history books about labor's contribution to changing laws and policies prohibiting child labor, reducing the work day to eight hours, gaining pay for overtime work, reducing or eliminating sweat shops, or bringing women and minorities into the workforce. Labor unions have been responsible for myriad changes in workers' lives which upgrade workers' standards of living. These benefits were often not easy to win and required prolonged strikes and work slowdowns in which thousands of workers suffered and died. We often forget, or maybe we've never thought too much about, these hard-fought battles of previous generations who labored long hours in unbearable conditions to simply make ends meet. We should remember that our current workplaces, most of which are relatively clean and safe, are not that way because employers love their employees so much. Our

workplaces offer these amenities because somewhere in previous generations, labor unions battled long and hard for safer working conditions, better
pay, and safer working environments. The laws and restrictions placed on
employers today which require limited hours, safeguards on moving machinery, proper lighting, clean air, and minimum wages result from legislation in
the form of the Fair Labor Standards Act (1938), minimum wage legislation,
and labor laws which balanced the power of workers and employers.

My experiences in the labor-management arena began in a paper cup and
plate manufacturing plant in Springfield, Missouri, which closed in 2005.
The plant's ownership changed hands any number of times since its incep-
tion in 1950. The plant was known as the Lily-Tulip Cup Corporation when I
began my employment and was one of the premier manufacturing facilities
in Missouri at that time. It was a spacious brick building on the city's north
side and was surrounded by acres of manicured lawns. The front entryway,
for supervisors and guests, was made to look like a huge paper cup printed
with the Lily-Tulip design called *greenleaf*, a sort of green vine printed
around the rim of the cup.

I began working there right out of high school. I am from a small town in
Southwest Missouri and from a large family. There was little expectation that
I would attend college after high school graduation, so I began working in the
plant on the night shift which ran from 1 am to 7 am. The plant manager ran
"women's shifts" and "men's shifts." Women worked only six hours each
day/night because they had other jobs at home to do such as care for the
house and children and cook. Men worked eight hours and overtime because
they had the primary responsibility of supporting the family. During the
1970s, the law changed which made it illegal to discriminate by working
different genders different hours, so women then began working eight-hour
shifts.

A number of men in the plant had been "talking" about organizing a
union. I can remember what are known as "captive audience" meetings being
held at the plant. In a large warehouse area, the employers would set out
hundreds of chairs to accommodate the four hundred workers per shift, and
the plant manager and other top executives of the corporation would rail
against the unions. They told us we didn't need a union because they would
take care of us by providing good wages and benefits. They touted their open
door policy to settle disputes which might arise, and therefore, there was no
need for the union's grievance and arbitration process. They explained they
may have to simply close the doors to the plant if a union were voted in as
our collective bargaining representative because the company could no longer remain financially stable if they paid union wages.

The organizers for the union, I found out later, had been threatened by all
sorts of intimidation tactics such as threatening phone calls to their homes.
Nevertheless, authorization cards were passed out, signed by over 31 percent

of the membership, sent to the National Labor Relations Board (NLRB) for certification, and certification was granted. Thus, the International Brotherhood of Electrical Workers, Local 1553 became the sole representative bargaining agent for the employees at the plant. Negotiations followed and a first contract was signed.

I didn't become very active in my union until some years later when I became a shop steward and eventually became the first female chief shop steward in the plant. There were around 1,400 employees at the time. Since that time, I held most positions within the union: negotiating committee member, executive board member, and secretary-treasurer. I was involved in sanctioned strikes and one *wildcat strike*, an illegal strike which is not sanctioned by the union, for which the employer was granted an injunction forcing the workers back into the plant. I know what it is like to be a union member, fight for my and other members' rights, and have management do their very best to discredit me and terminate my employment. I give this brief synopsis of my labor background to emphasis that my story is similar to many other stories of those involved in organized labor. The decline and eventual closure of the paper cup manufacturing facility in Springfield, Missouri, is comparable to thousands of other manufacturing plants across the nation which have been closed or downsized. The ripple effects of plant closures to the well-being of workers and their communities reverberate through broader economic and social environments for years. The unequal power dynamic which gives corporations clout to create these disruptions in the name of profit reinforces the inequality in the employment relationship. Corporate decisions to downsize or close factories have direct and indirect consequences for individuals, families, and communities. A discussion concerning the historical development of the labor movement then necessarily entails talking about factories and workers, laws and policies, employers and corporations, and the rise and decline of their power relationships.

Broadly speaking, the power dynamics of the employment relationship shift between workers, the proletariat, and the owners of production, the bourgeois. There are many stakeholders within these two divisions: individuals, leaders, groups, and coalitions with which organized labor and corporations have been associated. Our focus is to understand how these stakeholders have negotiated power to change the labor-management relationship over time. The previous discussions concerning workers' and labor's place within the social structure now shifts to a historical exploration of the origins of labor unions and a look at some of the major players who had a profound influence on organized labor's growth and demise.

THE FIRST AND SECOND INDUSTRIAL REVOLUTIONS

Society is generally thought to be divided into two classes, the working class or the proletariat, those who produce goods and provide services, and the owners of production or the bourgeois, often called the upper class or the aristocracy. The division of humans into classes is a holdover from the early centuries of European civilization in which landowners or masters in a feudal system governed their workers, or serfs, with an iron fist. Serfs performed the agricultural and mining duties while the masters simply oversaw their work. This master-serf system, in some form or fashion, was transferred to the United States in the form of masters and slaves in the southern regions of the United States and landowners and wage earners in the northern parts of the United States. The idea was largely intact until the beginning of the Industrial Revolution sometime around the latter part of the seventeenth century and is the forerunner of the division of work today.

The ideas of unions, or groups of workers coalescing for the purpose of bettering their lives, which began in Europe and Great Britain and attached itself to a political agenda, worked through the government and owners of production to facilitate change. This could occur in Europe and Great Britain because of the collective thinking of the populace. The mindset of individuals in countries outside of the United States is such that their goals are to do what is right and good for their families, their communities, and their countries. Each individual's welfare, though important, doesn't rank as a number one priority. This mindset allows individuals to work with and through elected and appointed officials and owners of production for the betterment of all. Consequently, government and business do what is best for the whole, not just parts of the whole. This is a difficult mindset for Americans to grasp. One of the main reasons this country was formed was for religious and economic freedoms. Rugged individualism was necessary for a revolt from England during this country's founding. The individual rights and liberties of Americans tend to trump collective actions; therefore, Americans are suspect of government and business, who they believe generally do not have their best interest at heart.

A firmly established market economy which had evolved from the previous idea of conditional rights associated with communal property was entrenched as exclusive ownership rights (Rifkin, 2014). The transition from a rural, communal-based subsistence economy in which the people belonged to the land had moved to a market-based agrarian economy in which the land now belonged to the people "in the form of real estate that was negotiable and exchangeable in the open marketplace" (Rifkin, 2014, p. 31). Individual labor, too, became a commodity in the marketplace.

The First Industrial Revolution, usually established as the period from 1760–1840, was known for transitioning from hand or craft manufacturing to machine manufacturing. The improved use of water, steam, and coal power to drive equipment facilitated a turning point in American history and influenced every aspect of daily life. Beginning in Great Britain and spreading to Western Europe and the United States, this time period witnessed the invention of Watt's steam engine, Whitney's cotton gin, and McCormick's mechanical reaper. These new machines allowed new types of commercial enterprises to gain footholds in the textile and grain industries which could then grow, deseed, bale, and sell for export King Cotton in the southern states, and grow, harvest, and produce wheat products in the northern states. Inventions during this period revolved around textiles and iron and steam engine technologies.

Embedded in this First Industrial Revolution prior to the Civil War was a period, 1820–1840, which came to be known as the Awakening Period of the American labor movement (Commons, 1910, pp. 224–226). This period was characterized by the idea that industrial organizations were driven by not only technological change but by distribution changes as well. This was a period when transportation was moving away from water ways, which was the original method of distribution, to railroads. The influx of immigrants provided cheap labor for building the roads, and the technological advent of the steam engine allowed trains to move quickly from the North to the South and the West to the East. New markets could more quickly be accessed with faster transportation. This new visionary idea of faster transportation to move goods accelerated the idea of capitalism, which was to produce and sell in the most efficient manner possible. Advanced technology, transportation, and new markets would give producers incentives to compete with one another. This conflicted with the Marxist notion that technological changes in production were the most important changes and would drive the workers to revolt.

Pre-Civil War unions were often not seen as legitimate organizations. They faced punishment by courts and growing competition from immigrant labor. Most unions existed among skilled workers, but unskilled textile workers also became involved. These collective efforts helped catapult Andrew Jackson into the White House in 1829. His successor, Martin Van Buren, issued an executive order decreasing the workday for federal employees to ten hours. In major U.S. cities, unions successfully used the *strike* to secure wage increases and union membership swelled. Poor economic conditions soon tipped the scales in favor of employers, and union membership waned.

A philosophical view of labor which emerged by the second quarter of the nineteenth century developed as an outgrowth of Karl Marx's idea that wealth could only be created when the form of a raw material was changed or formed into another product. For instance, when raw iron was made into ornamental iron bars for windows or when farmers fed livestock to fatten cattle for sale on the market, a change was facilitated to the input. Since the value of the changed raw material was orchestrated by workers, Marx felt workers, the proletariat, who *created wealth* for the owners of production, the bourgeois, should share in the profits from the sale of the goods. Marx reasoned the bourgeois simply *transferred* the goods from one entity to another entity, and though that transfer did add a cost to the goods in the chain of distribution, the added cost should not become an economic and moral burden on the worker. Marx predicted at some point in the future, workers would rise up in revolt and overthrow the owners of production thereby shedding the extra cost of transferring goods.

The Second Industrial Revolution, a period generally agreed to be from 1860–1910, was characterized by increased technology, economic progress, and rapid changes in transportation. Also known as the Technological Revolution, this period witnessed the introduction of Bessemer steel, steam-powered boats and ships, railroad expansion, large-scale manufacturing, electrification, mass production, and the assembly line. These new technologies, scientifically based, led to a time of great prosperity and expansion in the United States where the population tripled, and manufacturing mills were established along with existing textile mills. An increased demand for workers to man the factories and the mills saw an increase in foreign immigration as well as domestic movements from farms to urban areas. These demographic shifts were the result of increased product demand from domestic and foreign consumers. Owners of production, eager to supply consumers with products for which they could charge increasingly higher prices, hired workers for low wages in order to maintain profit margins. Since a steady supply of workers was always available, employees could continually reach production quotas as well as maintain a low wage threshold. Workers, working in unsafe, dangerous, and unsanitary work environments, found themselves producing profits for employers at the expense of their own well-being.

UNION FORMATION AND STRIKES

The National Labor Union

In 1866, a national organization of labor took steps to protect workers and their rights. The National Labor Union (NLU), under the direction of William Sylvis, proposed reform through political action by bringing all workers, skilled and unskilled, and social reformers together to reform labor as a whole. Sylvis, an avid supporter of labor unions and president of the Iron Molders' International Union, ceaselessly worked for political reform. The NLU advocated their general aims through the *Address to the Workingmen of the United States* which were the establishment of the eight-hour workday, consumer and producer cooperatives, reform of currency and banking laws, limitations on immigration, abolition of convict labor, provision of public lands to settlers, and the establishment of a cabinet-level Department of Labor. Membership was open to interested and sympathetic individuals, not just skilled tradesmen (Dubofsky, 2004). The NLU fought for women's voting rights, and suffragists figured prominently at the organization's national meetings. The NLU recognized working women by "pledg[ing] individual and undivided support to 'the sewing women, factory operatives, and daughters of toil'" (Dubofsky, 2004, p. 93). After its founder, Sylvis, died in 1869, the NLU lost traction and declined in 1872. Though the NLU was largely unsuccessful, many of its proposals, such as the eight-hour work day, continued as important battle cries. This shift in power from labor unions to businesses during the early 1870s propelled the country into a deep depression.

The years 1870 to 1930 were characterized by panics, recessions, and depressions. Recessions, which were known as panics prior to 1940, were caused by economic failures in the United States and abroad. Because there was no government intervention in the market prior to Roosevelt's administration, the *laissez-faire economic system*, which required the markets to adjust themselves, often had far-reaching consequences. Lack of confidence in the monetary structure of the time resulted in runs on banks in which individuals pulled out their money. Jay Cooke, an American financier, who backed the Northern Pacific Railroad in hopes of building a railroad to the Pacific coast, was bankrupted in 1870 when his bank overestimated its capital for funding the railroad. Employer-favored legislation contributed to the instability of the economy. The gap between employers and craft unions widened.

The Panic of 1873 resulted in closed factories and mines, thousands of unemployed workers, and falling wages. These harsh economic times undercut the ability of labor unions to survive as business took advantage of every opportunity to crush organizing efforts. Workers, with no legal recourse, were also ham-strung by their own inability to coalesce around issues important to the workingmen, and labor unions failed to adjust to the new industrialized environment by focusing on single issues such as the eight-hour day or the abolition of the wage system as had the NLU. Spokesmen for labor increasingly seemed to be disconnected from active workingmen who wanted a return to the pre-depression era when cooperation among workers yielded results. Strikes abounded, and workers often demonstrated, resulting in police intervention and brutality. Dubbed "The Great Upheaval," this period reflected the dissatisfaction and unrest fueling mass strikes and turmoil. The general populace grew concerned with the potential for explosive disturbances as well as the influx of European immigrants with Marxist ideologies and revolutionary ideas. Decrying anarchy as the undoing of democracy, conservative businesses and right-wing ideologues incorrectly assessed the situation as one of socialist and communist infiltration and overthrow instead of the more benign search for a more equitable balance between labor and capital.

Thompkins Square Riot

In many instances, violence against innocuous groups of individuals simply looking for ways to satisfy hunger and shelter needs was interpreted by local, state, and federal governments as attempts to overthrow government powers. One such event became known as the Thompkins Square Riot. In New York in 1874, workingmen from the International Workingmen's Association, mostly homeless, hungry, and unemployed, had secured a permit to hold a public meeting in Thompkins Square to visibly bring awareness to their plight. One hour prior to the meeting, city administrators revoked the workingmen's permit because "evidence that radical agitators were prepared to address the proposed gathering" (Dubofsky, 2004, p. 107) surfaced. Workingmen filled the square not knowing their permit was revoked, and mounted police stampeded the crowd beating them with clubs. Many were injured. Among those injured was a young man named Samuel Gompers whose experiences that day solidified in his mind the idea that only workingmen can protect other workingmen. Gompers later became the head of the American Federation of Labor (Dubofsky, 2004).

Another example of unrest occurred when the Miners' and Mine Laborers' Benevolent Association, a union of anthracite coal miners, walked out of the mines in Eastern Pennsylvania when the Anthracite Board of Trade cut previously agreed upon wages by 20 percent (Dubofsky, 2004). Called "the long strike," the Anthracite Board tried to force the miners back into the mine through starvation. This situation gave birth to a secret society of miners known as the Molly Maguires, radical Irish coal miners in Pennsylvania, who were charged with violence and property destruction. The decision for their punishment was based on the testimony of one Pinkerton detective, James McParlan, who went undercover to expose the Molly Maguires. Though there may have been a core group of Maguires responsible for some violence, the major industrialists and their hired agents, the Pinkerton Guards, killed and injured many innocent workers and their families. Owners of the mine as well as anti-labor railroad heads were later found to have instigated much of the destruction in order to provide an excuse to move in and squelch the rebels and the union's organizing efforts. The owners not only successfully halted union organization, but arrested and convicted twenty-four Molly Maguires (Dubofsky, 2004). There is little evidence left of the Maguires, so much of what we believe we know is speculation.

The Haymarket Riot

The great railroad strikes of 1877 followed with public opinion divided between the striking railroad workers and the railroad owners. The strikes were the result of significant wage cuts and paralyzed railroad traffic and delivery across the nation. Desperate strikers seized railroad property, tore up railroad lines, and looted railroad storehouses. President Rutherford Hayes called in state militia and federal troops to restore order, but by the time they arrived, the chaos had ceased, and many of the striking workers, knowing they were beat, went back to work. The public, having witnessed such violence and insurrection, shifted their opinion from sympathy for the strikers to support for the railroad owners. This swing to support railroad owners and discount grievances of the strikers reflected the traditional view of the employment relationship which posited workers should "submit to whatever conditions prevail[ed] in industry" (Dubofsky, 2004, p. 111) and was reminiscent of the Great Chain of Being which suggested all property was owned by God, and each individual had specific roles and responsibilities to play. Employers were energized as never before and sought to reestablish old conspiracy theories, suppress any labor activity, and brought in scabs to replace striking workers. This shifting of the power equation toward businesses and against labor organizing solidified in the workers' minds the need for sensible organizing and solidarity which would skirt uncontrolled retaliation by authorities yet tap into the great power of the collective.

Tensions between business and labor continued to escalate. In Chicago, Illinois, left-wing groups which included the Workingmen's Party, a combination of socialists and disgruntled members of the defunct International Workingmen's Party, Marxian socialists who promoted overthrow of capitalism, Lassalleans, who wanted to achieve success via political methods, and the Black International, a spin-off group of radicals who promoted revolution, proposed support of the generally accepted idea of an eight-hour work day. These operatives, spurred by miserable working conditions and ten- to fourteen-hour workdays, joined other supporters in solidarity on May 1, 1886, in Haymarket Square in the working district near the stockyards in Chicago. The strikers were peaceful yet jubilant. But on May 3, the situation turned ugly and found the police firing on a crowd of strikers engaged in attacking strikebreakers at Chicago's McCormick Harvester Plant. Four were killed and many wounded.

This spontaneous eruption was just what radials in the Black International were waiting for, and they encouraged the striking workers to "take up arms" (Brecher, 1997, p. 64). A meeting was set for May 4 to protest police brutality. Three thousand "German and Polish metal workers, cabinetmakers, and packing house employees" (Dubofsky, 2004, p. 112) met outside in Haymarket Square and listened to anarchist's speeches though the gathering remained calm. As rain fell and wind gusts increased, the crowd dispersed, leaving around 300 workers there. At that point, some 200 police descended on the workers and demanded the meeting stop. As the speakers halted talking, a bomb exploded among the police, wounding seventy, one fatally. The police retaliated by wounding many and killing one demonstrator. Panic ensued, and assumptions were made that the strikers had hurled the bomb, thus sentiment against labor once again turned negative. The mayor of Chicago, Carter Harrison, ordered the police to break up any dangerous gatherings, and sweeps of the city resulted in hundreds of anarchists and socialists being jailed. Hysteria against labor continued when seven of the anarchists seized for the Haymarket Riot were sentenced to death; four eventually were hanged and the remaining sentenced to prison. They were, in 1893, pardoned by Governor John Peter Altgeld who maintained the trial contained "malicious ferocity" (Brecher, 1997, p. 66) and was unfair. No evidence was ever found linking the striking workers to the violence, and organized labor vehemently denied any connections with the anarchists. Yet, public opinion against organized labor, fueled by fear of anarchy promoted by business, continued to strengthen. Though the strike was broken and the workers returned to the factory, the Haymarket Riots were an important step in eventually securing an eight-hour work day for wage earners (Foner, 1986).

The Knights of Labor

The Noble and Holy Order of the Knights of Labor, more commonly known as the Knights of Labor, was formed on December 9, 1869, as a secret society, labor organization, and fraternal lodge. Founded in the American Hose Company in Philadelphia in 1869 by nine tailors, the Knights promoted a union of skilled and unskilled workers, demanded an end to child and convict labor, equal pay for women, a progressive income tax, and cooperative employer-employee ownership of the mines and factories. Their vision was of an all-encompassing labor organization "that would make it possible for all the nation's workers [to form] in a single unified order, without regard to nationality, sex, creed, or color" (Dubofsky, 2004, p. 118). Led by Uriah S. Stephens and Terrence Powderly, the Knights, often known as *procedurists,* believed that corporations and greedy financial capitalists, through restriction of free trade and tax avoidance, and immigrants, who relied on government welfare, were draining the country's finances. The Knights became less secretive and agreed to make their name and objects public and to abolish their initiating oaths. Though most rituals associated with the order continued, the Knights entered their period of greatest growth.

The Knights were opposed to militancy and strikes, believing instead they could facilitate change through rational means by avoiding class struggle. Stephens and Powderly believed producer cooperatives could legitimately engender an industrial commonwealth in which "moral wealth rather than material wealth would be accepted as the true standard of individual and national greatness" (Dubofsky, 2004, p. 118). The Knights, an open organization encouraging blacks and women to join, promoted a humanitarian approach to organizing which was often at odds with workers' purposes for organizing to raise wages. This altruistic approach was acceptable to the Catholic Church which had a strong influence on ethnic populations and immigrants, yet the church feared the Knights' teaching might be inconsistent with the church's rhetoric. Terrance Powderly held meetings with Cardinal Gibbons to assuage the church's fears, and Catholics were also allowed to join with the Knights. The Knights disallowed professionals from joining, saying they were unproductive members of society. They also excluded Asians and supported the Chinese Exclusion Act of 1882.

Yet, the Knights' participation in strikes during the 1880s was relatively successful, and raised their status among the working class. The Knights supported and participated in a conflict with railroad magnate Jay Gould, a financier of the nineteenth century, when the Knights struck the Wabash Railroad and refused to handle rolling stock of the line when it was pulled by engines on other lines. Gould met with Powderly and agreed to call off his campaign against the Knights of Labor, which had caused the turmoil originally. These positive developments encouraged new membership, and a rush to join the Knights followed; by 1886 the Knights had over 700,000 members.

The unprecedented rise of the Knights' power was cause for concern among businesses and employers who prophesized the overthrow of the current economic and social order by a few men who "control the chief interests of five hundred thousand workingmen, and can at any moment take the means of livelihood from two and a half millions souls" (Dubofsky, 2004, p. 130). This very unfounded and overstated fear of the Knights' unlimited power was shared by workers who often pushed worker demands on employers and expected backing from the Knights. For instance, when workers made extravagant demands on Gould and his railroad officials, Gould brought to bear the power of strikebreakers and Pinkerton Guards and called on state governments for militia assistance. Railroad employers pushed back by refusing to compromise with the Knights whose actual participation in the strike was minimal. Powderly, faced with the loss of control over an unstructured organization grown to big too quickly, retreated and ordered the striking workers back to work. The ultimate rise to power of the Knights was also the beginning of their demise. Defeats in other railroads and packinghouses, the failure to secure legislation for the eight-hour workday, disorganized administrative blunders, and a lack of will on the part of Powderly to sanction strikes led to the disintegration of the Knights. The Knights' decline can be attributed to the unsuccessfulness of their strike activity, the growing dissention between skilled and unskilled workers, and the public negativity against labor unions during the late 1890s fueled by the Haymarket Riot of 1886. Power operatives in business and labor exerted strength during the Knights' reign and showcased the tremendous dynamics of public opinion and the collective. Many of the Knights' members chose to join Gompers's AFL which was founded in 1886.

The American Federation of Labor

The death of the Knights of Labor set the stage for a revival of craft unionism popular fifty years earlier. A more practical approach to unionism took form in the American Federation of Labor (AFL) founded in Columbus, Ohio, in 1886. Frustrated craft unionists who wished to preserve their crafts sought short-term solutions to decreased wages, long working hours, and dangerous working conditions. Whereas the Knights promoted an all-inclusive organization with a humanitarian approach to bring industrial cooperation between workers and business, the AFL envisioned trade unionism based on a business model known as the "new unionism." Proponents of the new unionism believed only workers standing up for themselves within the stable framework of a craft union could extract concessions from employers. They were uninterested in overthrowing the capitalist system as had been the National Labor Union and were more interested in working within the reigning economic system and recognizing short-term benefits for their members via bargaining with employers.

Samuel Gompers was elected as the first president of the AFL at the organizing conference. He was a cigar maker who emigrated to New York with his parents from London in 1863. Familiar with Marxist theory and socialism, he was influenced by the Knights of Labor and radical action punished by civil authorities, but disagreed with the Knights who wished to centralize power while Gompers wished national craft unions to retain their power. He paid close attention to the craft workers he represented. He sought gains through bargaining, not legislation. His long tenure with the AFL as its president is partly responsible for the *business model of unionism*, which services its members through a grievance and arbitration process. The AFL's goals are to win gains from employers by entering into a *collective bargaining agreement* (CBA) and rationalizing the workplace through labor contracts. This model places an emphasis on "bread and butter" issues such as wage and benefit increases through the collective bargaining process and less emphasis on membership gains through the political or legislative process.

He, along, with Adolph Strasser, formed the foundation of the American trade union. They accepted the capitalist system and worked within it so their response to social reforms was necessarily limited. The structural design of the federation was very pragmatic and preserved the autonomy of its members' international unions and national unions, made locals their subsidiary, and left dispute resolution to the federation. This served two purposes: 1) the leaders' focus is toward the job problems unique to the trade and the craft and 2) discipline is maintained over the local's activities. This allowed the AFL to present a more united front to employers. One of the reasons Gompers was so adamant about only organizing craft unions was the example set by the Knights.

The AFL is an umbrella organization for craft unions whose members are represented by different locals who share a community of interest centered on common materials, techniques, and tools of the trade. Though members may work for different employers, all craft workers are skilled workers who have a trade, as opposed to industrial workers who are unskilled or semi-skilled workers. Craft workers consider themselves as separate and apart from industrial workers; this *elitism* has caused fissures between skilled and unskilled workers, and employers are quick to capitalize on these prejudices and emotional biases. Though Gompers was adamant about only organizing craft unions after witnessing the collapse of the Knights who promoted inclusionary practices, the move toward elitism within the AFL contributed to its eventual downfall because it was seen as an exclusionary organization which didn't welcome women or minorities. The survival of the AFL was only made possible by its merger with the Congress of Industrial Relations (CIO) in 1955.

Vehelahn v. Guntner

The late 1800s was a time of great labor disputes in the United States. Many immigrants were in the workforce and were organizing. Some workers thought immigrants were taking their jobs, so the mood in the country was contentious. Many workers, immigrant and native as well, went on strike and picketed businesses for the purpose of limiting the business's ability to produce and sell products. These actions flew in the face of business owners who felt they had every right to sell products to whomever they could at any price the market would bear. This public display of insolence by workers was too much for business owners to accept, and their usual response to such action was to ask the courts to issue injunctions which forced strikers back to work. In *Vegelahn v. Guntner*, the union asked to court to allow legal strikes, pickets, and boycotts of a business as well as to release the stranglehold businesses had on *yellow-dog contracts*, a pledge from workers that they would not join a union during the extent of their employment. One such case found its way to the Supreme Court in Massachusetts.

A major decision came from the Massachusetts Supreme Court (1896) who ruled in *Vegelahn v. Guntner*, a labor-law decision, that the union was guilty of *an intentional tort*, which meant the union had coerced and intimidated employers by picketing the employer's business to persuade employees and applicants not to enter and to pressure workers to break employment contracts with the company in the hopes of gaining higher wages. During this time period, there was much labor unrest, and many immigrants in the workforce corporations used the courts to issue injunctions against unions who tried to collectively use their power to affect change (Surhone, 2010). Though the union lost, the case is famous for Justice Holmes's dissenting opinion and his argument called the *Countervailing Theory of Labor and Capital*. He equated the collective force used by workers (labor) as transient and necessary to compete against prevailing corporate strength (capital). He found it justifiable and desirable for collective action to "counter" the efforts of society to glean the most from its workers and saw unions as an equalizing power to corporate power. It would not be until 1932 with the passage of the *Norris-LaGuardia Act* that labor law would catch up to Justice Holmes's opinion.

Homestead Strike: 1892

Two major strikes occurred during the 1890s: the Homestead Strike of 1892 and the Pullman Strike of 1894. Industrial strife and labor unrest erupted in 1892 in a showdown between the Amalgamated Association of Iron, Steel, and Tin Workers of America (AA) and the Homestead Steel Works owned by anti-labor millionaire Andrew Carnegie and managed by his equally anti-labor general manager, Henry Frick. Carnegie introduced major technological changes to the Pittsburg Bessemer Steel Works which allowed for continuous production, speed-up, and the use of less skilled labor. Anticipating a strike when the contract ended in June 1892, as well as reacting to decreased steel prices for product, Frick increased inventory through the already established improved technological production.

The bitter relationship Frick had with the AA prior to the impending strike was exacerbated because early on Frick determined the functioning of the steel mill was inefficient with union and non-union workers. He maintained the union workers, in the minority, should not control the majority of non-union workers. To that end, he declared at the end of the present contract with AA, the plant would be non-union, and wages would be cut by 18 percent. The union workers, knowing a strike was eminent, marshaled forces and planned for the upcoming strike. The AA, in order to protect wages, hours, workloads, speeds, improve working conditions, and eliminate the dreaded yellow dog contract, formed the Advisory Committee which was to coordinate the strike, maintain the pickets, and keep strikebreakers from entering the premises to man production.

Frick, fully supported by Carnegie, determined to cut workers' wages and break the union, engaged the Pinkerton Guards to come to Homestead, Pennsylvania, via barges on the Monongahela River and stand by in case of violence. Frick tried to sneak the Pinkertons in during the night, but the communication system set up by the Advisory Committee, flares, whistles, and word of mouth, was sophisticated and within ten minutes of the Pinkertons' arrival, they were greeted by 10,000 striking workers. The Pinkertons, not allowed to disembark from the ship, stayed on the hot, miserable barge for days. Many of them mutinied because they had been misled about the nature of their work. The violence that ensued resulted in seven deaths and over 320 wounded and injured Pinkerton Guards. The local authority was powerless to maintain control in the face of such huge opposition by the striking workers, and the nation was stunned at such atrocious acts.

The local authorities pleaded with the state militia to take control which they eventually did. Though the strike breakers continued their valiant efforts, after about four months, they were disheartened and subdued. The militia began ferrying in small groups of strike breakers who manned production, but Frick had difficulty recruiting the skilled labor he needed for production. Often the skilled strike breakers were kidnapped and held hostage in the plant. Eventually winter came; morale was down, and men began filtering back into the plant. The once powerful AA was weakened. In retrospect, the workers were displaced and defeated by the new technology introduced into the plant which required fewer workers. The plant, in 1897, was running full steam with a 25 percent reduction in the work force.

The Pullman Car Strike: 1894

The Pullman Car Strike represented the dire situation in which workers found themselves during the 1890s. Employees of the Pullman Palace Car Company in Pullman, Illinois, lived and worked in a *company town* owned by George Pullman, paid rent to George Pullman, and were required to buy everything from Pullman's company store. According to Dubofsky (2004), town rents were "25 percent higher than in nearby communities" and "in most instances [the homes] had no bathtub and but one water faucet for every five families" (p. 159). Pullman instituted wage cuts three times during the 1893 depression and laid off "3,000 of it 5,800 workers" (Dubofsky, 2004, p. 159) without making comparable rent cuts; this angered workers because shareholders continued to receive dividends, and their pleas to Pullman for relief were met with rejection.

During 1894, the Pullman workers were organized by The American Railway Union (ARU), founded on June 30, 1893, in Chicago, Illinois, by Eugene Debs, five-time presidential candidate for the Socialist Party. The ARU became the largest industrial organized union in the United States. Its membership consisted of white railway workers below the rank of foreman. The Pullman employees formed a grievance committee for the purpose of visiting Pullman's manager and asking that the auditing clerks, who wished to join the union, be allowed to do so. Three members of the committee were fired, thus setting off a maelstrom of discontent. Though Debs tried to resist the workers' demands to strike, the rank and file prevailed. A strike against the Great Northern Railroad, headed by James Hill, ensued. The ARU, a very new organization which as yet didn't have a lodge, quickly organized and stopped all freight train traffic, forcing Hill to accept an arbitrator's decision which favored the union. This success brought scores of workers to the ranks of the ARU, swelling its membership to 150,000. This spirit of solidarity was the forerunner of the Great Pullman Strike of 1894. The workers banded together not because they believed they could necessarily win the strike, but because the wages they were being paid would not support their families. In essence, they could not afford to work for the railroad under those conditions.

Pullman refused to arbitrate; a convention committee of the ARU urged a boycott of the Pullman cars. The boycott started on June 26, 1894, when switchmen refused to switch Pullman cars. Soon all railroad service was stopped with 18,000 men on strike. The boycott extended to twenty-seven states and territories when 260,000 railroad workers, half not even ARU members, joined the strike. This strike represented one of immense magnitude, a battle between capital and labor. The paralysis of corporate power stirred the General Manager's Association (GMA) to call for help from the federal government. Grover Cleveland was more than happy to oblige saying that "it would have been criminal neglect of duty if those charged with the protection of governmental agencies and orderly obedience and submission to federal authority, had been remiss in preparations for an emergency in that quarter" (Brecher, 1997, p. 104).

Up to now a peaceful strike, the arrival of federal troops in Chicago on July 4, 1894, awakened the ire of past indignities in 10,000 immigrants, strikers, the unemployed and unskilled. The crowds threw switches, overturned boxcars, and blocked tracks. The total force called to put down the strike was 14,000. Thirteen people died, and fifty-three were injured. The conflict spread across the United State with violence in Colorado, New Mexico, and California. A general strike across the nation was advocated by the Chicago unions. The entire situation continued to escalate. A management strategy finally led to the end of the strike. Pullman cars were attached to mail cars. If uncoupled by workers, federal charges of mail interference could be brought. The strike ended on August 3, 1894, and Debs went to jail for six months. Pullman died in 1897 fearful that labor activists would desecrate this tomb. He had his coffin lined with lead and steel and had concrete poured over the burial ground for safekeeping. Two significant factors emerge from this strike. The first is the unprecedented solidarity of national unions to join together, and the second is that federal troops are willing to marshal forces with corporations against organized labor.

Strikes and work stoppages were the visible signs of growing discontent and high unemployment undergirded by a weak economy during the 1880s and 1890s. Dissatisfaction expressed by industrial workers, farmers, and skilled craftsmen, tired of business and government suppression, fomented the rise of Populism, the idea that wealth belonged to its creators and workers had a right to share in that wealth. The People's Party, also known as the Populist Party, formed in 1892 as a vehicle to restrict immigration, end the use of injunctions, enforce the eight-hour work day, and make illegal yellow-dog contracts and the use of thug armies such as the Pinkerton Guards. The platform of the People's Party, backed by the already weakened Knights of Labor, the NLU, and the ARU was osmosed into the Democratic platform in 1896 in an attempt by the Democrats to secure the labor vote. Republicans and conservative forces rallied their forces of capitalism and prevailed in the 1896 election of William McKinley to the presidency. The capitulation of power toward business once again demoralized labor which witnessed declining membership numbers, little pro-labor legislation, and the immense power of government to crush active strikes.

The Progressive Era

The industrial unrest which colored the late 1800s brought with it the sobering realization there must be better ways to ameliorate labor-management conflict than breaking strikes with federal militia which incurred high costs for business and threatened public safety. A new era of reform emerged encouraged by the institution of corporate responsibility and workplace regulations. National wealth increased as a result of monetary reform and lowered tariffs, yet the bulk of workers did not receive comparable wage raises. The influx of immigrants and the introduction of technology continued to produce an oversupply of labor which held down wages while coal mines, factories, and textile mills still exploited workers and maintained unsafe work environments with sweatshop conditions. The AFL, which had managed to divorce itself from the Populist movement by remaining neutral in the political fray, was the dominant labor organization in the early 1900s yet continued to primarily support a skilled workforce. The bulk of workers then functioned outside of organized labor. This period of reform came to be known as the Progressive Era and was the precursor to the notion that labor and management must find a way to coexist in order to further industrial peace, a necessary component of capitalism.

Toward that end, the National Civic Federation (NCF), an organization of business, labor, and consumers was formed in 1898 in Chicago, Illinois.

Founded by Ralph Easley, the NFC's aim as a conservative think-tank was to "counteract socialist electoral successes and emergent labor militancy by joining capital and trade-unionism in a patriotic effort to end industrial strife" (Federation). A nationwide association, the NCF, which began as the Chicago Civic Federation (CCF) in 1883 for the purpose of renovating Chicago society through cooperation and social efficiency, functioned on the premise that "organized labor cannot be destroyed without debasement of the masses" (Dubofsky, 2004, p. 172) and was willing to bring labor and management together in arbitration settlements. These efforts drew criticism from business organizations such as the National Association of Manufacturers (NAM) who wanted labor agreements abolished as well as from pro-union forces who felt any capitulation of labor's rights under arbitration would be trumped by conservative viewpoints of property rights. The NCF's influence was minimal, and the idea that capital and labor could peacefully coexist continued to be challenged. One example, though, of changing attitudes toward a more collaborative stance occurred in 1902 with the Anthracite Coal Strike.

The Anthracite Coal Strike

The coal miners in eastern Pennsylvania, mostly of mixed European descent, had difficulty organizing because the mine operators exploited their ethnic divisions. The United Mine Workers (UMW) managed to organize part of the miners and called a strike on May 9, 1902, to protest low wages, long hours, dangerous working conditions, increased injuries and deaths, and enforced requirements of company towns. A previous strike earlier in 1900 had resulted in a settlement by the mine operators which was little more than lip service to the miners' demands and more a political stunt to quell dissention during the upcoming 1902 election which propelled Theodore Roosevelt into power. The mine operators touted the strike as one of anarchy and exaggerated acts of violence which threatened public safety, yet the mine workers remained very passive and simply stayed away from the mines. Thousands of policemen converged on the mines to quash the strikers, but there was little for them to do; the ethnic divisions which had created divisiveness among the miners now joined them into a cohesive group fighting not only for their jobs but for their way of life.

Offers to arbitrate the strike were rejected by George Baer, spokesman for the operators, who wanted to break the union at all costs. Baer was a proponent of paternalistic management and stated, "The rights and interests of the laboring man will be protected and cared for—not by labor agitators, but by the Christian men to whom God in His infinite wisdom has given the control of the property interest of this country" (Dubofsky, 2004, p. 178). Public opinion swung between sympathy for the miners and the need for coal to power their homes and businesses. Roosevelt, encouraged by the miners' agreement to arbitrate and frustrated by Baer's obstinate refusal to arbitrate, ordered the government to take over the mines if the mine operators didn't comply with arbitration. Very reluctantly, the operators agreed to arbitration and conceded to a three-year contract, an eight- or nine-hour work day, a 10 percent wage increase, and a board to settle future disputes. The operators fell short of recognizing the UMW as a bargaining agent for the miners. These gains, though impressive, were to come under attack in the near future.

As the Progressive Era continued, business fought back as public opinion once again shifted toward capital. Employers increased the use of the tools such as yellow-dog contracts and blacklisting not yet legislatively outlawed. Antiunion campaigns levied by the NAM promoted individual choice in the form of an open shop, a firm in which one is not required to join or financially support a labor union as a condition of employment. Fearful that union recognition would lead to government dissolution and the end of free speech and liberty, these antiunion forces propagated the use of violence to achieve their cause. One salient example of antiunion animus culminated in the militia's attack on a tent settlement in the Ludlow, Colorado, mine fields in which eleven children and two women were burned to death in their tents after the militia, using machine guns to subdue the miners, then soaked the tent colony with oil and set it on fire. John D. Rockefeller, Jr., owner of the Colorado Fuel and Iron Company which owned the mines, justified the massacre as the only way the strike could be settled and the interests of capital retained.

The Erdman Act of 1898

The power assumed to be the purview of employers was generally fortified through anti-worker and antiunion legislation. To counter the effects of injunctions and employer power and more fairly balance the power between unions and management, the Erdman Act of 1898 was passed. The law prohibited discrimination against railroad employees based on union membership and was the first such law to move toward mediation in railroad labor disputes. It was held to be unconstitutional in 1908 under a claim of abridgement of personal liberty and property rights. (*Adair v. U.S.* 208 U.S. 161 (1908). The Erdman Act grew out of the American Railway Strike in 1894 in which Pullman managers used a blacklist system to keep striking workers from further employment. The Pullman managers would either refuse to provide letters of recommendation (service letters) for their employees or more covertly wrote letters on Crane stationary (Crane Brothers was the employer) with different watermarks depending on the status of the worker. If the worker was not a striker, he received a letter written on paper with a watermark sporting a crane with its head erect; if the worker was a striker, he received a letter written on paper sporting a watermark of a crane with a broken neck. Only detectable by holding the stationary to the light, the watermarks gave future employers a heads up as to the status of the potential employee. The Erdman Act only was used in the settlement of sixty-one cases from 1906–1913; most of the investigative features of the act were repealed, but voluntary arbitration remained intact.

The Industrial Workers of the World (IWW)

The Industrial Workers of the World was a radical labor organization formed in Chicago in June, 1905, by a convention of socialists, radical laborers, and anarchists for the purpose of abolishing the wage system. Eugene Debs and Big Bill Haywood were elected its leaders, and they welcomed all workers of all nationalities. Theirs was the first union to embrace social justice. The strength of the IWW lay in certain populations such as mining and timber towns. In these remote areas, workers were housed in company housing which gave employers extra leverage over their workers. If the worker lost his job, he also lost his home. Known as the *Wobblies*, they promoted industrial unionism of all workers and opposed the beliefs of Gompers and craft unionism, which, they said, divided the working class. Their philosophy stated the working class must be organized in order to abolish the wage system, take possession of the means of production, and live harmoniously with the Earth. The Wobblies believed that workers and employers had nothing in common and a struggle would continue until all workers collectively struck to abolish the wage system. Their historic mission was to do away with capitalism, so they were condemned by the public and the press for being against free markets and corporations. They did not favor political action. They participated in one successful textile workers strike in Lawrence, Massachusetts, in 1912 but lost a textile strike in New Jersey at the outset of WWI. The IWW's influence waned during WWI with their neutrality in the war effort; they argued war was only for capitalist gain, so public opinion then turned against them. The IWW is still in existence today with around 2000 on the rolls and about 900 dues-paying members.

SOCIAL ENVIRONMENT: EARLY TWENTIETH CENTURY

During the early 1900s, the industrial revolution was in full swing. Factories produced the goods individuals needed; hundreds of thousands of workers had left the rural farming areas and moved to the cities. European, Irish, Welsh, Chinese, British, and Polish *immigrants*, who worked for very low wages, streamed into the United States and made up a good part of the workers in factories. By the 1840s almost two million immigrants were in the United States, and by the 1850s, almost three million immigrants were in the

United States with one out of eight people foreign born (Rodgers, 1978). Most immigrants came to America, where land and urban and industrial job opportunities were plentiful, looking for a better life for themselves and their families. What they found were low wages and deplorable working conditions. Factories were miserably hot in the summer and freezing cold in the winter. The main mode of transportation for workers was walking, so thousands of workers, who generally lived near the factory, would pour out of their company-owned shanties in the dark at the start of their twelve- to fourteen-hour work day and return home after dark. They worked six days a week. Their working hours were a hold-over from the farmers' agricultural heritage in which farm workers worked from sunup until sundown. During the industrial revolution, the work day continued as it had on the farm. There still existed in the United States the idea that Sunday was the Sabbath, a day of rest, and factories closed down in observance. But the wheels of industry would start up again at midnight on Sunday evening, technically the end of the Sabbath. Workers had little time for themselves.

The deplorable working conditions of factory workers did not go unnoticed during this period. Writers, such as Rebecca Harding Davis and Upton Sinclair, published accounts of the often inhumane and tortuous plight of factory workers. Davis, born in 1831 in Pennsylvania, was the daughter of genteel and wealthy parents; she was home-educated in Wheeling, West Virginia, until the age of fourteen when she was sent to the Washington Female Seminary in Pennsylvania. After graduation, she returned to Wheeling to live with her parents for the next twelve years. While there she witnessed industrial capitalism and how the other half lived (Tichi, 1998). Though she never experienced the conditions in which most immigrants suffered, she sympathized with them and was aware of the cultural bias toward immigrants. In *Life in the Iron Mills* (1865), Davis describes the backbreaking labor performed by Huge Wolfe, a Welsh immigrant, necessary to forge the iron for the railroads. American anti-immigrant sentiment was fueled by a conspiratorial theory; it was feared immigrants would intermix with whites and dilute the race. The Welsh immigrants occupied the lowest rung on the social ladder because of their propensity to drink, their lack of education, and their difficulty with the English language. Huge, the protagonist in Davis's novel, had come to America with this father and cousin, Debra. They moved to Chicago and lived in a two-room cellar with a dirt floor. Their diet consisted of boiled potatoes and ale. Debra worked as a domestic, and Huge took a job at the iron mill. The story of Hugh and Deborah emphasizes the class divide in America, and Davis crafts her writing to reflect the hopelessness, despair, and exploitation suffered by immigrants living in unfamiliar territory.

Upton Sinclair's novel, *The Jungle* (1906), an expose on the meat-packing industry in Chicago, reflects the insufferable working conditions of workers butchering and processing meat for consumers. Born to a strict tee-totaling mother from a wealthy family and an alcoholic father whose family had lost their wealth during Reconstruction after the Civil War, Sinclair gained insight into the extremes of rich and poor life. Going undercover as a hired worker in a Chicago meatpacking house to research the meatpacking industry, Sinclair witnessed firsthand corrupt owners who cheated workers out of their pay, inspectors who were bribed into allowing sick cows, feces, and vermin to be used in the processing, oppressive heat and unsanitary working conditions, and exploitation of workers forced to live in company housing and purchase supplies from company stores. He vividly portrayed these injustices in *The Jungle* which became a best seller and led to a public awareness of the unsanitary and unsafe conditions in the slaughterhouses. Ironically, the public disgust with slaughterhouse conditions was not based on the horrendous working conditions of packinghouse employees but rather on the idea that consumers could be purchasing meat products at their local grocer contaminated with feces and vermin. As a result, the Pure Food and Drug Act was passed in 1906, a measure which created the Food and Drug Administration whose job was to monitor package labeling. The publishing of the book also led to a political coalition of labor and consumer interests that has remained strong within the Democratic Party through today.

Another event which brought public attention to deplorable and unsafe working conditions in the textile industry and galvanized public support in favor of safer laws was the Triangle Waist Fire in Manhattan, New York (Center, 2011). This major fire, considered to be one of the worst industrial accidents in U.S. history, broke out on Saturday afternoon, March 25, 1911, in the Ashe Building, an old nine-story structure, home to the Triangle Waist Company where primarily women workers, who belonged to the needle trades, sewed shirts and worked long hours for little pay in sweatshop conditions. The owners, Max Blanc and Isaac Harris, subcontracted the administration of the company to male supervisors as a tactic to pay low wages to the workers and divert more of the profits to themselves. When the fire erupted, the subcontractors tried unsuccessfully to put out the fire while demanding the women continue to work. The fire raged out of control and the women, with their escape routes blocked by locked doors and piled-up inventory, were consumed by fire and smoke inhalation. Many threw themselves out of upper stories onto the pavement and to their deaths. Those that did survive were permanently scarred and disfigured, marring future chances of marriage and family life. In all, 146 out of 500 women died that day.

This tragedy stirred public sentiment against worker abuses. The International Ladies Garment Workers' Union (ILGWA) Local 25 and the Women's Trade Union League (WTUL) to which some of the women had belonged, not only organized relief efforts for the victim's families, but petitioned New York's mayor to form safety committees to investigate workplaces to assure the safety of the workers. The fire emphasized the inadequacy of fire inspections, safety exits, and worker protections. Frances Perkins, who later became the Secretary of Labor in the Roosevelt Administration, watched the fire that day, an event that influenced her decision to become a worker's advocate. She assisted in the forthcoming investigation of the Triangle Waist Fire while executive secretary of the New York Committee on Safety. The incident is significant because it highlighted the inhumane working conditions to which industrial workers were subjected. The owners were indicted on seven counts of second-degree manslaughter under section 80 of the Labor code which mandated that factory doors remain unlocked during hours of work. Both owners were found innocent of any wrongdoing. Civil suits were brought against the factory owners in twenty-three cases; they settled three years later and paid $75 for each life lost.

Jacob Riis, the third of fifteen children and a Danish immigrant to the United States in 1870, was a photographer who chronicled the underbelly of New York City life with his photojournalism. Upon his arrival in the United States, he was penniless and lived in a police "tenement" house for several months. His only friend was a stray dog which a police officer beat to death. This introduction to the underbelly of New York City was probably the catalyst for his desire to "shut down" these tenements. He eventually obtained a job as a reporter for the police department in New York City, and began writing stories and taking pictures for a living. He invented the "flash" for cameras, allowing him to shoot photographs at night in which he captured desperate and disparaging scenes of poverty, urban industrial environments, and crime. Riis's work stirred public compassion for the inadequate and substandard living conditions of immigrants and the poor (Riis, 1890, 1997). Theodore Roosevelt, then mayor of New York City, praised Riis for his humanitarian work. Oddly enough, Riis did not embrace all ethnic groups or women. In his autobiography, *The Making of an American* (1901), he writes that he was going to allow his second wife a chapter in the book, but she spent too much time writing and was telling too many things, so he cut short her chapter, saying it was not good for a woman to say too much.

COURT DECISIONS, LEGISLATION, AND PUBLIC OPINION

The Boycott Cases

Court decisions during the early 1900s continued to favor employers as workers and unions continued attempts to regain some balance of power in the labor management relationship. Several cases revolved around *boycotts*, abstaining from purchasing a good or service as a means of intimidation or coercion in order to influence a firm's policies. The boycott cases such as

Danbury Hatters, Bucks Stove, and *Duplex Printing* followed upon the heels of focusing labor-related events that riveted public interest, the Passage of the Pure Food and Drug Act, the Triangle Waist Fire, and the published photography of Jacob Riis. Boycotting is another method, short of the strike, of putting pressure on an employer. These cases involved a "secondary boycott" which is boycotting a seller or a product, not just the manufacturer. These national boycott cases called to support strikes led to legal reversals for labor organizations.

Danbury, Connecticut, also known as "Hat City," was home to hat manufacturer, Dietrich Loewe, who refused to recognize the hatters' union, United Hatters' of North American (UHU). The hatters staged a nationwide strike and boycott assisted by the AFL. Having organized most of the hatters' shops in Connecticut, the union's goal was to organize the Danbury shop. Loewe sued the hatter's union for violation of the Sherman Antitrust Act by alleging the union boycott interfered with his firm's ability to effectively engage in interstate commerce, a right granted to them via the U.S. Constitution. The strike continued and was considered a secondary boycott of all firms producing hats.

In 1908, the Court ruled against the strikers, saying the UHU had violated the Sherman Antitrust Act because they had interfered with the firm's ability to move/sell product across state lines. Faced with the possibility of losing their homes, the workers' union organized a "Hatters' Day" asking for an hour's pay from members to help pay the fines. This ruling, known as the Danbury Hatters Case, had a detrimental effect on union tactics because it not only outlawed secondary boycotts but allowed individual union members to be held personally responsible for damages caused from boycotts (States, 1908, 1915).

The AFL chose to boycott the Buck's Stove and Range Company to force a test case before the Supreme Court in 1911 that would establish labor's right to assert its powers of collective action in the interest of the unionization of the U.S. economy. The test case was also capitulated into prominence by James Wallace Van Cleave, the president of Bucks Stove and Range Company and the National Association of Manufacturers (NAM), an industry trade group that lobbied for the rights of property and the rights of American business. Van Cleave wanted to crush the development of labor's power over secondary boycotts (States, 1911). According to Heimert (1953), Gompers was held in contempt of court, and the federal district court prohibited the boycott. "The conspiracy doctrine specter reappeared in the application of court injunctions halting union's actions. Strikes, union organizing and other activities were increasingly interpreted by the federal courts as restraints on interstate commerce and hence, prohibitable and punishable" (Heimert, 1953, pp. 224–226). Though the issue of secondary boycotts was favorably settled in the interests of business, Gompers, framing the issue as a constitutional God-given right of free speech, was encouraged with the passage of the Clayton Act in 1914, signed into law by President Woodrow Wilson, in which the courts announced "the labor of a human being was not a commodity or article of commerce" (Dubofsky, 2004, p. 190) and limited the federal court's injunctive powers (Bradford, 1856).

The Clayton Act removed unions from the jurisdiction of the Sherman Act, anti-trust legislation designed to break up big business monopolies such as Andrew Carnegie's Standard Oil and John Rockefeller's US Steel. The Clayton Act was hailed as the "industrial Magna Carta upon which the working people will rear their structure of individual freedom" (Michaelsen, 1953, pp. 971–972). The excitement over removing unions from the jurisdiction of the Sherman Act was short-lived because of the act's ambiguous wording allowing the Supreme Court to reinterpret that unions' actions could still be construed to restrain trade. The Court also said that strikes ended the employee-employer relationship and thereby removed the protection against injunctions for lawful employee activities. Thus the Clayton Act was ineffective.

The Duplex Printing case also weakened labor's claim against injunctions through the Clayton Act by further undermining labor's ability to conduct secondary boycotts. A Michigan-based corporation, the Duplex Printing Press Company, which made printing presses, was being struck by the International Association of Machinists (IAM) represented by Emil J. Deering and William Bramley. The IAM promoted a secondary boycott of the presses including anyone involved with hauling, handling, or installing the presses from the Michigan firm. The court found these actions interfered with Interstate Commerce and found in favor of the Michigan firm (States, 1921).

Public Opinions Begin to Change

While the general public remained less than enthusiastic in their support of trade unionism, many were nonetheless moved to sympathy for those whose plight was becoming suddenly more real and understandable to them. The fiasco at Haymarket Square and the trial that followed, the working conditions in the meatpacking industry, the threatened seizure of private homes to satisfy the judgment in the Danbury Hatters Case, and the working conditions that allowed men who were supervisors to sanction sweatshop conditions had a cumulative effect: The public began to feel that working conditions warranted for many people an organized advocacy for change. It became increasingly obvious unions could play a role in that advocacy (Fossum, 2005, p. 25). Some gains for labor followed even though the Clayton Act was less than effective. In 1915, the La Follette Seamen's Act, which limited working hours, guaranteed minimum standards of safety and cleanliness, and established the rights of crews to organize, passed (Bunker, 1995). Hailed as the Magna Carta of the seas, the legislation was in response to the sinking of the Titanic in 1912 (*Seamen's Act*, 2003). The Adamson's Act was enacted in 1916 as a measure to prevent railway workers from striking over the establishment of the eight-hour work day and overtime pay. President Wilson intervened in a challenge levied by the railroads to the Supreme Court that the legislation actually raised wages rather than limited hours by securing a promise from the railroad owners to honor the legislation. The Court eventually upheld the Adamson's Act (States, 1917). Immigration policy was also approved by Congress which restricted entry into the United States through a literacy test requiring emigrants be able to read their own language. The impetus for this legislation was the influx of poorly educated southern and eastern Europeans and Asians who were thought to be undesirable and exacerbated the idea of normative whiteness as the United Stated became embroiled in WWI ("Immigration Act of 1917," 1917).

Trade Union Success and Apathy

Prior to and during World War I, the prominence of the IWW was in decline. Their goal of abolishing the wage system didn't have much traction, and their radical activity was thought to be akin to that of the uprising in Russia called the Bolshevik Revolution in 1917. Low wages in the United States increased strike activity and inflation grew, and the public became concerned that labor might be gaining too much power. To reduce the number of strikes and to temper labor's power, the National War Labor Board was formed in 1918. Five representatives from labor and five from management formed the Board which acknowledged labor's right to organize and bargain collectively; by the end of WWI, even semiskilled laborers were earning as much as $1000 per year. The AFL's membership had grown to 4,000,000 by 1919 (Dubofsky, 2004).

The American Plan

The mid to late 1920s was a prosperous time for the United States. After the end of WWI with its immense loss of life and limb to American soldiers, war production ended, and American thoughts turned to peacetime and refraining from future wars. The underlying ideals of capitalism which promoted efficiency and consumerism were solidified by advances in the availability of credit, higher wages for skilled workers, and the general idea that most Americans now belonged to the middle class. But the news of Bolshevism and the communist threat emanating from Russia was a real concern. The IWW's demise and the charges of sedition levied against its leaders kept the thoughts of war in the American psyche. Employers associated union leaders with foreign subversives and questioned whether it was safe for workers to be represented by leaders who didn't actually live and work in their communities. The United States Steel Corporation branded union organizers in its Chicago mills as "German propagandists" and demanded that steel workers sign a Pledge of Patriotism vow prohibiting them from striking. Simultaneously, the exclusion of certain groups from mainstream America resulted in discrimination against minorities, women, and new immigrants who still held second-class citizenship in the white, patriarchal, Protestant-based middle class. The reality of divided classes was reflected in philosophical differences between labor and business. Workers viewed their lives as struggles in which hope of success was elusive, while businesses regarded their future as bright and prosperous. Yet, workers more or less accepted their situation as inevitable.

The toxic atmosphere toward organized labor was upheld by the courts and government. Labor, relegated to the status of a commodity, was simply another good to be sold by workers to employers. No protections were afforded workers in their quest for equality with employers in the labor-management relationship. Though the Supreme Court believed workers should receive a living wage, they also believed employers were not bound by law to provide any set wage. Thwarted by antiunion animus and nationalism, organized labor's membership remained stagnant or declined. Employers promoted an open shop which would allow employees to refuse to join the union, while unions promoted the closed shop which made union membership a condition of employment. The use of yellow-dog contracts was commonplace. This anti-labor environment birthed dogma known as the American Plan. The term was coined during a 1921 convention of Midwestern employers in Chicago which included the National Association of Manufacturers, chambers of commerce, and the League of Industrial Rights. The American Plan encouraged open-shop committees to protect citizens from outside labor organizers, reinforcing the idea of local control, and pitted the individualist nature of a true American against the socialist subversive of the collective. In firms where unions did emerge, employers encouraged company unions. As a result of the American Plan, union membership dropped from 5 million in 1920 to 3.5 million in 1923 (Dubofsky, 2004).

One bright spot did emerge in 1926 with the passage of the Railway Labor Act, the first major piece of labor law legislation in the United States. Because the crux of capitalism depended upon interstate commerce to transport goods across state lines, President Coolidge signed into law this legislation which was designed to reduce interruptions in the flow of goods between states and to increase industrial peace. The law guaranteed the right of railroad workers to organize, join a union, and elect bargaining representatives of their choosing without the interference or coercion of employees. The law provided a mechanism for settling major and minor disputes through mediation. Later, this Act would cover other transportation workers ("The Railway Labor Act," 1926).

The End of an Era

The 1920s might be called the decade of transition: transition from an agricultural to an industrial economy, transition from craft unionism to industrial unionism, and transition from a focus on skilled workers to a focus on the semi-skilled and unskilled worker. As businesses, courts, and the government mounted an effective assault against labor with injunctions, yellow-dog contracts, and open shops, the ever-present hand of patriarchy introduced a new form of company control known as *welfare capitalism*. The idea behind welfare capitalism was for the employer to take responsibility for the overall well-being of the employee and provide wages, working conditions, and workplace voice to labor, thus eliminating the need for an external representative union. This quasi-union was a way to undermine outside union interference with employer's ability to control the firm and the workforce. Skilled workers, in the short term, benefited from and grew to depend on company unions as their wages stabilized and their working conditions improved though the unskilled worker saw little change in his paycheck or his job. Employers gloated that welfare capitalism not only profited workers but contributed to industrial peace. But workers' dependence on company unions was short-lived with the approach of 1929's Stock Market Crash and the Great Depression which followed.

Chapter Three

Employment Relations in Historical Perspective, 1935–present

CHANGING OF THE GUARD

Politically, the AFL had failed to increase membership during the 1920s as it had failed to throw the labor vote behind Senator Robert La Follette of Wisconsin, presidential candidate who ran as an Independent candidate in 1924 when neither the Republican, or Democratic party backed labor. This crushing political defeat and the death of Samuel Gompers the same year provided an opportunity to change the direction of the labor movement, labor-management relationships, and public policy. Gompers had reigned supreme among labor for fifty years and was credited by labor and management for holding labor steady and preventing extremists from hijacking the labor movement. The reins of power were turned over to William Green who swore to follow Gompers's policies of trade unionism. His rise from miner to AFL president influenced his decision to also embrace industrial unionism as a way to maintain wages for skilled labor. Though Green believed allowing poverty wages for industrial workers would eventually affect the wages of skilled workers, he made no attempts to organize unskilled workers during his tenure. The complacency of the AFL during the decade of the 1920s was notable for its lackluster; the AFL's focus was on maintaining the status quo for skilled workers, ensuring industrial peace, and accepting welfare capitalism. Even after 1929 when the country was in the throes of industrial and economic collapse, the AFL continued to cooperate with the conservative political allies in an effort to upright a sinking national economy.

The courts generally found, in cases involving union organizing, striking, or bargaining, for the employers. But this public policy began to shift favorably toward unions in the 1930s. The shaping of public opinion toward unionism was the result of many phenomenon: the increased unemployment rate, the Stock Market Crash of 1929, and the overwhelming use of injunctive power by the courts. The only piece of federal legislation favorable to unions was the 1926 Railway Labor Act which replaced strikes with bargaining, arbitration, and mediation in the labor relationship between transportation industries and their workers. Until that point, collective bargaining agreements were only reached through voluntary efforts between labor and management. During the Hoover administration in 1932, the Norris-LaGuardia Act was passed which restricted the federal courts' power to issue injunctions against striking workers and prohibited the enforcement of yellow dog contracts by Section 2(5) of the Railway Labor Act and Section 3 of the Norris-LaGuardia Act (Twomey, 2010).

The Stock Market Crash of 1929 and the Great Depression had far-reaching effects for millions of unemployed workers struggling for survival. Numbers associated with rising unemployment, bank and factory closures, lost industrial production, and homelessness only partially reflect the direct and indirect repercussions Americans experienced during this bleak time in U.S. history. The administration of Herbert Hoover held fast to the philosophical dictum the free market would eventually right all the inequitable wrongs of capitalism and never entertained the idea of allowing government intervention to correct for market failures. Spurred by Hoover's encouragements that prosperity was just around the corner, Americans continued to believe recovery was possible. As long bread lines and soup kitchens emerged to feed millions of unemployed workers and "Hoovervilles," tent camps housing the homeless, sprang up, skilled and unskilled workers alike began to understand the severity and long-term consequences of the economic collapse. Yet, there remained a passivity among workers and unions which is difficult to explain. Little to no activity toward revolt was recorded, but political action among industrial workers did increase with the upcoming 1932 election of Roosevelt. The move away from revolution and militancy and toward a more nuanced and sophisticated approach to settling disputes was coming to fruition.

THE NEW DEAL

As Roosevelt swept into office, the necessity of focusing on the welfare of industrial workers took center stage. The validity of capitalism as an economic system which would always correct itself through the free market was disproved as evidenced by long years of joblessness, increased poverty and homelessness, and decreased production output. The idea that welfare capitalism would assure job stability, pension and health benefits, and good wages for skilled workers was undermined when capital could no longer maintain optimal production and discarded its premier program, resulting in decreased living standards for millions of workers. Roosevelt's administration was the first to underscore the necessity for labor to stand on equal footing with management in order to equalize the balance of power and ensure continued industrial peace and interstate commerce. The new policies which Roosevelt orchestrated were known as the New Deal and gave workers hope that years of adversities and reverses were coming to an end.

New Deal policies were a mix of economic measures designed to revive the economy through job creation and the restoration of Americans' confidence in banks and government. Forged by Roosevelt's Brain Trust, a group of advisors from academia and industry, the New Deal put forth several laws which included the Banking Act of 1933, the Emergency Federal Relief Administration of 1933, the Social Security Act of 1935, and what came to be known as Roosevelt's alphabet soup programs: the Works Progress Administration (WPA), the Civilian Conservation Corps (CCC), the Agricultural Adjustment Administration (AAA), and the National Industrial Recovery Act (NIRA). The NIRA was designed to create jobs and put individuals back to work. Roosevelt deemed the NRA "the most important and far-reaching legislation ever enacted by an American Congress" (Dubofsky, 2004, p. 251). The NIRA sought cooperative industrial practices by encouraging employers to set prices and industrial quotas through industrial codes. The agency formed to administer the NIRA was the National Recovery Administration (NRA). Countless industrial codes were established which made necessary multiple layers of bureaucracy to enforce and administer this law, making it very cumbersome and ineffective. Though many of the sections of the NRA were found unconstitutional by the Supreme Court in the following year, the bulwark of the legislation, Section 7(a), remained intact.

Section 7(a), which was reestablished in the Wagner Act of 1935 and remains the lynchpin of labor law, gave workers four rights: the ability to form and join a union, the right to collectively bargain, the right to be represented by a collective bargaining agent of their choice, and the right not to do any of those things. These provisions continue to be the heart and soul of labor's ability to organize today. Without Section 7(a), labor would indeed suffer. The National Relations Labor Board (NLRB), a five-person governing board appointed by the U.S. president, was created to administer and enforce the act. The prime duties of the NLRB were (and are) to certify union elections and adjudicate unjust labor charges. The Act also establishes the concept of exclusive representation. For instance, if a group of employees wish to join a union, that union, if certified, becomes the sole representative bargaining agent for those workers.

A new burst of union activity which saw millions of industrial workers join the ranks of organized labor began with the creation of Section 7(a); but the organizing euphoria was short-lived. The AFL's old guard, conscious of their mission to preserve craft unionism and their political allies within conservative government circles, marshalled their forces against the formation of industrial unions into its fold and adopted a policy of admitting newly formed unions through charters which gave little protection or clout to the new unions. Disenchanted with the AFL's intentional distance from them, new industrial unions, often filled with leaders favoring action over discourse, led successful nation-wide strikes in Toledo, Ohio, San Francisco, California, and Minneapolis-St. Paul, Minnesota. The militant nature of industrial workers in automobiles, textiles, and steel was anathema to the AFL's notion of pacifism. The initial gains industrial workers made in 1933 were dwindling away because of employers' reluctance to recognize collective bargaining rights, the hesitancy of the AFL to actively organize the industrial workforce, and the government's reluctance to provide protections for striking workers.

Business and industry did not embrace the newly granted power of labor and did everything in their power to stall its advances. The tension between employers and workers escalated because employers thought the Wagner Act would soon be found unconstitutional as had the NIRA. Businesses, particularly in steel, automobiles, and rubber, began to arm themselves against the potential of striking workers by massing an arsenal of machine guns, ammunition, and tear gas with which to assault encroaching strikers. Employer intransigence also included resisting labor's power through a public relations plan known as the Mohawk Valley Formula. This plan included fostering company unions, exploiting the difference between the AFL and the CIO, associating the leaders of labor, Walter Reuther and John Lewis, with communism and foreign influence, suggesting that a worker's freedom of choice was being compromised by the closed shop, calling the police to break up picket lines, enlisting community interests against local unions, and spending money to put anti-union legislators in office. This war-like aggression of business against labor, exposed by the La Follette Civil Liberties Committee, startled even conservatives who defended labor's rights to unionize.

Roosevelt, on the other hand, continued to justify his support of the Wagner Act because it leveraged the power of labor to stand on equal footing with management, a necessary balance for industrial peace. Public opinion, too, was on the side of labor. The public was sympathetic to the worker's plight after a century of "conspiracy laws, enforcement of yellow-dog contracts, judicial interpretations of liberty that actually nullified the individual worker's freedom, and the arbitrary use of injunctions" (Dubofsky, 2004, p. 261). Industrial unionism, the organization of all skill levels under one union, didn't really catch on prior to 1930 because of immigration which provided an unlimited supply of cheap labor, a disinterest within the AFL of organizing the unskilled, rapid industrialization which proved a fertile ground for organizing efforts, and the revolutionary mindset of industrialism.

This was very different than the approach taken by Gompers who promoted the organization of only skilled workers into craft unions through an apprenticeship with a skilled craftsman or some familiar connection. By 1935, the atmosphere was changing largely due to the Depression and legislation concerning labor-management relations.

The ability of labor to stand firm against the power of business was solidified when the Supreme Court in 1937 found the Wagner Act constitutional. Employers fully expected the Wagner Act to be found unconstitutional as had been the NIRA, and their opposition to the Wagner Act was not without validity. The American Plan, the Mohawk Valley Formula, and the illegality of the NIRA gave employers a sense that sentiment and legislation favorable to unions would never stand for long. Employers believed that unions would add major costs to their companies, an idea not without merit, so their resistance to legislation favoring organized labor was primarily for economic reasons. Employers' full-blown assault against the Act was challenged in Court in *NLRB v. Jones and Laughlin Steel Corp.* 301 U.S.1 (1937) ("NLRB v. Jones and Laughlin Steel Corporation," 1937). Chief Justice Hughes, delivering the opinion of the Court, said Jones and Laughlin Steel Corporation engaged in unfair labor practices by discriminating against members of the Beaver Valley Lodge No. 200, which was affiliated with the Amalgamated Association of Iron, Steel and Tin Workers of America, by coercing, intimidating, and interfering with the members' right to self-organize. The Court said this violation affected national, state, and local manufacturing by impeding interstate commerce and was, therefore, subject to the Commerce Clause, Article 1, Section 8, Clause 3 of the U.S. Constitution ("Commerce Clause," 1992) which is interpreted to give Congress the power to regulate interstate commerce.

The power of labor was further strengthened with the passage of the Fair Labor Standards Act of 1938 (FLSA) which set a minimum wage of 25 cents per hour, a forty-four hour standard work week, and a prohibition against the labor of children under the age of sixteen. With the passage of the FLSA, the judicial, legislative, and executive powers of government had successfully reversed centuries of discriminatory power against labor and set in motion a recognition that the long-term well-being of society depended on a balanced industrial relations policy which assured the longevity of democracy and capitalism.

The new authority granted to labor became somewhat problematic for craft unionism because of its long-held belief in the organization of craft workers at the expense of industrial workers. The philosophical debate centered on whether to embrace the opportunity to organize the unorganized and grow labor's ranks which would require diverting resources to mobilizing and away from political action or to maintain the status quo and strengthen craft unionism as a way to prevent discord among labor's ranks and grow union ranks from within. This polarized dichotomy was publically show-cased in the arguments between William Green, the AFL's president and John Lewis, president of the United Mine Workers (UMW), an ardent spokesman for organizing the unskilled worker. Barrages of name calling, disparaging remarks, and hateful comments were hurled like missiles be-tween Green, who defended craft unionism and portrayed Lewis as a dictator who wanted to control all of organized labor, and Lewis, who, stifled in efforts to organize the unskilled as members of the AFL, described Green as a failure who did not understand the national implications for the labor movement.

The AFL convention, the governing body of the federation held every five years, met in 1935 in Atlantic City, New Jersey. The tension between shifting resources toward organizing the masses versus maintaining trade unionism took center stage. Green, following the auspices of his predecessor, Gompers, continued to stand firm in trade-union tradition while Lewis un-equivocally denounced traditional policy and waxed eloquently in his sup-port for mass organization. The emotional intenseness of the two sides was epitomized when the verbiage escalated to fever pitch with Lewis engaging in a fist fight with William Hutcheson, president of the Carpenters Union and advocate for trade unionism. This irreconcilable split between trade unionism and industrial unionism led to Lewis's break with the AFL during the 1935 convention, and along with Phillip Murray of the UMW, formed the Con-gress of Industrial Organization (CIO) in order to promote the recognition and acceptance of mass industrial organizing and modern collective bargain-ing.

The United Automobile Workers (UAW), originally formed as a federal union under the AFL, broke ranks with the AFL and joined the CIO. Under the leadership of Homer Martin, the auto workers, who commanded higher wages than other manufacturers but suffered from tedious jobs and fatigue, sought recognition from General Motors (GM). In a series of sit-down strikes, the workers eventually won recognition of their union and GM agreed not to discriminate against union members. The sit down strike was a new tool employed by workers in which they simply did not leave the factory after their shifts, but, rather, sat down on the factory floors. To oust the sitting workers, GM would need to use force and that might mean a bloody and politically unacceptable scene. The strike began on December 30, 1936, and ended on February 11, 1937, with the Treaty of Detroit, a collective bargaining agreement recognizing the UAW as the bargaining representative of the GM workers for the term of the agreement. For the first time in history, an industrial union had won over an open-shop agreement. The impact of this agreement reverberated throughout the auto industry and beyond and was the catalyst for future unionization efforts in other industries.

The CIO also set out to organize in the textile, steel, and rubber industries. The steelworkers established the Steelworkers' Organizing Committee (SWOC) in 1936 which actively held meetings, distributed literature, and canvassed in attempts to organize. Their victories, though, were not without trouble. In the spring of 1937, SWOC called a strike in multiple steel plants which resulted in thousands of steel workers walking off the job. The strike was successfully thwarted by antiunion tactics such as attacks against picketers, tear gassing of union buildings, and encounters with police and militia. Though strikers went back to work, dissention continued to swell, and violence erupted at a peaceful picnic and parade at the Republic Steel Mill on Memorial Day in 1937. An unprovoked police attack upon the workers and their families resulted in forty injuries; ten strikers were killed by the Chicago police (Hogan, 2014). Known as the Memorial Day Massacre, the event did little to gain support for organized labor because of the resurgence of strong public antiunion animus against industrial unionism and the CIO.

Labor Power Fluctuates

Differences between the philosophical approaches to organizing became more pronounced as labor gained power. The CIO succeeded in bringing hundreds of thousands of new workers under the tent of organized labor which is something the AFL had never done. The exclusionary practices of the AFL which generally rejected the unskilled, minorities and women from its ranks, acted as a sifting mechanism for potential craft unionists who wanted to maintain purity within the federation. The inclusionary practices of the CIO, on the other hand, welcomed all workers in the ranks. The CIO was well aware of the importance of government intervention in worker protections via common and statutory law whereas the AFL had more or less shunned the intrusion of government in laws which would assure minimum wages, pensions, and unemployment insurance. The CIO realized political involvement was necessary to hold on to existing economic gains which were now intricately woven into social gains while the AFL believed political involvement was best left to politicians. The chasm between the AFL and the CIO was too great for their ranks to be joined, and the stalemate between the two continued. Jurisdictional disputes between labor unions over turf became commonplace when unions engaged in raiding each other's ranks for members. This practice, which saw simultaneous representation by two unions who asserted their members were entitled by contract to perform certain work, was outlawed in several states.

Once again, public opinion about labor began to shift in a negative direction. Industrial workers voted en masse for Roosevelt in 1936 because they felt his policies had allowed them economic and social recovery and more or less hitched their wagon to the Democratic Party while the CIO publicized and promised their support for candidates and policies which supported labor. Conservatives proclaimed the CIO was the breeding ground and conduit for socialism and communism. Lewis, who didn't see communism as a threat to labor, capitalized on the ability of communism to bring more workers into the industrial unionized fold. The discovery some union staff positions were held by communists who didn't support Roosevelt's nonaggression pact in 1939 allowed employers to brand labor as socialist and non-patriotic. The public continued to be concerned a communist element had infiltrated the CIO's ranks and that leftists would emerge in both union and political leadership positions. Lewis, who could deliver labor's vote to Roosevelt's 1940 presidential election, expected reciprocity from Roosevelt in the form of support for labor's causes but became disgruntled with the Roosevelt administration for a perceived lack of support in return for the campaign assistance given by labor in 1936 and shifted his support to Republican challenger, Wendell Wilkie. Lewis believed New Deal policies had failed to provide government assistance for the CIO and threatened to leave the presidency of the CIO if Roosevelt were elected a third term. Roosevelt was reelected, and Lewis left his position as CIO president though he retained the presidency of the UMW. Lewis's successor, Philip Murray, threw his support behind Roosevelt's policy of extending aid to the Allies. This attack against organized labor might have been quite successful if WWII had not begun in 1941.

WORLD WAR II BEGINS

As Europe marched toward war with Germany, the United States debated over whether to take an interventionist approach and provide support for the Allies or take an isolationist approach to safeguard Americans. The war focus shifted the nation's attention to foreign policy and away from domestic policy. European war orders increased the need for new production in defense industries which created the need for more U.S. workers to produce ammunitions, planes, and other supplies. Economic recovery including decreased unemployment, wage increases, and the need for skilled workers followed and spurred a national recovery which New Deal policies had been unable do. The AFL, the CIO, and industry promised to cooperate with business during WWII in order to meet the production needs of the war, but labor, recalling the backlash it experienced after WWI, warned business it expected a continuation of New Deal policies maintaining and strengthening collective bargaining. During 1940, labor and management did cooperate, but the truce was short-lived. A growing concern over labor's power continued to grow, and business once again dug in its heels to halt labor's progress. Strike activity rose as more than "4,300 strikes began during 1941 involving 8 percent of the workforce" (Fossum, 2005, p. 49), and the public viewed labor's demands as secondary to national defense. Fearing decreased production and the inability to deliver wartime goods to Europe, Roosevelt established the National Defense Mediation Board (NDMB), which only had power to produce non-binding resolutions, to settle labor disputes. The NDMB was able to resolve a major miner's strike which threatened to shut down coal production and pitted Lewis against Roosevelt, who was toying with the idea of supporting antistrike legislation, but overall had little effect in inducing industrial peace. The growing tide of negativity against labor was stalled with the Japanese attack on Pearl Harbor, Hawaii, on December 7, 1941. The United States had entered WWII.

Wartime prosperity endured, and for the next four years, Americans saw full employment, higher wages, and job security. Replacing male workers serving in the Armed Forces, women and minorities entered the workforce in droves and manned the skilled factory jobs which produced wartime equipment, planes, and tanks. The workforce and the government, united in their efforts to save democracy and eradicate communism, cooperated as never before and agreed to a no-strike/no-lockout provision during the war, diplomatic conflict resolution, and, by Executive Order, the establishment of the National War Labor Board (NWLB) to resolve unsettled disputes leading to the disruption of wartime production. From 1941 to 1945, fewer man hours were lost to strikes and work stoppages than during any previous time period in American history. Though strike activity did occur during this period, the intensity and longevity of the strikes was diminished. The NWLB instituted the maintenance of membership principle which required union workers to pay dues to their union as a condition of employment and a cost-of-living raise commensurate with the cost-of-living index. The passage of the Economic Stabilization Act of 1942 stymied the cost-of-living raises when congressional approval resulted in only a 15 percent wage increase. As living costs skyrocketed, unions and workers rebelled against the lower wage raises, setting the stage for future labor unrest.

Though no-strike pledges were made, strike activity escalated in 1945. Fossum (2002) writes 4,750 strikes involving 3,470,000 workers lost 38 million work days that year (p. 49). Fearful strikes would cripple national security, Congress passed the War Labor Disputes Act which allowed the government to seize striking plants in defense industries, required a thirty-day notice to the NWLB prior to a strike, and required the NWLB to monitor the strikes. The war experience allowed benefits to take the place of wage increases thus becoming part of labor contracts. Opportunities were also given to women and minorities, who manned the mills. As the war came to a close, labor and employers again clashed, and even more strike activity occurred. The effects of these strikes were wage increases in the coal, rail, steel, and auto industries spurred by labor leaders like Walter Reuther, strike leader of the UAW who played a dominant role in the dispute between General Motors (GM) and the UAW, and John Lewis, president of the UMW.

Truman created a fact-finding board to investigate charges levied by both sides in labor disputes as a way to circumvent strikes which would cripple the postwar economy; the board helped to settle disputes in most industries other than mining. When Lewis and Truman squared off in a conflict over operation of the coal mines, Truman was granted an injunction against striking miners, and the government took over the mines. The Supreme Court sided with Truman, and the miners went back to work. Subsequently a later contract between the UMW and the mine owners met most of the miners' demands. Another strike between the railway workers and the railway owners was narrowly averted when Truman threatened to take over the railways. Even though a settlement was reached, Truman proposed Congressional legislation which would allow injunctions against strikers, eliminate strikers' seniority rights, and conscript strikers in the armed services. Though the legislation didn't survive Senatorial approval, labor vehemently disapproved of and condemned Truman's actions.

Changing the Balance of Power

The postwar accord reflected a more powerful labor than at any other point in history. The postwar industrial landscape featured highly productive firms with rising profits, lower unemployment and poverty rates, and the ability to accumulate capital. Business and labor fleshed out collective bargaining agreements which ensured business a stable and skilled workforce for the duration of the contract and ensured labor a steady standard of living for an industrial workforce. But business complained there now existed an inability on their part to effectively manage operations, and they sought to once against shift the balance of power in their favor. After the strike activity during WWII and the subsequent wage increases experienced by industry, employers felt organized labor's power needed clarifying, and the public sided with business and conservatives who believed labor had too much power. The Wagner Act of 1935, which addressed employers' unfair labor practices but did not address union's unfair labor practices, was amended to reflect union's unfair labor practices in the Labor Management Relations Act, known by its sponsors as the Taft-Hartley Act in 1947. This legislation expanded employee rights to refrain from union activity beyond membership or paying dues. Taft-Hartley was also the seed bed for right-to-work legislation which effectively disemboweled the closed shop. To administer this legislation, the Federal Mediation and Conciliation Service (FMCS) was created to settle unresolved contractual disputes. Secondary boycotts became illegal. Corporations and labor unions were enjoined from making political contributions, and federal employers were forbidden to strike. Unions, naturally, opposed the legislation because it took away protections they deemed vital to their existence. The legislation was passed over Truman's veto, and the government became the referee between employers and labor.

Even though Taft-Hartley proved very unpopular with rank and file workers, the actual number of strikes and lost work days decreased considerably during 1947. A tight labor market, rising wages, and growing union membership served as a backdrop for improved labor management relationships which saw business profits and workers' wages rise. In return for long-term contracts which promised companies a dedicated and knowledgeable workforce, business provided cost of living adjustments and forms of unemployment insurance as well as health care and pension protections, and vacation and holiday benefits. Labor, remembering their stinging defeat after WWI as well as after Taft-Hartley, continued to rail against the provisions of the Taft-Hartley Act through legislative efforts to amend or rescind the Act. Labor also recognized that a greater involvement in politics through a cooperative stance between the AFL and the CIO was necessary if labor was to maintain and advance the gains it had so painstakingly won. Both fully supported Truman's foreign policy which impeded further Soviet imperialism and communist aggression and distanced themselves from communist influences within their ranks. On the domestic front, the AFL and the CIO marshalled their forces behind social welfare legislation, helped expand the social security program, and raised the minimum wage established by the Fair Labor Standards Act. Both labor federations now supported industrial unionism as foundational to the labor movement and were soon to experience internal organizational changes which would lead to further cooperation.

Reassessment and Merger

The old guard in the AFL and the CIO, William Green and Phillip Murray, died unexpectedly of natural causes in November, 1952. The time was ripe for new leaders who had different visions for the emergence of the labor movement. George Meany, long-time secretary-treasurer of the AFL, and Walter Reuther, president of the UAW, took over the presidencies of the AFL and the CIO, respectively. Both men were visionaries who believed the success and longevity of their federations was dependent upon a more cooperative stance. The two leaders first agreed to a two-year no-raid provision which discouraged union piracy and then moved toward forming a committee to explore a potential merger. The time for marshaling the forces of the craft unions and the industrial unions was at hand. During 1955, the AFL merged with the CIO to form the *AFL-CIO*, a federation which would direct labor's energies toward unity. Meany took the reins of the AFL's presidency while Reuther became vice president of the Industrial Union Department formed to ensure the organization of the unskilled. The goals of the AFL-

CIO were to organize the unorganized, rout out corruption and communist infiltration, and eliminate racial discrimination. Because Taft-Hartley had increased labor's need to take a more proactive stance in legislative activity, monies and energy were channeled into electing pro-labor candidates to office. Labor and management negotiated more contracts covering more years to provide stability to the employment relationship. Most large corporations, during this period, were resigned to labor's power; thus, wages and productivity increased along with the living standards of many Americans. The effect of the merger was to increase the harmony between labor and capital so much so that labor leaders and business executives were vested in ensuring business remain profitable in order for labor to extract concessions from them during contract negotiations. This organizational reformation of labor's structure led to labor's increased interest in preserving gains won for their members while relegating gains through social programs to the back burner.

A Less Militant Approach

The new direction in which Meany and Reuther drove the labor movement was a reaction to a different economic, social, and political landscape characterized by a growing national economy, an increased introduction of technology into the workplace, and the threat of communism. Workers, especially those working under union contracts, enjoyed higher wages, better benefits, and increased living standards yet were faced with potential unemployment as business augmented production lines with new forms of technology which reduced the need for human capital. As jobs in mining, manufacturing, and transportation industries manned by blue collar workers declined, jobs in retail, service, and government sectors held by white collar workers increased. Job growth developed along parallel tracks with white males holding blue collar, better-paid jobs and women and minorities holding service industry and lower-paid jobs. There seemed to be little interest among blue and white collar workers to unionize when business was amiable to providing good pay and benefits in return for employee loyalty to the firm. Union membership reached its zenith in 1956 with around 35 percent of the workforce organized but began to decline in 1957. The effects of Taft-Hartley which allowed states to determine their own right-to-work status provided cover for southern and western states to outlaw closed or union shops, making it more difficult for workers to engage in union activities. Labor threw its full support behind political candidates who favored labor policies and established the *Committee on Political Education* (COPE) as a mechanism to fund such support, but the results were disappointing as efforts to repeal or amend Taft-Hartley were unsuccessful, and membership numbers continued to decline.

Equally disturbing for organized labor were the charges levied against unions for their real and perceived internal corruption and association with organized crime which undermined American's faith in organized labor. The AFL-CIO's attempt to purge from its ranks the likes of Dave Beck and Jimmy Hoffa, Teamster presidents who engaged in racketeering, tax evasion, jury tampering, embezzlement, and violence did little to bring the Teamsters in line with acceptable federation practices. The AFL-CIO wanted changes in their internal oversight operations with which the Teamsters, the Bakers, and the Laundry Workers didn't agree. They were expelled from the federation in 1957. The criminal actions of the Teamsters' international leaders, though, should not reflect on the thousands of locals across the country which performed their duties admirably.

Yet, public opinion is difficult to control, and organized labor received a black eye because of these actions. Corruption in the Bakery and Confectionery Workers Union, the United Textile Workers, and other unions confirmed to the government and the public that organized labor could not effectively police itself and needed external oversight. This discovery led to legislation which placed strict financial guidelines on organized labor and gave the government fiduciary oversight over unions. Known as the Landrum-Griffin Act or the Labor-Management Reporting and Disclosure Act (LMRDA) of 1959, the legislation also strengthened the laws governing secondary boycotts and picketing, controlled ex-felons and Communists from holding union office for five years after their release, and could place a wayward union into trusteeship if its financial affairs were not in order. The intent of the bill was to protect the rank and file from unscrupulous financial dealings, but the reality of the bill was closely monitored financial oversight to which no other organization must submit. Incorporated in the LMRDA was a Workers' Bill of Rights which allowed the rank and file to be more transparent, democratic, and responsive in the conduct of union affairs and promised discipline for misuse of funds. The effect of this legislation was to more deeply involve the government in internal union affairs and expose the limited power of the AFL-CIO to control its membership. In 1989 the Justice Department, via the Racketeer Influenced and Corrupt Organization Act (RICO), gained oversight over Teamster elections and financial operation through 1996.

The battle between labor and management over control of the work processes and the introduction of technology continued throughout the late 1950s and early 1960s as epitomized by a major strike in the steel industry. The USW adamantly refused to concede on issues of wages and work rules during the summer of 1959 and walked off the job. President Eisenhower, under the umbrella of Taft-Hartley, ordered the courts to issue an injunction against the striking workers forcing them to return to work. Confident another strike would occur when the injunction ended, US Steel settled with the USW in a compromise which retained work rules and increased wages, pensions, and insurance. This victory symbolized the strength labor could muster against business but was in no way a precursor of the things to come. Unions, faced with technological introductions which eliminated workers' jobs, accepted guarantees of earnings rather than guarantees of jobs. This tactic ensured current workers an income in lieu of income for future workers or future jobs. This constraint on blue collar and trade-oriented jobs shifted uneducated and unskilled workers into lower-paying service jobs with horrible working conditions while highly skilled workers continued to gravitate toward white collar, professional jobs.

Automation and guaranteed income constraints affected minority workers more than it affected white workers. Minority workers who had blue collar jobs were squeezed out of the workforce through automation, and unskilled, uneducated minorities were relegated to the ranks of lower-paying jobs. Women, a growing segment of the workforce and generally noted as pink collar workers, also worked for low wages as did teenagers. Millions of these workers lived in poverty and were often known as "the other America," a massive number of citizens outside the set of unionized and professional workers to whom Kennedy and the Great Frontier and Johnson and the War on Poverty directed their social, progressive programs of job training and public works. Union workers were among the few whose wages and benefits increased as did their standard of living. The income levels between unionized workers and some professional workers blurred though there still existed social divisions between blue and white collar workers. Blue collar workers tended to join fraternal orders, supported traditional male-female social roles, spent time at home with their families, and gravitated toward left-leaning politics, while white collar workers preferred civic organizations, affective relationships, and right-leaning political affiliations. This then was the indistinct backdrop for Civil Rights legislation supported by labor. Though the AFL-CIO had internally engaged in exclusionary practices throughout its existence, it presented a united front in the fight for voter enfranchisement and applauded President Johnson when he signed the Voting Rights Act in 1965.

The decade of the 1960s proved to be a tumultuous time for the United States with the assassination of President John Kennedy, Martin Luther King, and Senator Robert Kennedy. Other significant events included the riots at the 1968 Democratic convention in Chicago and the entry of the United States into the Vietnam War when the USS *Maddox*, conducting an intelligence mission, was attacked in the Gulf of Tonkin by three North Vietnamese torpedo boats. Labor relations, couched in the social and political unrest during this time, moved away from the rather peaceful accord labor and management had enjoyed for the last three decades in which "a relative balance of power, mutual acceptance of conflicting interests, and compensation gains offset by rising productivity and profits" (Hogler, 2004, p. 170) provided an environment of relative stability. This accord was soon to be displaced by economic upheavals featuring rising inflation, higher unemployment, a shift from well-paid manufacturing jobs to lower-paying service jobs, and employer animus toward unions.

LABOR IN CRISIS AND TRANSITION

The 1970s were a complex and difficult time for organized labor. Productivity was high but wages were declining. The reasons for this economic turnaround from previous decades were the energy (oil) crisis in which oil shortages and price increases caused Americans to tighten their belts in energy conservation, the Vietnam War's costs, inflation, unemployment of 10 percent, and the influx of automobiles, steel, electronics, and textile imports from abroad. President Nixon attempted to combat inflation by setting wage and price controls which temporarily helped, but when the controls were lifted, inflation returned with a vengeance. Exacerbating inflation was an oil embargo imposed on the United States by the Organization of Petroleum Exporting Countries (OPEC) nations, a group of Persian Gulf Arab countries embroiled in conflict with Israel, who elevated the price of crude oil to such extremes that an energy crisis ensued in the United States, raising petroleum-based product prices even higher. As the Watergate scandal forced Nixon from office and ushered Gerald Ford into the presidency, economic conditions worsened, unemployment rose, poverty increased, and purchasing power parity declined.

The decade of the 1970s saw American workers' standard of living decrease, forcing multiple family members into the workforce. The two-wage-earner family became the norm, and the idea of a living wage was fast becoming elusive. Husbands often worked two jobs, while wives often worked outside the household. Consequently the workforce began to change as more women and younger workers manned the available factory and service jobs. Home life changed as well with fewer hours devoted to family time and more hours devoted to work. Heavily industrialized industries such as automobiles and steel were greatly affected by import competition from Asian markets who could produce and sell quality products to U.S. consumers more cheaply than could U.S. producers. In order to compete with foreign producers, new technologies and automation were introduced into manufacturing processes, resulting in the need for fewer workers. Mass layoffs and plant closings followed, leaving cities and towns which depended on manufacturing as their life blood little more than ghost towns. The deindustrialization of the United States was underway.

One important feature of U.S. deindustrialization was the antiunion animus of employers toward organized labor. Employer strategies to discourage and prevent their employees from forming unions increased in intensity as businesses searched for ways to reduce costs and increase profits. Firms began moving operations abroad in search of cheap labor and fewer environmental regulations. Offshoring production decimated the electronic, textile and garment industries and resulted in the losses of hundreds of thousands of unionized jobs. The exodus of American workers from these industries created a space for resurgent sweatshops on the east and west coasts into which immigrants, legal and illegal, were funneled, paid slave wages, and worked in inhuman conditions.

President Carter, faced with domestic economic stagnation, capital fluidity, electronic communication exchanges, and global competition, attempted to placate his three most important constituencies, labor, women, and minorities, but was faced with economic challenges of inflation and rising interest rates. He chose to implement policies which had little cost such as promoting equal rights for women but failed to deliver on high-cost issues such as job training and creation and improved social transfer payments for those in poverty, thus alienating labor and minorities. His efforts to pass labor law legislation in a Democratic Congress and Senate which would have strengthened the NLRA failed and signaled the declining role of organized labor in the Democratic Party. As tensions tightened between labor, government, and management, Carter lost his 1980 presidential reelection bid to Ronald Reagan.

Reagan was swept into office by Reagan Republicans and Democrats who were mostly white Protestant consumers who detested government handouts, obeyed the law, believed in gun rights, and paid their taxes. Capitalizing on fears that organized labor was a special interest group whose wage and benefit demands would cripple the economic structure of free-market capitalism, Reagan, a former actor, union member, and head of the Screen Writers' Guild, appealed to race-conscious voters that white workers and their tax dollars were being exploited by "welfare parasites" (Dubofsky, 2004, p. 389), union wages came at the expense of non-union workers, and Latin American and Asian immigrants, legal and illegal, were taking American jobs.

Reagan, along with Paul Volcker, Carter's head of the Federal Reserve, implemented fiscal and monetary policies which came to be known as Reaganomics in which deficit spending and enormous defense expenditures initially created a recession but eventually curtailed inflation and lowered unemployment while simultaneously producing stagnant wages and incomes. These policies shepherded in an economic period of wealth and income disparity not seen since the 1920s. Reagan proposed and passed a huge personal and corporate income tax cut. A by-product of this tax cut was to make business expenditures very costly. The Federal Reserve Bank raised short-term interest rates well above 15 percent in an effort to control the money supply and thereby inflation. These reverse Robin Hood strategies essentially took away from the poor and gave to the rich.

Reagan also effectively undermined the strike as a tool for organized labor in 1981 during the Professional Air Traffic Controllers Organization (PATCO) strike, when he fired all the air traffic controllers and replaced them with strikebreakers under the *MacKay Radio* decision of 1938. Employers then came to believe that if the president was willing to replace economic strikers, they would face little resistance if they adopted the same practices. Unions had no experience with this defensive position; after all, the labor accord had lasted from 1930 until 1980. Coupled with the changing structure of labor's metamorphose from a manufacturing base to a knowledge base, labor's ability to respond was significantly diminished.

Juridical interpretations and court appointments also affected labor's ability to respond to corporate attacks against union organizing and mobilizing. Findings against labor in unfair labor practice and representative election cases continued to increase with the presidential appointments of antiunion board members to the NLRB during the Reagan and subsequent Bush administrations. Federal judges rendered verdicts against the rights of workers and for the rights of property owners, and Supreme Court decisions mandated the use of grievance and arbitration machinery, if it existed, in place of strikes, brought unions under anti-trust legislation, increased the use of injunctions which had been mostly outlawed by Norris-LaGuardia in 1932, and generally weakened the rights of workers to act collectively.

Some gains for unions existed in the public sector which saw its membership increase to 36 percent in 1978 (Dubofsky, 2004, p. 391). Public workers such as teachers, firefighters, policemen, and federal and state employees joined the American Federation of State, County, and Municipal Employees (AFSCME), the American Federation of Teachers (AFT), the National Education Association (NEA), and the American Federation of Government Employees (AFGE). Since females primarily dominated these public institutions, women moved into leadership roles and introduced the concept of "comparable worth," the notion that gender should not play a role in wage-rate discrepancies for similar jobs and that women's job concerns are family and worker concerns. These ideas led to conversations about employment law, work regulations, and benefits for all workers.

Organized labor's ability to grow continued to diminish as manufacturing jobs declined, firms offered comparable wages, benefits, and job security to workers in lieu of unionizing, and employers moved into a global competitive arena in which offshoring and outsourcing became the norm. Practicing an alternative form of industrial relations, many high-tech firms offered to workers pseudo-union benefits such as various forms of internal job security, higher wages, health insurance, and company retirement plans. In return for employee loyalty, these firms adopted and practiced forms of participatory management such as shared decision making between management and labor, shifting job assignments, and teamwork. Borrowed from the Japanese and known as the Toyota Model, this organizational work structure eliminated layers of bureaucracy between upper management and lower-level workers streamlining the manufacturing process by reducing production time, errors, and redundancy, and practiced what is known as lean, mean manufacturing. Successfully used in the Asian auto market to reduce research, development, inventory, and delivery costs, the Toyota Model was touted as profit maximizing by reducing the cost of labor and warehousing and was implemented in many U.S. manufacturing firms.

The influx of Japanese automobiles into the American market and the Japanese auto transplants situated in the United States using nonunion American workers forced U.S. auto makers to adopt the Toyota Model. Because U.S. auto makers could produce more vehicles than they could sell, the Big Three, General Motors, Ford, and Chrysler, shed excess capacity, downsized, and laid off workers in order to be more competitive with the Japanese who provided job security to their workforce in exchange for labor flexibility. This tactic diminished the UAW's ability to use the strike as a weapon during contract negotiations, furthering weakening the union's position in the auto market.

Another reason labor's ability to unionize declined was the view that workers could achieve redress of their grievances through litigation rather than union action. Title VII of the Civil Rights Act of 1964 banned employment discrimination on the basis of race and sex and defined protected groups of people who could benefit from this protection, so aggrieved workers could now, individually or collectively, seek solutions through the courts and not organized labor. Many workers felt this to be quicker and more satisfactory than a grievance and arbitration procedure.

Federal industrial deregulation played a huge part in organized labor's inability to organize and successfully negotiate contracts in the transportation, communication, and energy industries. Deregulation removes governmental barriers such as environmental and financial restrictions on industries and opens the door for participation, thus increasing competition. The argument for deregulation is that business can operate more efficiently and at a lower cost if not required to comply with costly regulations such as safe disposal of hazardous waste or consumer protection. Arguments against deregulation are that it causes wide volatility in markets and provides an unreliable product source. Regulations prevent environmental degradation and financial instability, maintain a standard of quality for services, and create a level playing field for competition. Anti-union rhetoric was similar to the early 1900 mantra that the free market could and would correct any imperfections in the economic system and should be left to do so.

Business used an arsenal of strategies to prevent unions from forming or growing by engendering a corporate culture in which management and labor were all one big family; using alternative industrial relations and modern human resources management, business dangled company-funded retirement plans, health and wellness clubs, and internal job security before employees, and then hired anti-union attorneys and union-busting consultants to convince workers unions were detrimental to their relationship with the firm. Coupled with the anti-union animus of conservative legislators and growing public anathema against unions, labor seemed unable to marshal even enough power to protect its workers' interests.

During the decade of the 1990s and under the administration of President Clinton, several attempts to pass pro-union legislation failed, yet policies which lowered the federal deficit and interest rates and increased tax rates for the wealthy set the stage for a tight labor market in which unemployment fell, and the median family income rose. Yet incomes did not necessarily increase because of higher wages but from working more hours, working overtime, or increasing the number of family members in the workforce. Increased work loads of American workers, who now worked more hours per year than their foreign counterparts, had the indirect consequence of producing higher individual and family stress levels resulting in physical and mental exhaustion, child and elder care issues, and a consumptive drive to "keep up with the Joneses." Consequently debt levels increased as never before. The wealth and income disparity experienced during this period widened exponentially as CEOs of major firms raked in 300 times more than the average wage earner. According to the Census Bureau, the share of aggregate income for the top 20 percent of earners in 1990 was 46.6 percent and rose to 51 percent in 2012 while the top 5 percent of earners in that group earned 18.5 percent in 1990 and 22.3 percent in 2012 (Bureau, Census, 2012). The aggregate income for the lowest 20 percent of earners in 1990 was 3.8 percent and dropped to 3.2 percent in 2012 (Bureau, Census, 2012). Wealth disparities reflected an even greater gap. But greater income and wealth inequity didn't seem to stir American workers to action. The labor movement did have a few successes in industries immune to offshoring and outsourcing such as health and hospitality, but the majority of labor's efforts in transportation, steel, automobiles, and construction were unproductive.

LABOR'S STRUCTURAL AND ORGANIZATIONAL RESPONSE

A new strategy for revitalization of the labor movement surfaced in 1995 at the AFL-CIO convention in Las Vegas, Nevada. Held every five years to elect officers, introduce policy changes, and amend organizational structure, the convention, the guiding law of the federation, replaced retiring President Lane Kirkland with John Sweeney, former president of the Service Employees International Union (SEIU). Noted for increasing membership in the SEIU through mobilization tactics and representation of large numbers of women and minorities, Sweeney's expansive agenda called for more money to be channeled into mobilization drives, more training for student organizers, a Center for Strategic Campaigns to help coordinate national contract campaigns, and stronger outreach to central labor councils and state federations. He also eliminated some constitutional and administrative departments. Yet union membership did not increase during Sweeney's first term in office and few inroads were made politically with the Democratic Party.

Dissatisfaction soon set in with Sweeny's policies which were seen as punishing those who did not support his election. A group headed by Andy Stern, current president of the SEIU and friend of Sweeny, broke away from the AFL-CIO and formed the New Unity Partnership (NUP) as did the Teamsters, the Laborers, the United Food and Commercial Workers (UFCW), and the Carpenters. The NUP recommended structural, organizational, and financial changes which would consolidate or eliminate departments, channel even more money into organizing, and merge smaller unions into larger unions. Stern abandoned the NUP prior to the 2005 convention saying its purpose of promoting discussion had been fulfilled. He then announced the formation of the Change to Win Coalition (CWC) comprised of the SEIU, Teamsters, UFCW, the Laborers, the Carpenters, UFW, and UNITE-HERE. During the 2005 convention, the Teamsters, the UFCW, UNITE-HERE, and the SEIU disaffiliated with the AFL-CIO and the other members boycotted the convention. These unions regrouped under a new Change to Win federation. Sweeney retired in 2009 and Richard Trumka became president of the AFL-CIO.

The beginning of the new millennium saw an end to economic prosperity, primarily resulting from higher oil prices and lagging wages, as Republicans took over the White House, the Congress, and the Senate. The AFL-CIO had supported Al Gore, Clinton's Vice President, in his 2000 presidential election bid against George Bush. The results of the vote hinged on a close vote in Florida which triggered a recount. The infamous "hanging chads," indentations on ballots which voters punched with a stylus, were subjected to individual scrutiny by election officials in four counties. Ballot counts were litigated by Florida's Supreme Court and the U.S. Supreme Court which found in favor of Bush thus giving Florida's Electoral College votes to Bush even though Gore won the popular vote. Bush felt no compunction to associate with the AFL-CIO, and the first year of the Bush presidency saw a 10 percent tax cut for the wealthiest Americans. This then was the economic landscape as America entered the fall of 2001.

The disastrous event of September 11, 2001, in which terrorists demolished the World Trade Center in New York City had profound effects upon American workers and the institutions which govern them. A symbol of American financial security and power, the World Trade Center represented American's national and international strength in financial markets. The phrase "Bent but not Broken" surfaced on posters and billboards to reflect that though the Twin Towers may have been destroyed, American resilience and spirit could not be diminished. Yet 3,000 people lost their lives that day, and hundreds of thousands more lost jobs and financial stability. Of necessity, national attention was diverted from domestic economic issues to fighting terrorism on an international scale. To worsen matters, the stock market, predicated on creative accounting practices based on fictitious holdings by "high tech" firms, took a nose dive, catapulting major corporations like Enron and Worldcom into bankruptcy. With internal corporate fraud exposed as well as public disclosure of the lavish salaries corporate officials enjoyed, investor confidence dwindled and profits fell. A domino effect ensued with thousands of firms shedding excess capacity, downsizing, or closing their doors. Fifteen million Americans found themselves out of work over the next several years, and America entered into the Great Recession, a period of time from 2007–2010 comparable to the Great Depression of the 1930s.

The Great Recession was the perfect backdrop for President Bush to continue his onslaught against organized labor. The creation of the Department of Homeland Security in 2003, which consolidated twenty-two federal departments and agencies in order to streamline and coordinate a national strategy for safeguarding the country, allowed the President to waive collective bargaining rights and civil service rules for thousands of federal workers and move toward the privatization of thousands of federal jobs in the name of national security. The administration claimed collective bargaining was incompatible with the fight against terrorism which necessitated a flexible workforce. Republican animus against union rights for federal employees, the appointment of anti-union board members and judges to the NLRB and the courts, and the systematic move toward privatization and tax cuts for the wealthy further weakened labor's ability to gain power in the labor management relationship.

The election of President Barack Obama in 2008 signaled a turn in the economic policies which had so devastated the United States in the previous eight years. Unemployment averaging 10 percent, millions of home foreclosures and medical bankruptcies, and increasing levels of poverty served as a testament to the previous administration's misguided policies. Working with a Democratic Congress and Senate, President Obama attempted to pass the Employee Free Choice Act (EFCA) in 2010 which would have amended the NLRA by establishing a more efficient system enabling workers to form, join, or assist labor organizations and impose financial sanctions on employers committing unfair labor practices during organizing drives, but the legislation failed to receive enough votes for passage. The AFL-CIO's relationship with Obama cooled somewhat after failure to pass the EFCA, resulting in less support for the Democratic Party in Obama's 2012 reelection campaign. Also antagonistic relationships between the Obama administration and the AFL-CIO resulted from Obama's support of existing free-trade agreements and expanding free-trade agreements with Panama, Columbia, and South Korea which focus on global trade and the free market instead of job creation, a stalwart concern of labor.

The state of the American labor movement remains in flux as efforts by employers and conservatives favoring globalization and the free market to dismantle organized labor remain on the corporate agenda. Most likely, organized labor will continue to be pummeled by federal and state anti-union and anti-worker legislation in the name of capitalism and globalization. As long as corporations are able to exercise almost total control of the labor management relationship, labor unions, workers' associations, and work councils will remain weak. Labor is not without its occasional success in organizing, but on the whole, the labor movement needs to rethink it strategies for survival. Coupling with other social movements, such as women's, immigrants', or minorities' rights movements would be a step in the right direction. Moving away from site-specific organizing and organizing by general industry, such as all textile workers or all metal workers, might also prove beneficial. The collective is a powerful force, and labor unions must learn to tap into that power if they are to regain their former position of influence and clout in the labor management relationship.

Chapter Four

Theoretical Models Associated with the Labor Movement

THE COMPULSORY NATURE OF UNIONISM

Theorizing about the labor movement requires us to analyze the labor movement's evolution over time through "two main lines of development. One . . . is concerned with . . . forces shaping the program of the labor movement and assessing its social and economic functions . . . and the other is concerned with the economic consequences of union behavior in the market" (Perlman, 1960, p. 338). Developing a theory of the labor movement embodies asking such questions as how did the movement originate? What factors, both external and internal, affected the labor movement's pattern of growth? Since there exist many different labor movement forms in many different industries and countries, a labor movement theory must be broad enough to capture all the differences (Larson, 1987). What are the labor movement's goals and relationships to economic systems, and why do individuals join unions? What benefits do individuals gain from associating with labor organizations?

Labor organizations, much like any other organization, are strengthened or weakened by external factors such as social and political institutional changes, technology introductions, changes in market structures and economic systems, and social mores and beliefs as well as by internal factors such as individual and group behavior, the informal or formal nature of the group, and the voluntary adherence or participation of members to the group's interests. This complex interaction of competing external and internal forces makes the development of a theory of the labor movement more difficult because each force does not act in isolation. The history of the labor movement, painstakingly documented over the last two hundred years, does not necessarily enlighten a theory of the labor movement. Though historical events tell us what happened when, they do not paint a broad picture of the complex environment in which the events were situated nor do historical events capture the interworking of group dynamics and their effect on labor unions in different contexts. The history and theory of the labor movement then are two distinct entities, yet one cannot be explained without the other. An exploration of the ways in which internal and external forces and competing interests mediated the organization of labor unions helps to clarify how groups of socially inferior individuals, specifically workers, form groups known as labor unions in order to achieve the goals of wealth redistribution in a capitalist economic system which would shift the balance of power in the employment relationship toward labor in order to improve living standards, maintain workplace protection from unfair management practices, and find due process and voice in employment.

The ability of individuals to form groups to further their collective interests is implicitly and explicitly accepted as standard group behavior by most academics including economists (Olson, 1971). Olson (1971) writes that logically speaking collectives such as corporations seek higher profits to pacify stockholders, consumers seek lower prices, and workers seek higher wages, better benefits, and a workplace voice (1971). Rational self-interested group behavior in which all group members are better off if the objective of the group is achieved would seem to follow naturally from the premise that groups would act in support of the group's objective. This view is based on the assumption that individuals seek to maximize their own utility or interest. But in reality, groups, as well as individuals, do not always act in their own best interests as evidenced by corporations that go bankrupt, consumers who pay more for a good or service than it is worth, or workers who work for poverty wages. Unless there exists some form of coercion or separate incentive which compels group members to act in concert, they often choose not to act in the best interest of the group. Individuals who could advance their own interests without joining the group would surely do so. The incentive then to join the group is to further an individual interest which cannot be furthered without partnership with the group.

Since labor unions are economic organizations, they are sometimes referred to as pressure groups because they put pressure on legislators, their members, the business community, and so forth to achieve their goals. Some scholars believe the pressure group acts as a buffer between capitalism and socialism and should play a larger role because it is beneficial. Olson (1970) writes that John Commons believed that representation via pressure groups would be a more representative form of government than the current system of geographical representation because they affected American economic policy. Common's argument was that the current *laissez-faire* environment of capitalism did not confer fair results, created haves versus have-nots, and this inequity resulted from the unbalanced bargaining power of the groups.

Since powerful men controlled the legislature through which the policies were made, pressure groups could exert influence on these men to change the policies through lobbying. Commons believed economic interests would be served by interest groups promoting their own long-term interests and that economic pressure groups, more representative of the people's wishes than was the Congress, were the catalysts for change in a pluralistic society, one in which political power is distributed among a large number of groups. He believed the job of the legislature was to ensure the existence of voluntary associations such as "labor unions, farmers' cooperatives, business cooperatives, and political parties (Olson, 1970, p. 116).

As economic organizations, labor unions require compulsory membership in order to provide services to its members. A comparison of the obligatory membership in groups will help explain the nature of compulsory membership. The U.S. government is one such entity that requires compulsory membership in the form of taxation. American citizens must pay a variety of taxes which fund public goods and services called collective and noncollective goods. *Collective goods* are sometimes called nonrivaled or nonexclusive goods because one individual's use of the good does not detract from another individual's use of the good. For example, the military protection our government provides is available to every citizen in the United States. We pay for this service through our tax system. Not every individual in the United States pays taxes. Some citizens are disabled, too young, or otherwise not required to pay taxes, yet they enjoy the same military protection as do the tax-paying citizens. It would be impossible for a private firm to provide military protection to every citizen of the United States because it would not be profitable for them to do so. Not every citizen could afford to pay for this service, yet it is a service necessary for the survival of the United States. Therefore, military defense is a collective good made available by the government for the benefit of the entire citizenry of the United States.

Another collective good provided by our government is clean air. Clean air is essential for the survival of the U.S. citizenry. It is too costly for a private firm to provide clean air because all citizens could not afford to pay for the product. Therefore, our government makes laws to protect clean air through environmental regulations which prohibit pollution. Clean air is a collective good which is nonrivaled and nonexclusive because one person breathing clean air does not detract or take away from another person breathing clean air. The same is true of a scenic view along a highway or river. Our government may limit the number of advertising signs along a roadway or prohibit the building of certain structures near a pristine river in order for U.S. citizens to enjoy scenic views. One individual's use of that view does not detract from another individual's use of the view, so the scenic view is a collective good. There are many examples of collective goods provided by our government: public schools, interstate highways, public libraries, prisons, and so on.

Labor unions also provide collective goods for their members. These goods are nonrivaled and nonexclusive which means that one member's use of the good doesn't detract from another member's use of the good. For instance, some collective goods labor unions provide are improved wages, shorter working hours, better working conditions, workplace voice, and due process. One worker's improved wage, shorter work shift, or clean and safe work environment does not take away from another worker's improved wage or clean environment. Labor unions also provide *selective incentives* or private benefits in addition to collective goods. An example of a selective incentive would be jobs. Labor unions work to keep jobs for workers through wage competition and job security. They do this by negotiating collective bargaining agreements or contracts between labor and management which ensure workers belonging to the union maintain high wage scales and seniority (tenure) on the job.

Noncollective goods, on the other hand, are also provided by the government. These goods could be provided by private enterprise, but for some reason, private enterprise doesn't deem them profitable enough to undertake. Electricity is one example. In certain places in the United States, electricity is provided by a government provider and not a private firm. One reason for this might be that in very rural areas, it is not cost effective for a private firm to clear timber and build an infrastructure grid in order to provide electricity for a small number of citizens. The onus of electricity provision might then fall to the government which then also charges the rural citizens for the provision of electricity. There are also instances in which private firms "bid" or otherwise take over the provision of noncollective goods. For instance, in some states, privatized interests now administer state license bureaus, public school lunchrooms, toll roads, and prison telephone systems. Deemed cost-cutting measures by state governments looking for ways in which to save money, public employees are replaced with private employees.

The ability of the government and labor unions to provide collective and noncollective goods to citizens and union members lies in the nature of compulsory membership. This suggests an element of coercion within the group. Without taxes, the government could not provide public goods to its citizens and their well-being would be compromised. Without union dues, labor unions would not be able to provide services to their members thus compromising their members' well-being. This explains the compulsory nature of a labor union. No union member has the incentive to work for or in a labor union unless the union can provide some collective or noncollective good that can't be provided by some other organization. Labor unions provide collective goods (jobs) through selective incentives (better wages, hours, and working conditions) to their members. Therefore, the main function of a labor organization is to provide for its members better wages, hours, and working conditions, workplace voice, and due process. But labor unions have another function as well and that is using their organization's power as an economic and political group. This function is a by-product of a greater function. Labor unions can exert great political pressure because they have millions of members who potentially vote. This strength then lies in their ability to influence governmental policies which inform labor law. The concept of a labor organization providing this function is known as the "by-product theory" of large groups. The political power of unions is then a by-product of their nonpolitical activities. Olson (1970) explains this as the *by-product theory* and writes that an individual has no incentive to voluntarily "sacrifice time or money to help an organization obtain a collective good unless (1) he is coerced into paying dues . . . , or (2) he has to support his group in order to obtain some other noncollective benefit" (p. 134).

The compulsory membership of labor unions has always been a point of contention for those who argue that unions are outdated and useless today. After all, they argue, if workers wished to join a labor union, they would do so, and maintaining compulsory membership is somehow undemocratic. This leads to the idea that all compulsory membership is bad. In fact, there are many professional organizations which compel their members to join and pay dues: the American Medical Association, state bar associations for attorneys, farm cooperatives, and so forth. The role of coercion must be weighed against the benefits, collective and noncollective goods, provided by the organization. Labor unions not only provide collective goods in the form of jobs and noncollective goods such as better wages, hours, working conditions, voice, and due process but provide a by-product, a pressure group which can politically influence legislators to vote for labor-friendly policies. This by-product theory helps explain why labor unions are structured through a federated system such as the ALF-CIO. A federation is a meta-organization of organizations. Many national, international, and local union organizations choose to belong to the AFL-CIO because of the benefits they receive. The by-product theory applies to the AFL-CIO because membership in the federation is not compulsory. Labor unions can belong or not belong to the federation. If labor unions choose to belong to the AFL-CIO, they receive benefits they would not otherwise receive such as a powerful lobby in Washington D.C., access to one of the biggest mailing lists in existence, and the backing of influential and powerful union leaders.

The compulsory nature of union membership and the closed shop are currently in a state of flux as states reassess their position on right-to-work legislation. Regardless, traditional compulsory union membership has been an integral part of labor movement theory and its effect on the future of the labor movement remains in question.

THEORIES OF THE LABOR MOVEMENT

Marxism

Probably the best known theory of the labor movement is Marxism, named after its founder, Karl Marx, a nineteenth-century philosopher, political activist, socialist, economist, and historian. He was born in 1818 and died in 1893. His most well-known work is his *Communist Manifesto* coauthored with Fredrick Engels and written in 1848. The first line of the Manifesto reads, "The history of all hitherto existing society is the history of class struggles" (Marx, 2012). Marx understood the economic system of capitalism to be inherently flawed and thought it would implode from within. He believed that the nature of capitalism, which rests on the creation of wealth by workers who are exploited for their labor by the owners of production, would be destroyed and replaced by a classless society in which everyone was equal.

Marx based his philosophy on the labor theory of value which says labor is the source of value. He argued "the laws of history tended to make the most materially productive group in society emerge as dominant" (Perlman, 1960, p. 339) , and, consequently, the laboring classes would eventually rule. Marx based his thinking on his view of human nature as being adaptable and separate from history. An individual's place in society is a result of an individual's life experience, education, and the environment in which that individual has lived. An individual adapts or changes to fit into a social environment because he has the ability to actively think and create human consciousness. Marx calls an individual's ability to change "nature," the process of transformation "labour," and the capacity to transform nature, "labour power." Marx believed human work was a social activity, and the conditions under which one worked were determined by the social context. Knowing the mode of production had changed from feudal times to a capitalist mode of production, Marx realized the relationship workers have with production is more objective than subjective. In other words, workers were not in control of their own relationship to production. Capitalism's built-in system of privatization incorporated workers as inputs or cogs in the wheels. Owners of production had access to land, natural resources, and technology while workers had only access to their labor power. He defined these distinct separations between workers and owners of production as social disruption. He described separating or giving up one's ownership of his own labor as alienation which he equates with giving up one's own nature, a spiritual loss. This loss is mitigated by the things people produce and consequently use. The use of goods dictates the social context in which people live. Therefore, the goods that are produced, exchanged, and circulated by the worker are really reflections of the social relationships between workers and the owners of production. He saw this as a vicious cycle only to be broken by revolution.

Marx believed that class was a result of the relationship individuals had to the means of production and not that class was determined by wealth alone. He principally divided humans into two social classes: the bourgeoisie or owners of production who buy labor power from workers and exploit them and the proletariat or workers, who sell their labor power, which adds value to a product, to the owners of production. The excess value of the good created by workers is sold and creates a profit for the bourgeoisie. Other classes which Marx designated were the lumpenproletariat, criminals and vagabonds who had no economic stake and sold themselves to the highest bidder; landlords, who retained some of their wealth and were very important; and peasantry and farmers, who were disorganized and incapable of affecting change and would probably bleed into the proletariat or landlord class.

Marx was not intentionally a social reformer and was not primarily interested in materially improving the lives of downtrodden workers per se. He believed the revolution of the working class was the vehicle which would ultimately be the salvation of the industrial labor class, yet his Marxist philosophy came to illuminate the grave inequities between the classes and served as a catalyst for pinpointing all that was awry in the bourgeoisie. Even those who philosophically disagreed with Marx used his schema as a social reform platform for improving the social and economic conditions of the working class.

Marx believed capitalism to be an exploitive system which would mold workers into revolutionaries who would use trade unions as the mechanism of self-defense. Overthrowing and taking over the means of production from the bourgeoisie would be the first step in emancipating the working class from the oppression of economic dependence and insecurity heaped on them by the owners of production. This would require the class struggle to further organize along political lines in order to form a socialist society in which the means of production are socialized. Trade unions would support workers' economic interests, train workers to organize, and help develop class consciousness in anticipation of the revolution.

There are many variations of Marxism but most of them share the same properties that capitalism is a system by which owners of production exploit workers; the dominant ideology of an individual's consciousness is shaped by the economic environment; class is determined by one's relationship to the means of production; social relations and material conditions are pliable; class struggle drives historical change; and the current class structure will be replaced by a class structure which manages society for the good of all. The versions of Marxism evolving from his original mantra of revolution are concerned with "the basic Marxian question of an inferior group's rise to power" (Perlman, 1960, p. 340) , but scholars vary on the idea of achieving the results of emancipation and enlightenment via revolution and how that revolution would successfully occur.

Historical Materialism

Marx developed a theory of socioeconomic development called *historical materialism* in which society and the economy were understood to be determined by changes in the material conditions under which people need to live and survive. Historical materialism was based on the premise that humans need to systematically produce and reproduce materials necessary for their existence; this Marx called production relations or the economic base of society which was founded on property ownership. From this economic base, culture, laws, and political institutions as well as ideologies, social mores, and morality arose. These paradigms constitute society's superstructure and are known as coherence. *Coherence* reflects the modifications each generation makes to the economic inheritance from the preceding generation and suggests human history results from the struggle between social classes based on an economic structure and not some supernatural force or historic accident. Historical materialism is now an approach to the study of society, economics, and history which explores the causes and developments by which humans collectively produce necessities for survival and views political institutions and social classes as vestiges of economic activity.

Within the collective of human work, there exists a division of labor; some workers earn wages while others own the means of production. The structure of the society and class divisions are dictated by production relations which are determined by the modes of production: primitive communism as seen in tribal societies; feudalism as seen when the aristocracy is the ruling class, and merchants develop into capitalists; slavery as developed when the tribe became a city-state and aristocracy was born; socialism when workers gain class consciousness and overthrow the capitalists and control the state; and capitalism when capitalists are the ruling class and employ the working class (Marx, 1859). Production modes are influenced by new technologies, accumulation of capital, and capacity. The difference between capitalism and all other production modes is that the state acts as a force separating politics from economics and manages conflict stemming from property rights.

Labor and Social Reform within the Capitalist System

Sidney and Beatrice Webb, British socialist reformers who studied industrial society and trade unions, took exception to Marx's claim that the bourgeois class must be eliminated in order for the working class to make gains. They instead believed that trade unions were economic institutions whose main objective was to better the wages and working conditions of wage earners. Members of the British Fabian Society, a left-wing think tank dedicated to the gradual reform of capitalism through trade unions and legislation, the Webbs fashioned a "'common sense' creed of hope for improved working and living conditions" (Perlman, 1960) by suggesting the entire working class could "be materially improved by the growth of trade unionism and by limited political action" (Perlman, 1960, p. 341).

The Webbs deduced that labor unions fashioned their goals in response to the social, political, and economic environments in which they were situated. For instance, during the 1700s, labor unions believed workers had a legal right or sole claim to a particular trade and subsequently had a natural right to protect that claim. This "vested interest" doctrine led to trade apprenticeships which tried to control the labor supply through limiting the number of workers who could gravitate into a particular trade. But this approach was at odds with the premise of industrial efficiency which sought "the best man for the job" regardless of a worker's vested interest in the trade as well as serving to discourage union membership. Labor unions' method for resolving the problem of attracting potential recruits was offering "mutual insurance," in the form of unemployment, health, and pension benefits (Larson, 1987; Perlman, 1960).

The doctrine of supply and demand in the free-market economic system of capitalism during the 1800s challenged labor unions to find ways to protect workers from simply being considered inputs into a production system. Collective bargaining surfaced as the method by which standard wage rates and conditions of employment were contractually codified. Collective bargaining ran counter to the idea of contractual freedom in which workers and employers freely enter into an unwritten employment contract and either party can exit the relationship at any time, so the public would often intervene by seeking and securing state intervention through legislation limiting workers' rights to collectively bargaining (Larson, 1987; Perlman, 1960).

Another issue arising during the 1900s was community concern over the number of low-wage workers not protected by collective bargaining agreements who were unable to fully participate in community life because their community engagement was limited by their strength in the labor pool or their ability to join a labor union. This concern led unionists to adopt the "living wage" doctrine as a supplement to the supply and demand model. The idea behind the living wage doctrine was that all workers should be able to earn enough wages for a sufficient living which would benefit communities and industrial efficiency. The method to resolve this issue was establishing "legal enactment," a national minimum wage which would legally ensure no workers fell below a certain income level. Unions then turned their attention to the passage of minimum wage laws (Larson, 1987; Perlman, 1960).

The Webbs's work provided a framework for the analysis of group be-havior and choices made by workers whose inferior power was a barrier and an opportunity for workers' alternatives in the superstructures which dictated workers' economic and moral choices. Sticklers for detailed knowledge about the British working class, they felt trade unions were essential to protect the working class whether they functioned under capitalism, social-ism, or government control. According to Perlman (1960), the Webbs's writ-ings marked "the beginning of the empirical analysis of the materially iden-tifiable labor movement" (p. 341).

John R. Commons was a labor historian and institutional economist at the University of Wisconsin-Madison. Commons, in the vein of Sydney and Beatrice Webb, initially believed labor unions should and could gain benefits for workers within a capitalist system through "reinterpreting the meaning of property, with job rights becoming the new form" (Perlman, 1960, p. 342). Attempting to move unionism from under the umbrella of Marxian socialism, Commons refuted the idea that "surplus value and the mode of production" (Larson, 1987, p. 245) were causes of inequality between the working class and the owning class or that exploitation of workers by owners of production existed. He rather explained these phenomenon as market reflexes. A propo-nent of labor unions who felt them to be necessary to represent workers during negotiations, Commons advocated for social harmony at the bargain-ing table where representatives of labor, capital, government, and academics could compromise within the parameters of capitalism which assumed a free market economy. His ideas were reminiscent of corporate liberalism, and his viewpoints volleyed between progressivism as described by Gompers's bread and butter unionism, the evils of Marxist revolution, and an acceptance of property owners as a "legitimate interest group" (Larson, 1987, p. 247). For a fuller discussion of Commons and his theories, see the Introduction.

Syndicalism

Selig Perlman also developed a revolutionary theory of the labor movement known as *Syndicalism*. Syndicalism derives from the French word *syndica-lisme* which means trade unionism (Larson, 1987). Perlman, an economist and labor historian trained in Europe and heavily influenced by German historical sociologists, developed his philosophy of the labor movement as a result of studying with John Commons while at the University of Madison, Wisconsin, during the early 1900s. This relationship helped shape Perlman's belief that U.S. trade unions must focus solely on bettering wages and work-ing conditions and not class revolution because the marketplace was the source of conflict between owners of production and workers and not a capitalist economic system. Perlman believed workers should work within the existing economic system in the form of direct action at the point of production through trade unions to interrupt or stop the flow of production which would ultimately decrease the firms' profits and eventually cause capitalism to collapse.

Marx and Perlman agreed some type of social organization was necessary for workers to coalesce under trade unionism but disagreed about whether "private ownership, traditional western parliamentarianism . . . , [or] cultural pluralism" (Perlman, 1960, p. 342) was the best framework in which trade unions should operate and whether workers under a specific framework would revolt, accept social evolution, or maintain the status quo of the political system.

The differences between Marxism and Syndicalism lie in the methods of revolution and the nature of the revolution in the future. Marx insisted political avenues were necessary for revolution while Perlman believed differing individual politics divided workers even when those workers were held together by an economic community of interest. Perlman's belief that direct action was the best revolutionary tactic could take the form of strikes, work slowdowns, or sabotage. Regardless of the tactic used or its success or failure, workers would become acquainted with revolutionary tactics which could further be refined for subsequent direct action as well as awaken class consciousness in greater numbers of workers and instill in those workers the need for revolution (Larson, 1984).

Perlman (1968) is responsible for the development of *business unionism*, an approach which uses trade unions as the first step toward socialism (Perlman, 1922). Devoid of political activism, this model focused on collective bargaining agreements among craft workers and their employers as far superior to industrial unionism and the organization of unskilled workers into labor unions. Business unionism was supported by Gompers and the AFL which initially shied away from political activity.

Perlman (1968) believed there existed a difference in the mentality of the trade unions and that of the intellectuals. Intellectuals, as outsiders, didn't really understand the workers' plight and therefore intellectuals like Marx should not influence the labor movement. "If given the opportunity to exist legally and to develop a leadership from among its own ranks, the trade union's mentality will eventually come to dominate" (Perlman, 1968). He believed those who came up through the ranks of trade unions would be wise and practical enough to "see through" the ideologies of Marx and be content to win for workers what they could through the business unionism. Though Perlman turned out to be wrong, he holds a significant place in the development of labor history.

A Theory of Industrial Relations

Around the late 1940s, a new approach to developing a theory of the labor movement surfaced when John Dunlop, labor scholar, labor economist, and Secretary of Labor under the Ford administration, developed a framework known as the industrial relations system which proposed past theorists had neglected the important components of new technologies, changing product and factor markets, and the role of government (Dunlop, 1958). Unlike his Marxist counterparts and veering away from Commons's, the Webbs's, and Perlman's focus on labor relations within a capitalist economic system, Dunlop argued changes in labor's position currently called for a contemporary exploration of the relationship between different forms of economic systems and their workers, the government, and the community from the vantage point of the individual rather than the group (Kerr, 1955). This shift meant labor unions, no longer considered an inferior group, would only play an important industrial role when collective bargaining agreements were present; labor unions would have less impact only when they played a political role. Dunlop also suggested labor union collusion with other social movements of similar purpose could have a positive effect on "raising inferior groups and/or redistributing wealth and income (Perlman, 1960, p. 345).

The institutional changes of income and wealth inequality, social mobility, and the move from a manufacturing base to a service base undoubtedly had an effect on the direction of the labor movement during the fifties and sixties as witnessed by more interest in mechanisms which regulated the market than the previous focus on social and political forces. As new technology was introduced into the firm, and fewer workers were on payrolls, traditional theories of the labor movement, influenced by capitalist market forces, gave rise to new questions about labor's place and effect in and on the market. The labor union's ability to affect wages within and across industries was an example of the questions with which economists were concerned. Some economists believed unions had the ability to change wages if they acted as a monopoly but their actions usually were accompanied by socially adverse effects such as reducing the number of jobs in the firm or hurting other workers (Machlup, 1952). Others believed that under certain conditions, unions improved wage rates but preferred government intervention in the market rather than countervailing market power (Galbraith, 1956). Still others concentrated on the various forms of trade unions and their ability to change wage rates (Cartter, 1959; Dunlop, 1950) as well as empirical verification of links between labor unions and wage rate increases. Dunlop (1958) concluded other factors such as productivity and output changes and market forces had more effect on wage rates than did trade unions.

The New Left Labor Movement Theory

Andre Gorz, a French and Austrian social philosopher born in 1923, fostered a labor theory of the guaranteed basic income; he wrote about this theory in his book *Critique of Economic Reason* (1989). He subscribed to the New Left Movement, a radical leftist political movement especially active during the 1960s and 1970s which disavowed Marxist's theory of revolution and class struggle, the Establishment, and the labor movement and subscribed to student activism and young intellectuals as the change agents. He based his theory on the idea that workers should receive a basic income throughout their lives which allowed them leisure time to do with as they wished (Gorz, 1989). He likened this future guaranteed benefit to the monies a worker now receives for holiday or vacation pay. This future income would be based on the socially produced wealth to which each individual is entitled by virtue of their participation in the social process of production. The trade unions of France and Germany, during the 1980s, adopted Gorz's theory and utilized the 35-hour work week as a basis for hours of work. This helped address the issue of unemployment and provided more leisure time for workers to spend with their families, pursue educational endeavors, or do whatever they chose. The idea behind this theory is to provide a better quality of life for trade union members.

Stanley Aronowitz, a political activist born in 1933 and professor of sociology at CUNY Graduate Center in New York posits "unions must become social movements" (Aronowitz, 2005, p. 286) which address the concerns of workers in a democratic organization that practices union democracy in order to survive and grow. Aronowitz believes unions, who continue to remain subordinate to capital and the Democratic Party cannot survive in their present form and to regain their independence must form an independent labor-oriented catalyst that invests in union democracy, a more transparent process for unionization, and social justice for all. In this form of social movement unionism, the workers organize whether they obtain a union contract in the future or not. Workers can join the "labor movement as individuals, and groups that do not have an immediate chance of winning a majority to strike or petition for a representation election should be invited to be part of labor movements" (Aronowitz, 2005, p. 289). Moving the formation of this social movement from a vertical structure in which the AFL-CIO and leaders of national and international unions make all the decisions to a more lateral structure in which Central Labor Councils or work councils composed of concerned workers make choices about issues important to them would broaden the reach of the movement to any worker or any race or gender and would bring to the forefront specific labor and social issues and provide a forum for debate about how to develop a vision for our current globalized environment.

SOCIAL MOVEMENT UNIONISM

Social movements are collective actions. They are the result of large groups of people joining forces to correct injustices, fight oppression, or otherwise change an objectionable environment. There have been throughout history many notable social movements such as the social movement to abolish slavery, the social movement to ensure civil rights for all citizens, and the social movement to correct injustices against women. Labor has also been involved in social movements, and these large collective actions have changed the conditions under which workers labor. The shelf life of social movements lasts only as long as the stamina from the collective exists or the anticipated change occurs. This section explores how social movements take root and survive and the value of social movements to the renewal of the labor movement as a viable collective representing workers.

Social movements didn't really exist prior to the late eighteenth century. There have been campaigns, various forms of political action, special interest groups, demonstrations, rallies, concerted public and private mobilizing efforts, and petition drives, but these efforts do not constitute a social movement (Tilly, 2005). Social movements do not exist forever. They spring up, fulfill their purpose, and then fade away. Social movements sprang up in the beginning of the nineteenth century because this was a period in history when ideas like individual rights, freedom of speech, and civil disobedience were in vogue. Conditions must be "right" for a social movement to exist, and this usually means some type of polarization or collective challenge to the status quo. For instance, huge disparities between the wealthy and the poor or blatant injustices between classes could foster a social movement. Born when there is a convergence of an oppressive climate, huge numbers of individuals who share like backgrounds and experiences, and some type of conduit through which affected individuals can express their despair, social movements in the United States coalesced around student protests, welfare rights, women's liberation, and the Civil Rights Movement. Social movements are closely connected to democratic political systems and are a popular expression of dissent (Tilly, 2004).

Social movements do not simply spring up overnight. Even if there are thousands of citizens discontented with the status quo, there doesn't exist a social movement until those discontented citizens can communicate with one another. Just how do these social movements begin? What spark ignites the fires of social movement unionism? How do activists who share similar concerns come together and reach other people? There exist data which explain the beginnings of social movement unionism (Freeman, 1999). This data is pulled from the social movements of the sixties and seventies: civil rights, student protest, welfare rights, and women's liberation (Freeman, 1971). This data suggests that there must exist "recurrent elements" within the environment before social movements can form. One of the main elements that must exist is a communications infrastructure.

A communications network through which activists can respond to a crisis is necessary if the crisis information is to be generalized to a broader constituency. Otherwise, the crisis remains localized, and the activity goes no further than the original core activist group. If there is no communication, there is no social movement. Therefore, one of two things must happen for a social movement to materialize: 1) there must be a preexisting form of communication through which discontented citizens can channel their concerns, protests, demonstrations, rallies, and so on, or 2) there must be organizing efforts between small groups of discontented citizens to form communication channels through which a broader audience can be connected.

If a communications network is in place, it must be one in which new ideas can be disseminated to people with similar backgrounds, interests, class, and experiences. Like-minded individuals are more likely to respond to new ideas if they share such commonalities. Given the existence of such a communications network, some focusing event must occur which spurs a nucleus of discontented citizens to reach out to others through the network. This event and its ramifications galvanize others into action, and a social movement is born. If no solid communications network exists, then organizers must build one, which usually takes time and dilutes the impetus of the movement.

Such a communications network existed prior to the Civil Rights Movement. Freeman (1971) relates there were actually two focusing events that preceded the beginning of the Civil Rights Movement. One is the arrest of Rosa Parks for "sitting down" in the front seat of the bus reserved for white riders in Montgomery, Alabama, in 1955, and the second is the "sit-in" of four freshmen at a lunch counter at A&T College in Greenboro, North Carolina, in 1960, which resulted in the formation of the Student Non-Violent Coordinating Committee (SNCC). Some history explains why these two focusing events could be deemed the catalyst for the Civil Rights Movement.

Within the South, there are two main institutions, the church and the black college, which acted as communication networks for the black community. These two institutions provided leadership to the community in the form of preachers and teachers. Preachers were the most important and were held at a higher status than were teachers because the church and religion touched the lives of all blacks, while schools only touched the lives of some blacks. Preachers were also more economically separated from whites than were teachers who worked in the public school system and received their paychecks from the government. Blacks, throughout American history, used the church as their social network, particularly during the period of slavery. Though not all churches represented all blacks, the blacks that were represented became the activist pool from which agitators were selected. The black church had male leadership, but the church's population was largely middle-aged female and lower class. The black colleges were populated by middle-class, black intellectuals.

There existed within the South several organizations which had existing communication networks but failed to launch the civil rights social movement. One was the very wealthy Urban League whose members were black and white. It functioned more as a social service agency. Secondly, there was the National Association for the Advancement of Colored People (NAACP) which primarily pursued change through litigation. A major accomplishment of the NAACP was the abolition of segregation in *Brown v. Board of Education* (1954). This court decision laid the groundwork for the Civil Rights Movement. The third organization was the Congress of Racial Equality (CORE) which adopted a non-violent direct approach to racial problems. Originally formed in the North, CORE was not situated to lead a southern movement because it had no southern roots.

Prior to Rosa Parks's defiance on a Montgomery, Alabama, bus, there had been conversations between black leaders and city leadership about inequality within the city busing system. Most blacks rode buses to work, to the store, and other places because they did not own cars. Buses were blacks' main mode of transportation, and blacks made up the "paying ridership" of the bus system. If blacks chose not to ride the public transportation system, then white bus owners would suffer. Hints of a boycott of the busing system had circulated through Montgomery and led city leaders and black pastors to discuss the busing situation. No resolution to the segregated seating on buses surfaced.

Blacks were particularly disturbed and resentful about the busing situation. They were forced to pay their fares at the front of the bus and then reenter the bus at the rear. White drivers harassed black passengers and often drove away when blacks were attempting to reboard at the rear. Blacks had to sit behind a moveable mobile barrier which divided the bus into a white section and a black section. The moveable barrier could be pushed back to make room for more white passengers.

On December 1, 1955, Rosa Parks, a seamstress and former secretary of the NAACP, sat down in the white only section of a bus. The driver demanded she move to the black only section, and she refused. She was subsequently arrested and jailed. She called E. D. Nixon, president of the local NAACP chapter. Nixon not only posted her bail, he called influential women in Montgomery who belonged to the Women's Political Council (WPC). These women actually suggested that the bus boycott proceed as a one-day boycott to coincide with Parks's trial scheduled for December 5, 1955. The WPC printed up 52,000 fliers and disseminated them to blacks in Montgomery. They also notified Ralph Abernathy, pastor of the First Baptist Church and Martin Luther King Jr., minister at Dexter Avenue Baptist Church. Abernathy and King, along with fifty other pastors, black and white, endorsed the boycott and planned a massive rally for the evening of December 5. The NAACP, looking for a test case concerning segregation to take to the Supreme Court, began preparing a legal challenge.

The trial ended with Parks's conviction of violating segregated seating laws. Black leaders agreed to extend the bus boycott and formed the Montgomery Improvement Association (MIA) with Martin Luther King as the president. On December 5, 1955, 7000 blacks met at Holt Street Baptist Church and were inspired by King's address which included the admonition, "There comes a time when people get tired of being trampled over by the iron feet of oppression" (King, 1960, p. 284). That month a 381-day boycott began. Over 42,000 blacks took taxis, carpooled, and walked to their destinations. Facing hostile terrain in Montgomery, blacks adopted a credo of nonviolent resistance. Taxi drivers were threatened by police for giving discount fares to blacks or were arrested for going too fast or too slow. Encouraged by King to persevere, blacks leaders continued to meet with civic leaders presenting their modest demands for bus seating equality. They were always met with refusal (Freeman, 1971).

White opposition escalated. Boycott leaders were terrorized; vigilante groups bombed black homes and churches, and police sweeps arrested leaders including King. The newly formed MIA filed a federal suit against bus segregation, and the issue of civil rights took center stage on the national scene. During the summer, the Supreme Court of the United States ruled segregation unconstitutional. The ruling was to take effect December 20, 1956. That night, King, Abernathy, and others rode the city buses in Montgomery. The bus boycott kick-started the Civil Rights Movement and propelled the movement into the national spotlight. King was heralded as a great leader; his picture appeared on Time magazine, and he was catapulted into the public eye. Further coordinated efforts to continue anti-segregation protests resulted in the formation of the Southern Christian Leadership Conference (SCLC). The SCLC's efforts were primarily continued through the network of established churches.

The coordinated efforts of the MIA and the bus boycott were successful because of the communications network in existence in black churches. The church provided the ideal conduit through which communication could flow on a regular basis to the masses. When blacks held meetings, registered voters, or socialized, they went to black churches. The SCLC was responsible for the formation of the Student Nonviolent Coordinating Committee (SNCC), a youth group interested in non-violent action in desegregation efforts. Black southern colleges tended to be the primary drawing ground for participants. Sit-ins were becoming popular through the South as a type of non-violent protest against segregation. An alma mater of Shaw University, Ella Baker, also a member of the SCLC, coordinated resources for the sit-ins which included meeting space at Shaw and money from the SCLC. The space which was created by the SCLC allowed the youth group to morph into the SNCC.

The Civil Rights Movement hails from two different focusing events, Rosa Parks's refusal to remain in a segregated bus seat and a student sit-in at a white lunch counter. These tactics are very different though they move in the same strategic direction, that of focusing attention on injustice. Most social movements are not controlled by some hierarchy. The college students held no prominent positions; they simply felt the sting of injustice and protested. Rosa Parks was not a visible high-profile leader, but rather a small of statue, soft-spoken female. Both of the actions taken were broadcast to a larger audience by communication networks within black southern churches. Once the realization occurred that these events had far-reaching and broader implications, national news media carried the message to the entire world.

Social movements can be started by planned action or spontaneous action; they can be leader oriented or grassroots oriented. The sit-in was a more or less spontaneous action by a group of college students. The bus boycott was a planned effort by black community and church leaders who capitalized on the defiant act of Rosa Parks. A communications network was in place through which the Civil Rights Movement could progress. Other resources, tangible and intangible, were also in play which helped this movement to grow. Tangible resources include money, space for meetings, and publications. Intangible resources include people, time, and commitment. Social movements need both to survive.

Money is an important component of any social movement. Funds have to materialize from somewhere. Donations or fund-raisers account for most of the movement's income. If money is abundant, then space for meetings can be purchased. Space can also be donated. If there is little money and no available donated space, then publicity for the movement can help raise money in order to rent space. People are a most valuable intangible resource. Social movements are usually strong on people and weak on money. People bring to the social movement various specialized and unspecialized skills. It is unlikely there existed enough money to pay young people to register voters in the South during the Jim Crow era. This was a dangerous job and risky job. But thousands of young people responded to the call to register voters because they believed in the social movement's cause, fighting injustice.

Knowledge concerning the origins of social movements must be tied into the labor movement. The labor movement and unions are not synonymous but rather are two distinct entities. A union is an institution, "a legally constituted collective bargaining agent that represents workers in complex economic and juridical relations with employers and government" (Clawson, 1999, p. 109). The labor movement, on the other hand, is a "fluid formation whose very existence depends on high-risk activism, mass solidarity, and collective experiences with transformational possibilities" (Clawson, 1999, p. 109). The union's existence, therefore, depends on the existence of a labor movement. The last fifteen to twenty years of employer dominance has made the existence of the labor movement more difficult to sustain. The long *post-war accord* between labor and management, an unwritten assumption between labor and management in which labor and management accepted each other, fostered a climate in which worker discontent grew commensurate with employer power.

Because of current weakened labor laws, extreme employer resistance to unions, and an economic climate which encourages globalization including free trade, privatization, deregulation, deunionization, and dehumanization, the labor movement is in a state of flux. The existence of organized labor may very well depend upon the revitalization of the labor movement. Scholars and labor leaders have made suggestions as to how best to facilitate the labor movement's transformation. Labor's response has been multi-faceted: militancy, organizing efforts, pacifying efforts, and reestablishing labor as a valued partner.

MILITANCY AND SOCIAL MOVEMENTS

The labor movement has adopted pages from the playbook of the Civil Rights Movement, according to Isaac and Christiansen (2002). Both the Civil Rights Movement and the labor movement felt existing injustices must be corrected, and both chose forms of militant action to affect that change. Perhaps a definition of militancy is in order here. *Militant action* is direct, confrontational, disruptive action which alters the current landscape and may be violent or passive, but it must somehow attempt to alter, disrupt, or change existing conditions. In the Civil Rights Movement, black southern citizens participated in bus boycotts and sit-ins as a form of passive non-violent resistance to the status quo. Their militant actions resulted in changes in the law concerning segregation in public transportation. Within the labor movement, militant action has taken the forms of strikes which were often very violent strikes, worker resistance to employer pressure through work-to-rule actions, work slow-downs, or sabotage, or indirect employer pressure through contract or corporate campaigns (Issac, 2002). During the New Deal era, militant action fostered the passage of the NLRA in 1935. Since then, labor laws have weakened as has worker militancy.

Issac and Christianson (2002) hypothesize that "the civil rights movement revitalized labor militancy through protest 'demonstration effects'" and "through social movement organization growth, which was more efficacious than were 'demonstration effects'" (p. 728). The direction of a movement is driven by increased activity and participation which can be diffused or spread from one movement to another. Issac and Christianson (2002) believe that labor borrowed from the Civil Rights Movement the idea that protests and demonstrations could be legitimized through militant and sometimes violent action and that even though one focusing event such as a crisis, protest, or demonstration was not sustainable through long periods of time, the social unrest associated with that protest was sustainable for long periods of time.

The intangible resource of people is necessary for continued social movement activism. Because people are workers, they often reside in both the world of labor and the world of civil rights. Even workers who were not living in the south and were not exposed to Jim Crow were sympathetic to workers whose rights were violated in the workplace. This diffusion of concern between the Civil Rights Movement and the labor movement fostered a borrowing of ideas between movements.

Organizing Efforts

Most union members are familiar with the business model of unionism in which the unions service their needs such as contract negotiations and grievance handling. Due to decreased density and decreased union power, most scholars and labor leaders believe the switch to a mobilizing or organizing model of unionism will help shore up declining numbers and revitalize the labor movement. Moving from a business model of unionism to a mobilizing model of unionism has met with some resistance. One example of this is the move toward engaging workers to process their own grievances instead of relying on a staff representative or steward to process the grievance. The idea behind having workers process their own grievances is to engage workers more fully in the grievance process and free up staff to attend to organizing functions. Workers, still immersed in the servicing model of unionism, are used to having a representative service the grievance and feel entitled to steward or staff representation as a fee for service (dues), so they often do not embrace the organizing model because it requires effort on their part to learn how to maneuver through the grievance process. It also requires staff to train workers in grievance processing and handling. Therefore, the staff's time is spent in training workers in the grievance process instead of organizing new members. The suggestion that workers must be educated to help service their own grievances and become more politically involved has met with some resistance.

Pacifying Efforts

Some firms now embrace what are known as participatory management systems, systems in which labor may be invited to sit at the table. These programs range from quality circles to team production systems. Management's goal is to involve employees in decision-making processes in order to transform workplace relationships in hopes of greater production outputs. Usually group processes and nonadversarial relationships are stressed. Sometimes workers welcome this invitation believing they can affect workplace conditions, gain dignity, and have a voice in their working lives. More often than not, these workers are disappointed in the outcomes of their participatory endeavors, and generally there is a greater deskilling of the workforce than an upgrading of skills (Milkman, 1997). The end result is a greater distrust of management than before the engagement of participatory management systems.

The idea of employee involvement (EI) is one of mutual trust between labor and management. EI programs portray an image of a unified team working together to further employee's interests. This very notion that workers' interests are the same as managements' interest is disconcerting. It is in management's interest to move toward programs which quell worker resistance. Remember, the goal of management from the very earliest times has been to wrest control of the work process away from workers. EI programs are simply a modern-day extension of this earlier goal.

Reestablishing Labor as a Valued Partner

One of the most important aspects of the labor movement is reestablishing labor as a valued member of the labor management relationship. The current laws were designed to protect full time, nonsupervisory, long-term manufacturing employees who worked for a single employer. The changing landscape of work today reflects a much different picture—that of contingent, temporary, short-term service sector employees who are often given supervisory duties. Our current system of industrial unionism is unsuitable to many workplaces which "demand new forms of employee organization and representation" . . . "some of these possibilities might include occupational organizing, community-based actions, and connections to other social movements" (Clawson, 1999, p. 112).

Clawson and Clawson (1999) provide some suggestions concerning new forms of unionism, though they conclude these are speculative. *Occupational organizing*, sometimes known as *industrial organizing*, entails organizing around a specific occupation or trade. Large unions such as the International Brotherhood of Electrical Workers (IBEW) and the United Auto Workers (UAW) use this approach. The focus of bargaining is moved from the individual employer to an industry-wide structure. This structure presumes that most employees are union members. Another form of occupational unionism is known as *associational unionism*, a professional grouping of workers bound together to pressure employers. Associational unionism occupies a "space somewhere between a current union and professional association" (p.

113). The National Educational Association (NEA) is an associational union. *Community-based unionism* is seen in the form of Central Labor Councils (CLC), the local arms of the AFL-CIO which include representatives from local unions within some geographic area. CLCs, though weak for many years, have been resurging after AFL-CIO leadership changes in 1995. John Sweeney, president of the AFL-CIO, believed CLCs were an obvious conduit for political mobilization, new ways of organizing, and reaching into the community.

Community organizations are another form of unionism or collective action which circumvent labor law and are protected by the First Amendment. A community organization is largely based on coalitions consisting of various groups who share similar concerns and believe that by binding together, they can facilitate change and fight injustice. The groups might be labor, environmental, civic, or faith-based, and their agenda might be varied as well. For instance, if a group of workers wanted to put pressure on an employer to change working conditions, they would solicit help from other groups in the coalitions who would benefit from the employer's change of conditions as well. Publicizing an employers' practice of storing hazardous waste from the worksite in unapproved containers in an open lot next to the production facility puts community and environmental pressure on the employer to dispose of the waste in a safer manner. The community organization functions on reciprocity; if one group needs assistance, then all groups respond.

The labor movement faces strong challenges today because the movement, particularly during the seventies and eighties, did not join forces with social movements of that time: the Civil Rights Movement, women's movements, environmental movements, antiwar movements, and welfare rights movements. These are lost opportunities and were due in part to the isolationist nature of business-model unionism, lack of organizing efforts, and labor's refusal to participate against corporate greed. Some scholars believe that unions can once again reclaim their power by allying with other social movements who fight corporate greed and domination and encourage social justice. By building alliances with other prevalent social movements, labor could once again strengthen its position with management.

Labor must also take care of some internal housekeeping. Shifting more resources into organizing drives to build union density, instituting union democracy with all unions, and shifting the power from the top of the labor structure to the rank and file are necessary components of revitalization. Strengthening the labor movement requires all the components necessary for the formation and sustaining of a social movement: a communications network through which the masses can be contacted, tangible resources such as money, space, and publishing ability, and intangible resources such as people, time, and commitment. The infusion of tangible and intangible resources into the revitalization of the labor movement is of paramount importance.

Chapter Five

The Current State of the U.S. Employment Relationship

POVERTY, WEALTH AND INCOME INEQUITIES, AND EQUALITY VERSUS EQUITY

The economic system of capitalism under which we now function has created some vast income and wealth inequities within the United States. The theory of competition, which encourages producers to operate with profit margins in mind, drives businesses to consider the capital, raw material, and labor costs of production. Since capital costs are usually long-term investments such as new buildings, additions to existing buildings, and updated equipment, they cannot be easily changed or modified. If would be difficult to spend large sums of money on renovating work space or bringing in updated and more sophisticated equipment if the space were only to be used for a short while. So capital investments are usually part of a long-term strategic plan as is the return on these investments. Producers usually have little impact on the price of raw materials used in their product's manufacture, so raw material costs are usually absorbed by the producer. There may exist a cheaper substitute for a raw material used in the production of a product which a firm could purchase and still maintain the quality of their product, but without this option, firms/producers have to pay the cost of the inputs. Firms/producers do have some control over the labor component of their product. Obviously the product cannot be manufactured without some workers, but the number necessary to add value to the product in its manufacture can vary. Non-union workers can be hired/kept/fired at the producer's will. Investments in new technology dictate the number of workers necessary to produce some level of outputs. Firms/producers are always looking for ways to cut costs, thus increasing their profit margin, and labor is the first arena to which producers look for cost containment.

Over the course of labor history, many workers' jobs were sacrificed in the name of the bottom line, and firms adopted terminology such as "freed up commodities" to describe workers who have been "kicked to the curb" through a lay-off or termination situation. These workers who lost their jobs were no longer able to support their families, pay their mortgages, or contribute economically to their communities. They often relied, if they were eligible and met certain government requirements, on social welfare services such as unemployment, food stamps, and public assistance, for long periods of time. If these workers were not eligible for government assistance, they relied on charitable organizations, friends, or family for assistance. They not only suffered the long-term direct economic consequences of job loss but suffered the indirect consequences of job loss such as mental despair and depression, marital and familial discord, child and elder care problems, and/or physical disorders.

Job loss and unemployed, underemployed, or low-wage workers contribute to the wealth and income inequality in our society. A society that focuses primarily on profit margins and bottom lines creates an environment in which the wage and wealth gap continually widens and in which a very small portion of the population own most of the nation's wealth while the majority of the nation's citizens own very little of the nation's wealth. Government rules which regulate wealth distribution such as tax policies are very important in determining who in the United States owns wealth and receives income. An examination of wealth and income inequality in the United States reflects how trade, economic, monetary, and fiscal policies contribute to income and wealth disparity. These policies are of great concern to workers who deal with the fallout from wealth and income inequality on a daily basis. The issue of fairness in the allocation of goods and services and the process by which wealth and income are distributed lead to discussions concerning equality versus equity and the implications for a nation which pursues policies of inequality. First, we turn to income inequality.

We are all concerned about the fairness of our economic system and the social problems resulting from inequality in total income, regardless of the source. There are three sources of income: earned income, unearned income, and social transfer payments. Earned income is wages and salaries individuals earn by selling their labor to owners of production. Unearned income is the result of capital investments, interest income or profit, or rental income from land and natural resources. These types of income are also known as *nonlabor income* or *property income.* Some individuals such as Warren Buffet and Bill Gates have a great deal of income from labor and property. Some households also receive social transfer payments or welfare. Transfer payments are forms of governmental payments such as Social Security, unemployment insurance, or earned income tax credits. Those individuals and families who have limited incomes below certain numeric amounts are said to be in *poverty*. Poverty is the state of being without, often associated with need, hardship, and lack of resources across a wide range of circumstances. The repercussions of poverty have long-term economic, political, and social consequences for individuals, families, and society in terms of the nation's health, education, environment, housing, crime, homelessness, and the ability of the United States to maintain its position as a world leader. A closer look at poverty in the U.S. reveals the extent to which Americans are in poverty, how poverty is measured, and what policies are in place to alleviate poverty for some working Americans.

POVERTY IN THE UNITED STATES

The *poverty line* is the income level below which a family is considered to be in poverty. The official poverty line as reported by the U.S. government is determined by the income of all family members considered to be in a household. This income includes any earnings such as wages from a job, unemployment, workers' compensation, Social Security benefits, veterans' benefits, and pensions and unearned incomes such as rents, royalties, income from trusts and estates, assistance from outside the home, and other miscellaneous sources (Bureau, 2014) but does not include noncash benefits such as food stamps, housing subsidies, or capital gains or losses and is based on a before-tax status. *Poverty thresholds*, originally designed under the Johnson administration by Mollie Orshansky as a way to determine who would receive public assistance in the War on Poverty, were based on U.S. Department of Agriculture food budgets for families under economic stress and the portion of a family's income which was spent on food. Orshansky's research found a family of three spent about one third of their after-tax budget on food. She calculated the dollar costs of the least expensive food budget for nutritional food developed by the Department of Agriculture and multiplied by three. This cost became the official working definition of poverty adopted by the Office of Economic Opportunity in 1965 (Fisher, 2003). The assumption is that a family needs at least three times its food budget to pay for housing, clothing, transportation, and other basic requirements. Poverty thresholds are updated yearly by the Census Bureau and are usually used for statistical purposes such as determining the number of people in poverty. Poverty thresholds are used to establish *poverty guidelines* which determine eligibility for social transfer payments.

There is some concern over how poverty statistics are measured because the current calculation does not take into account key government policies such as the tax credits and social transfer payments which alter a family's disposable income, rising standards of living occurring after 1965, expenses necessary to hold a job and earn income, such as child care and transportation costs, rising medical and insurance costs, changes in family structure such as cohabitation among unmarried adults or child support payments, or geographic difference in prices across the country (Short, 2011). The National Academy of Sciences (NAS) convened a Panel on Poverty and Family Assistance which assessed the weaknesses of the current system and made recommendations which gave a more contemporary picture of social and economic realities regarding the poor (Citro, 1995). The work of the NAS in conjunction with the Interagency Technical Working Group (ITWG) resulted in suggestions for Supplemental Poverty Measures (SPM) which define a different population in poverty including larger proportions of the elderly, working families, and married couples. These new supplemental measurements may well affect the way poverty lines, rates, and thresholds are calculated, but because the SPM are not officially in place at the time this book goes to publication, the current official poverty measures are used in all following calculations.

In January 2014 the poverty guideline for one single person is an annual income of $11,670 (*2014 Poverty guidelines*, 2014). A family of two earning $15,730 and a family of four earning $23,850 are considered in poverty (*2014 Poverty guidelines*, 2014). Adding an additional $4,060 per family member allows the computation of poverty lines for any size family. The *poverty rate* is another measure which reflects the percentage of families whose incomes fall below the poverty line given their family status (Hall, 2003). The official poverty rate in the United States in 2012 was 15 percent (Danziger, 2014), and there were 46.2 million people in poverty (Denavas-Walt, 2011). Poverty statistics allow us not only to see what level of income relegates individuals to poverty status but which groups of individuals more often fall into poverty. Poverty statistics are important because they increase policymakers' awareness of individuals at the bottom of the economic ladder. Of grave concern is the unequal distribution of poverty among different groups in the population.

Long-term trends in poverty suggest the overall poverty rate has increased since the 1970s and has never dipped below 11.1 percent (Danziger, 2014). More disturbing is that special subgroups of individuals, children, minorities, the elderly, the less educated, and female heads of households suffer poverty more than their white, male, educated counterparts. When President Johnson declared a War on Poverty in 1964, he instituted anti-poverty measures such as Medicare and Medicaid to expand medical coverage and health care for the elderly, increase social security benefits, and introduce Supplemental Security Income (SSI) to offset the reduced earning power of older Americans. Though poverty in the ranks of the aged declined significantly over the next forty years, the overall poverty rate remained stagnant or increased, leaving future administrations to blame the War on Poverty for an increase instead of a decline in the poverty rate. President Reagan declared that "Poverty won the War" (Reagan, 1986), and, reverting to the Theory of Social Traditionalism in which victims are blamed for their situations because they are lazy and slothful, blamed dependence on social programs as the cause. A closer look at the causes of poverty, though, reveal that economic benefits are not shared by all groups, an important reason poverty increased for most groups since the 1970s.

Increases in the number of workers who worked over six months per year characterized as being in poverty or workers characterized as being near poverty, also known as the working poor, grew 1,900,000 from 2007 to 2011 ("A profile of the working poor, 2011," 2011). Of the total labor force which grew from 153,124,000 in 2007 to 155,389,000 in 2013, almost three million workers and their families were in poverty while over four million were among the working poor. The working poor are defined as those who work at least twenty-seven weeks per year in a full-time wage or salary position or are looking for work yet their incomes fall below the poverty line. The working poor make up about 7 percent of the total workforce. Blacks (13.3 percent) and Hispanics (12.9 percent) were among the working poor more so than Whites (6.1 percent) or Asians (5.6 percent) (Research, 2013). Blacks, Hispanics, women, the young, and the undereducated tend to be in poverty and among the working poor more so than White and Asian men. In 2011, 14.4 percent of part-time workers and 4.2 percent of full-time workers were among the working poor (Research, 2013). See table 5.1.

The statistics about the poor and the working poor are gathered via the American Community Survey (ACS) which collects data each year from a sampling of addresses representing diverse areas of the country. Individuals at these addresses are asked to respond to survey questions which cover race, age, education, sex, and home ownership. The Census Bureau is mandated

Table 5.1.   Civilian Labor Force (non-institutionalized, in thousands).

	1973	2007	2009	2013
Total Labor Force	89,429	153,124	154,142	155,389
Unemployed	4,365	7,078	14,825	11,460
Unemployment Rate	4.9	4.6	9.3	7.4
In Poverty	22,973	37,276	43,569	46,200
Poverty Rate	11.1	13	14.8	15
Working Poor	No data	4,401	8,913	7,935

Author's Analysis: Bureau of Labor Statistics.

by the U.S. Constitution to collect this information under Title 13 of the U.S. Code of the Census Act in order for federal agencies to determine an equitable distribution of resources to the states. The states then use this statistically analyzed data to provide information on which communities can base governing decisions such as development and expansion, reassessment of existing programs, and expenditures among competing community and civic organizations. The ACS also provides data on many variables including race, age, gender, education, and labor force status (*American community survey information guide*, 2013). As reflected in the ACS, poverty rates for American Indians and African Americans were 27 percent and 25.8 percent respectively, followed by Native Hawaiians and other Pacific Islanders at 17.6 percent. Asian poverty rates were 11.7 percent, while Whites had a poverty rate of 11.6 percent (Macartney, 2013). See figure 5.1.

There exist differences in poverty rates between races and ethnicities, genders, age groups, and regions in the country. As indicated in table 5.2, Whites and Whites who identify as non-Hispanic are in poverty less than Blacks and Hispanics who identify as any race. Poverty rates also differ between genders in all age groups. Females over age sixty-five had a 10.7 percent poverty rate while men aged sixty-five experienced a 6.2 percent rate. The poverty rates for females between the ages of eighteen and sixty-four and females under eighteen years of age was 15.5 percent and 22.2 percent respectively while their male counterparts experienced poverty rates of 11.8 percent and 21.6 percent. Poverty tends to be concentrated in the South with 16 percent of the population below the poverty line and is less pervasive in the Midwest and the Northwest. Poverty increased in numbers and percentages in forty-four states from 2000 to 2012 (Denavas-Walt, 2011,

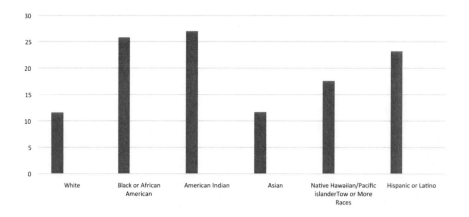

Figure 5.1. Poverty Rates by Race and Hispanic or Latino Origin: 2007–2011. Author's Analysis: American Community Survey.

p. 15). "In 2012, the number of people in poverty increased to about 48.8 million or 15.9 percent" (Bishaw, 2013). See table 5.2.

According to the Bureau of Labor Statistics, there are three labor market problems which contribute to a worker's inability to earn above poverty wages: low earnings, periods of unemployment, and involuntary part-time employment ("A profile of the working poor, 2011," 2011). The majority of the working poor experienced at least one of these major problems during 2011. Low wages for 4.4 million workers employed full time relegated these workers into the working poor category. Long periods of unemployment continued to affect about 4.9 million workers, especially the 1.7 million without work for over ninety-nine weeks. In 2012, 8.1 million workers remained in involuntary part-time employment as a result of unfavorable business conditions or lack of work which reflected double the number working in involuntary part-time positions prior to the 2007 recession. Overall, the employment and unemployment measures in the 2012 U.S. labor market

Table 5.2.   People in Poverty by Selected Characteristics: 2011.

Characteristic	Total	Number in Poverty	Percent in Poverty
People	308,456	48,247	15.6
Race/Hispanic Origin			
White	241,334	30,849	12.8
White, not Hispanic	194,960	19,171	9.8
Black	39,609	10,929	27.6
Asian	16,086	1,973	12.3
Hispanic/any race	52,279	13,244	25.3
Sex			
Male	150,990	20,501	13.6
Female	157,466	25,746	16.4
Age			
Under 18	73,737	16,134	21.9
18 to 64 years	193,213	26,492	13.7
65 years and older	41,507	3,620	8.7
Region			
Northwest	54,977	7,208	13.1
Midwest	66,023	9,221	14
South	114,936	18,380	16
West	72,520	11,437	15.8

Author's Analysis: Bureau of Labor Statistic.

continued slowly to improve "although the proportion of unemployed people who had been jobless for long periods continued to be high by historical standards" (Williamson, 2013, p. 20).

Work rates, wages, family composition, education, and immigration are major causes of poverty (*Combating poverty: Understanding new challenges for families*, 2012). Prior to the Great Recession in 2007 work rates for men and women were higher though wages were falling so consequently workers were working longer and earning less. The unequal distribution of poverty among Blacks and Hispanics is notable. One reason for this particular manifestation of unequal poverty is the lower wages commanded by nonwhite groups. This may be due to *discrimination* in wage rates and differences in education levels. Also blacks and Hispanics have less nonlabor income than do whites (Hall, 2003, p. 365).

Women, including single mothers, entered the workforce in droves after WWII, and with the passage of welfare reform under the Clinton Administration, single mothers' work rate participation increased by 40 percent. Many of these women entered or remained in the low-wage service industry, so their incomes were minimal. Incomes have fallen or remained stagnant for most of the population except the top 10 percent who saw a 32 percent increase in earnings after 2007 (Macartney, 2013). Families headed by single females continue to be in poverty more than any other subgroup of the population which means poverty rates for children continue to increase.

The lack of educational credentials is a major factor determining employment and earnings. For example, in 2012, of the 12.5 million eighteen- to twenty-four-year-olds enrolled in college, 7.2 million were White, 2.4 million were Hispanic, 1.7 million were Black, and 915,000 were Asian. Hispanics have made the most gains in college enrollment; their participation between 1996 and 2012 increased by 240 percent, while Black enrollment increased by 72 percent, and White enrollment increased 12 percent. Hispanic enrollment in the eighteen- to twenty-four-year-old age group surpassed White enrollment by 2 percent in 2012. The 2014 U.S. Supreme Court decision which banned the consideration of race in public college admission decisions may have an impact on minority college enrollment and diversity on college campuses. (*Table 1. Enrollment status of the population 3 years old and over, by sex, age, race, Hispanic origin, foreign born, and foreign-born parentage: October, 2012*, 2012). In 2013, 19 percent of Whites and 21 percent of non-Hispanic Whites had bachelor's degrees, while 12.6 percent of Blacks and 29 percent of Asians had college degrees (*Educational attainment*, 2013). Those without a college degree earn significantly less than their counterparts with college degrees, and those with a high school diploma or less are usually relegated to low-paying jobs. Educational levels speak to a worker's ability to be upwardly mobile, so without an education, workers' chances of moving into a higher paying classification remain static.

Immigration, both legal and illegal, continues to be problematic because of immigrants' lower educational levels, skills, and abilities which relegate them to low-paying jobs and poverty status. According to Borjas (2006), the poverty rate among immigrants is about 6 percent higher than among native-born Americans. If the poverty rate for immigrants could be lowered to reflect the national poverty rate, around 1.9 million people would be affected (Borjas, 2006).

WEALTH AND INCOME INEQUALITIES

Measures of Wealth and Wealth Distribution

Wealth is the value of everything one owns minus one's debts. The things one owns such as a home, a car, and other valuables are called assets and from those assets are deducted debts or liabities to derive one's *net worth*. For purposes of describing the distribution of wealth, economists more narrowly define wealth as *marketable assets*, the value of stocks, bonds, and real estate minus debts and libalitilies to derive one's net worth. The fluidity of marketable assets allows them to be traded, transferred, or turned into cash quickley (Domhoff, 2013). *Financial wealth* or *non-income wealth* is an economic concept which reflects one's net worth minus one's net equity in one's home or owner-occupied dwelling. Since the equity in one's home is usually a resource not available for immediate cash conversion, financial wealth discounts home equity and only relies on resources for immediate comsumption or investment (Wolff, 2004).

The United States has one of the greatest wealth inequalities in the world because most of the wealth is highly concentrated in the top 1 percent of the population. In 2010, the top 1 percent of households owned 35.4 percent of all privately held wealth while the next 19 percent held 53.5 percent of the wealth. This translates into the top 20 percent of the population owning 89 percent of the wealth. The remaining 80 percent of the population owned only 11 percent of the wealth. When considering financial wealth, the dispariety is even greater because the top 1 percent hold 42.1 percent while the bottom 80 percent own only 4.7 percent (Wolff, 2012). According to Domhoff (2013), "financial wealth is what counts as far as the control of income-producing assets, [so] we can say that just 10 percent of the people own the United States of America" (p. 3). This is a sobering statistic when viewed from a global perspective. The World Institute for Development Economics Research (2006), an arm of United Nations University, produced data which reflected the top 10 percent of the world's adults control 85 percent of the global household wealth (not just financial wealth) in comparison to 69.8 percent of the top 10 percent for the United States. The only other democratised industrial country with greater wealth inequality is Switzerzerland with the top 10 percent of adults owning 71.3 percent of the wealth (Davies, 2006; Levine, 2012). Some of the reasons other countries have less wealth disparity than the U.S. are the appropriation of larger social transfer payments to the poorest populations, progressive tax rates which extract fewer taxes from the poor and more taxes from the rich, and more equality in the income distribution of earnings (Levine, 2012). See table 5.3.

The distribution of wealth is important because wealth equals economic wellbeing and financial and psychological security for oneself and one's heirs and may bestow political influence on the wealthy. The amount of wealth necessary for economic wellbeing is a matter of debate among policymakers who determine tax policy, transfer payments, and investments. The role of redistribution in fiscal, economic, and monetary policies continues among Congressional officials who support and oppose higher or lower taxes and more or fewer social transfer payments in order to ensure long-term economic growth. Wealth also provides income each year because it is nonlabor income or *unearned income* such as owning shares of stock and receiving portions of the firms' profits, owning bonds and receiving some of the firm's interest payments, or owning apartments and receiving some of the rents. Because individuals with low wages seldom own wealth, the increase in wealth for a few individuals adds to the total income inequality.

For purposes of exploring wealth and income disparities, the U.S. population is divided into quintiles each representing 20 percent of U.S. households. Each quintile or fifth of U.S. households should account for 20 percent of aggregate wealth and income. Over the last several decades, the Congressional Budget Office (CBO), drawing data from the Census Bureau, has documented the stagnent share of income for the bottom quintile at around 4 percent and the top quintile at over 50 percent. This means those in the top quintile continue to move further away from the remaining quintiles, thus increasing the wealth and income gap already in existence (Levine, 2012).

Table 5.3.   **Wealth Distribution by Quintile (non-home) 1983–2010.**

Year	Bottom–Fourth	Fifth	Top 1%
2010	4.7	53.5	42.1
2001	8.7	51.5	39.7
1992	7.7	46.7	45.6
1983	8.7	48.4	42.9

Source: Domhoff (2013).

Measures of Income and Income Distribution

Income is the wages and salaries people earn from selling their labor in the marketplace and from the dividends, interest, and rent/royalties from financial investments, savings, and owned properties. *Income inequality* is the unequal distribution of a group's share of total income which is different than its share of the population (Levine, 2012). For purposes of measuring income inequality, economists use the concept of *money income* which "includes wages and salaries, interest, dividends, rent, payments from pensions and retirement savings accounts, and nonmeans-tested cash income (e.g., Social Security, unemployment compensation, and veterans' payment)" (Levine, 2012, p. 2). Money income does not include social transfer payments or capital gains and is figured on a pretax basis. In 2012 the lowest quintile received 3.2 percent of money income; the second quintile received 8.3 percent, the middle quintile received 14.4 percent, the fourth quintile received 23 percent, and the highest quintile received 51 percent of the money income. The top 5 percent within the top quintile received 22.3 percent of that quintile's money income. Table 5.4 reflects the decrease in each of the four lower quintile's aggregate income from 1970 to 2012 with the exception of the fourth quintile from 1970–1980. The fifth quintile reflects a continuing increase in aggregate income since 1970. See table 5.4.

Some economists believe that basing income distribution on money income does not provide an accurate analysis of a household's economic well-being. They argue that members in a household often share resources such as utilities, a homemaker's contribution in unpaid work to the family in the form of childcare, cooking, and cleaning are not monetarily valued, the business cycle's effect or seasonal adjustments to work are discounted, and the number and age of family members living in the household wildly changes. These variables make capturing a definitive share of aggregate income for each quintile somewhat subjective yet alternative measures which statistically account for these variations yield very similar results (Burkhauser, 2009).

Table 5.4. Income Distribution by Quintile: 1970–2012.

Year	Bottom	Second	Third	Fourth	Fifth	Top 5%
2012	3.2	8.3	14.4	23	51	22.3
2000	3.6	8.9	14.8	23	19.8	22.1
1990	3.8	9.6	15.9	24	46.6	18.5
1980	4.2	10.2	16.8	24.7	44.1	16.5
1970	4.1	10.8	17.4	24.5	43.3	16.6

Author's Analysis: U.S. Census Bureau.

Income inequality arises largely from wage inequality. Reasons for wage inequality are many and varied, but a few of them are the differences in abilities that individuals have, differences in *human capital* (investments in education), and the economy of the superstars (higher wages for those in the limelight: actors/actresses/CEOs/NFL/NBA players, etc.). The increasing introduction of technology has probably increased the relative rewards for those with higher-than-average ability and education. The telecommunications revolution including the Internet has created instant information dissemination and retrieval thereby allowing superstars to reach bigger audiences and achieve even higher incomes.

Trends in Income Distribution

Explanations for the continuing increases in income inequality revolve around the debate over the effects of globalization and the need for new technological improvements. Competition in a globalized economy with workers worldwide has reduced the need for less-skilled American workers who find their wages stagnating or declining, thus contributing to income inequality (Levine, 2012). The information technology currently available has displaced many low-wage workers whose jobs are now being done by robots or computers. The offshoring and outsourcing of digitized work increases the scarcity of many jobs once held by skilled U.S. workers who are not immune to job loss caused by globalization. The increasing need for technically skilled workers to man the high-tech and green jobs of the future requires further education and training in order to command higher wages (Goldin, 2007). This segmentation within the labor market increases the demand for highly trained technical workers, decreases the demand for semi-skilled workers in industry and administration, and maintains the demand for low-skilled workers in the service arena (Autor, 2003; Freeman, 2009). Contributing to these disparities is the decline of labor unions and the weakening of labor laws which protected workers as well as changing demographics such as aging baby boomers.

Deficiencies in Measuring Equality

There exist problems with how we measure income and wealth in the United States. The measures we use should tell us something about the economic well-being of individuals and groups so that policy makers and legislators can design policies most beneficial to more individuals. Our inequality measures suffer from some deficiencies because they are based on income earned by various individuals and groups. For example, the United States exercises a *progressive income tax system* in which higher-income households pay a greater share of their earning for taxes, but U.S. sales, gasoline, and other taxes are *regressive taxes* for which all users pay the same tax. Since lower-income workers usually consume more goods and services which are regressively taxed, they end up paying a larger share of their income for taxes than do those with higher earnings. Since our income measures are based on pretax dollars, the availability of income may be overstated. In other words, there may be less available income to spend than is reflected in our measures.

Another problem with income measurement is that government transfer payments or welfare payments such as food stamps, subsidized housing, free or reduced school lunches, and free medical care in the form of Medicaid are ignored in the calculation. These programs increase the share of income going to individuals at the bottom of income earnings but are not counted as income, so inequality may be overstated. Also ignored are fringe benefit packages and income from *capital gains,* which mainly benefit the middle and upper classes. If fringe benefits and income from capital gains were included in inequality measures, a greater portion of total income going to the middle and top income classes would be included and our income measure would be understated.

POLICIES TO ALLEVIATE POVERTY: MINIMUM WAGE AND THE EARNED INCOME TAX CREDIT

The Minimum Wage

One policy to correct the inequality in income is known as the federal *minimum wage* law. The federal minimum wage is a codified wage below which no employer can pay certain employees; it was enacted in 1938 as part of the Fair Labor Standards Act. At that time, it was 25 cents per hour and affected about 43 percent of industries. In 2008, the federal minimum wage was $6.55 per hour and rose to $7.25 per hour in July 2009 ("Wages: Minimum wage," 2012). Hall and Leiberman (2003) write that 90 percent of the workforce is covered by minimum wage laws. The question then becomes, "Does the federal minimum wage create greater equality among workers?"

According to the Bureau of Labor Statistics, there were 75.9 million American workers or 58.8 percent of all wage and salary workers over the age of sixteen who were paid hourly. About 1.5 million were paid the prevailing minimum wage of $7.25 per hour while 1.8 million were paid below that figure. These workers make up 4.3 percent of all hourly paid workers. There are some inconsistencies in the collection of this data which comes from the Current Population Survey (CPS), a national monthly survey under the auspices of the U.S. Census Bureau for the Bureau of Labor Statistics (BLS). Each month the CPS surveys one quarter of 60,000 households and asks respondents their hourly wage; the CPS does not ask respondents if they are covered by federal minimum wage laws. This may skew some responses because workers may over or under report their wage, not take into account overtime they may work, or may not report tips and commissions ("Characteristics of minimum wage workers, 2013," 2014). Also, this survey excludes salaried and other workers not paid by the hour even if their earnings would result in comparable minimum wages if figured by the hour. Consequently, the total number of workers affected by minimum wage is probably underestimated.

To understand the effects of minimum wage laws, it is necessary to look at three groups of workers in labor markets: skilled, unskilled covered by minimum wage, and unskilled not covered by minimum wage. When minimum wage laws are enacted, all eligible employees must be paid at least the minimum wage. Let's say that a firm is going to hire twenty workers at $30 per hour. All workers available for those openings will want to take those jobs because each worker wants to maximize his or her own utility (make the most money they can). The firm will have a large talent pool from which to choose because all available workers are, at this point, in the talent pool. So the firm picks the best and the brightest from the talent pool and hires twenty workers, and pays them $30 per hour. Another firm wishes to hire twenty workers at $20 per hour, so that firm chooses from those available in the talent pool. Again, because each worker wishes to maximize his or her own utility, all the workers in the talent pool want to gravitate toward the $20 per hour job. But the firm only needs twenty workers, so they choose the best and the brightest left in the talent pool. Another firm wishes to hire forty workers, and because there is a minimum wage law in effect, they must pay their workers $7.25 per hour. All available workers left in the talent pool want to gravitate toward the minimum wage job because it pays more than any other available job. The firm chooses forty workers from the talent pool. This gravitation toward the highest-paying jobs means that there is less demand from employers for workers at each successive level. Since no one can force a firm to hire more workers than it wishes to hire, there is always an excess of workers wishing to work (excess labor supply). Those who do not find work at minimum wage or above are relegated to working for below minimum wage or remain unemployed. Thus the effect of the minimum wage impacts the sector not covered by the law. Increased competition for jobs drives down the wages of all workers, even those already employed before the minimum wage was in effect.

Skilled workers are also affected by the minimum wage. When the wage of unskilled labor rises in the labor market covered by minimum wage legislation, firms will begin to substitute skilled workers and capital equipment (translate technological investments) for unskilled labor. Skilled labor is needed to design, produce, and repair the capital investments.

Minimum wage legislation sets off several events. As a result of minimum wage legislation, some unskilled workers benefit in the form of higher pay. Other unskilled workers are harmed by being forced into lower-paying positions. The only group who truly benefits is skilled workers. It is no surprise that labor unions are among the biggest supporters of minimum wage legislation.

About half of all minimum wage workers are below the age of twenty-five ("Characteristics of minimum wage workers, 2013," 2014). These workers tend to be less educated, work in the service, leisure, or hospitality industry, are unmarried, and work part time. The typical stereotype of the young, low-wage earner is different from the reality of low-wage earners over the age of twenty-five who are disproportionately female, between the ages of twenty-five and fifty-four, married, work thirty-five hours a week or more, and support families ("Characteristics of minimum wage workers, 2013," 2014).

In 1980, earning the minimum wage, which was $3.10 at that time, "was enough to lift a single parent out of poverty . . . but today's minimum wage is not enough for single parents to reach even the most basic threshold of adequate living standards" (Cooper and Hall, 2013). Currently a minimum wage worker earns about 37 percent of the wages commanded by an average American production worker (Cooper and Hall, 2013). If minimum wage "had kept pace with productivity, it would be almost $18.75 today" (Cooper and Hall, 2013). A hike in the minimum wage to $10.10 would affect 88 percent of low-wage workers twenty years of age and older, 54 percent of whom work full time, 69 percent whose families make less than $60,000 yearly, and over 25 percent who have children ("Characteristics of minimum wage workers, 2013," 2014; Cooper and Hall, 2013). The Fair Minimum Wage Act of 2013, legislation to incrementally raise the minimum wage to $10.10 per hour and tie it to inflation, met defeat in the House of Representatives in 2014. The inability of the value of the minimum wage to keep up with inflation has contributed to the unequal income inequality in the United States (Mishel, 2013).

Earned Income Tax Credit

Another policy to reduce the inequality in income is known as the *earned income tax credit* (EITC). The EITC is a federal income tax credit for low-income workers who are eligible for and claim the credit; the credit rewards those who leave welfare and move into work positions, encourages an increase in work hours, and offsets federal payroll and income taxes ("Policy basics: The earned income tax credit," 2014). Twenty-four states and the District of Columbia now also administer their own EITC (Magg, 2014). The credit reduces the amount of tax an individual owes and may be returned to the worker in the form of a refund at tax time. The EITC has been widely praised for its success in supporting work and reducing poverty, is the largest cash program next to the Supplemental Nutritional Assistance Program (SNAP) or food stamp program, and is credited with lifting "6.5 million people out of poverty, including 3 million children" (Magg, 2014). The federal EITC also has been proven effective in encouraging work among welfare recipients, especially single mothers, because only those who work can claim the credit. The EITC has support from across the political spectrum.

There are some concerns associated with the EITC. The complexity of the EITC may force low-income workers to seek help in tax preparation, contribute to the high error rate in improper refunds, and reduce the credit to some married couples with children because of their higher income. The EITC for childless workers or noncustodial workers who work full-time hours at minimum wage is too small to lift those workers out of poverty and may actually tax them into poverty ("Policy basics: The earned income tax credit," 2014). Steps to authorize higher threshold limits for those eligible for the EITC have been put in place through 2017 to address some of these issues. Proposed reforms to the EITC include increasing the credit for childless workers, consolidating the EITC with other tax provisions which benefit children, and parsing out the EITC through work incentives or child-rearing costs (Magg, 2014).

The EITC is a wage *subsidy*. Subsidies increase the cost of doing business and can be thought of as a *negative tax*. The societal implication of providing a subsidy depends upon to whom the subsidy is given. In this case, the subsidy is being given to low-wage workers who in turn may use the subsidy for consuming goods and services or savings. Recipients of the subsidy could purchase goods and services they normally could not afford. If consumer purchases are substantial enough, producers might increase the quantity or quality of the production of goods and services. Without the EITC, the consumer will pay market price. The consumer pays a higher price for goods when subsidies exist because the government will pick up part of the cost. Consumers are willing to buy more if they receive the subsidy, but the actual consumer outlay is lower because the government pays the extra amount.

The decisions made by policy makers to reduce or extend tax credits or subsidies to certain segments of the population to a large degree are dictated by political winds and may be influenced by the lobbyists and special interest groups legislators are trying to appease. The debate often revolves around what is economically feasible, will do the least harm, and is politically viable. Within this vortex of considerations, the issues of equality versus equity arise. Since all workers are not considered equal because of skills, abilities, and talents, should those workers receive compensation in the form of opportunities, education, and training in order to elevate their ability to command higher wages and move up in the distribution of income or should all workers receive equal opportunities regardless of their standing in the income distribution? What society determines to be fair and equitable in the distribution of income has far-reaching consequences for workers, their families and communities, and the nation.

EQUALITY VERSUS EQUITY: THE ROLE OF FAIRNESS

Confusing *equality,* which means everyone gets the same thing, with *equity,* which implies fair and equal treatment, is a common mistake. Equality, which implies sameness, is a separate issue from equity which denotes impartiality and justness. The issues of fairness and income inequality are interpreted differently.

Fairness may be a difficult concept to define. Most of us have some idea about what is fair and what is not fair. Theoretically we generally assume that reasonable people in policy-making positions will craft policies most beneficial to most individuals most of the time. But in reality, policies shift with the political party in power at a given time. Therefore, our policies may change from conservative to liberal or vice versa at each changing of the guard. Often highly emotional disputes arise over policy changes because many policy changes do not seem fair to certain segments of the population. Economics, a field emphasizing positive, descriptive, and predictive issues, usually avoids discussions of fairness because fairness may have arbitrary meanings. What may seem fair to one person may not seem fair to another. Individual ideas of fairness are usually associated with individual belief and value systems; this is often contentious ground upon which to focus a policy debate. Nevertheless, the debate concerning income inequality usually revolves around fairness issues. The debate within the field of economics which incorporates value judgments in economic decisions is known as *normative economics* and looks at what the economy *should be like* or what particular policy actions *should be recommended* to achieve a desirable goal.

The field of economics which determines policy on efficiency economics alone is known as *value-free economics.* Value-free economics does not make value judgments about what the economy should be like or what particular policy actions should be recommended to achieve a desirable goal. The point in measuring income inequality is to compare some standard of "what should be" to "what is." So the measurement of "what is" reflects the state of our economy at some given point in time. This measurement allows us to look at the policies which are in place and decide if the policies need to be changed based upon our satisfaction with "what is." This "what is" and "what should be" debate is based on the difference between two distinct premises: *efficiency* and *equity.*

Efficiency is strictly the use of resources to gain the most benefit, is associated with *cost-benefit analysis* and *rational choice theory*, and primarily looks at issues dealing with the bottom line or profit margin. Equity, on the other hand, looks at the fairness issue and takes into account *compensating wage differentials* and *property income* and revolves around what is fair or just. Equity issues spill over into social well-being, not simply economic well-being.

There are some issues of fairness or equity upon which most individuals agree. By understanding the causes of income inequality, policy makers can craft policies to help avoid income and wealth distributions which seem unfair. For example, most individuals would agree compensating wage differentials, receiving higher pay for jobs which incur risk, are environmentally unsafe, or require certification/licensure, are fair. If a worker must assume greater risk in a job, acquire more education for a job, or work longer hours in unpleasant circumstances in a job, then that worker should receive higher wages. Therefore eliminating wage differentials to make jobs more equal would be less equitable.

The same holds true for some property income or unearned income. Some Americans may have sacrificed, worked long years, assumed risk, or saved, to acquire wealth. It would be unfair to construct policies which decrease the wealth of those Americans. These examples suggest that inequality resulting from choices individuals make is generally regarded as fair.

What about inequality that arises not from choices individuals make but from *opportunities* individuals may have? Are differing opportunities inherently unjust or inequitable? There certainly exist some forms of unjust opportunities such as restricted opportunities in firms' discriminatory hiring practices. Therefore, social policy is directed toward resolving or weakening the barriers to hiring for victims of employment discrimination. If discrimination is perceived to occur anyway, the individual has a right to due process through a court system.

In other cases, there seems to be no general consensus about fairness. Americans who inherit large amounts of wealth are often perceived as socially evil because they have an unfair advantage from birth. Others may believe that one's property is one's to do with as one chooses. So passing inheritance on to one's heirs is appropriate. This argument extends to inherited talent, intelligence, beauty, and physical strength.

Americans attempt to resolve these democratic issues in a voting booth. Once Americans decide on their goals, policy makers design policies to reflect those goals. Understanding the impact of policies on various groups and the opportunity costs for making various choices helps us formulate policy. The consequence of each action taken by policy makers must be considered. Can there be a marriage between efficiency and equity? Can these two issues be resolved so they coexist in the United States to the benefit of all Americans? Policy makers must be aware that long-term benefits of social justice must not be sacrificed for short-term profits in this age of new global economic growth. Decisions about income distribution and life chances or opportunities which affect millions of Americans must be carefully crafted. The fallout from those policies filters down to affect all Americans in their everyday existence. Therefore, the importance of placing responsible people in policy-making positions is paramount. Understanding the differences in equality and equity helps us recognize and respond to the variances in wealth and income inequality inherent in an economic system of capitalism which dispenses rewards on an efficiency basis.

Chapter Six

The Evolution of the Employment Relationship

Work defines us. Work is an activity central to our lives and defines who we are and what we do. Humans identify with their work, with their coworkers, and with their employers. When adults are asked to identify themselves, they respond with their name and job or career. Our family lives, our leisure time, and our social agenda are often dictated by our work schedule. Work is such an integral component of our daily lives that when work changes or ceases, humans have difficulty adjusting. Our work then is our anchor in an economic sea of chaos; it allows us to feel secure and safe from financial storms of poverty, debt, and insecurity. Work then is defined as paid employment for the purposes of our discussion. Though there is great value in unpaid work such as household labor or volunteer activities in an informal economy, we limit our exploration of work to that of paid employment in the formal economy. This necessarily confines our discussion to the employment relationship between employers who pay for their employees' labor and those employees.

STANDARD AND NONSTANDARD EMPLOYMENT RELATIONSHIPS

When we talk about an employment relationship, we're talking about the relationship between employees and employers. This relationship is socially constructed in a political process (Gonos, 1997, p. 1213; 1998) and suggests there exists a *standard employment relationship* characterized by the exchange of a worker's labor for some sort of employer compensation based on hours worked, using the employer's capital, and under the employer's control mediated only by some agreed upon stipulations such as a collective bargaining agreement (Kalleberg, 2000). This standard employment relationship becomes the norm for most workers who depend on their work for continued employment, protection from unsafe working conditions through health and safety laws, defense from wage and hour exploitation through the Fair Labor Standards Act, shields from discrimination and unfair treatment through the National Labor Relations Act and federal anti-discrimination laws, and the provision of a social safety net in the form of unemployment, social security, and parental and medical leave benefits. In the standard employment relationship, workers enjoy full-time employment which allows them to buy homes, educate their children, save for retirement, and invest in their future.

There also exists a *non-standard employment relationship* which includes part-time, contingency, sub-contracted, day labor, on-call, contract, freelance, and self-employment work. These non-standard employment relationships are less likely to provide employment security and often avoid legal obligations of employers by engaging an intermediary to hire, fire, discipline, and pay employees; therefore, the employers do not assume the responsibility of extracting social security or unemployment insurance deductions from a worker's wages, ensure continued employment, or control the activity of the workers or the work process. This non-standard employment relationship is often known as *precarious work* and becomes the dominant employment relationship in the United States beginning in 1970. Precarious work directly impacts job and economic insecurity and inequality for workers and indirectly impacts individual, family, and community security (Kalleberg, 2009). Addressing the employment relationship through the various lenses of gender, race, ethnicity, civil rights, economic and social justice, family insecurity, work-life balances, emigration and immigration, and politics allows us to understand the implications of macro forces such as structural and organizational changes in work relationships as well as micro forces such as worker agency. Understanding the challenges and opportunities faced by employers and employees in this relationship helps create policy mechanisms beneficial to all stakeholders.

Precarious work is "uncertain, unpredictable, and risky from the point of view of the worker" (Kalleberg, 2009, p. 2). The free-market economy lends itself to precarious work because competition drives down prices and wages. When wages decline, workers lose money and are less able to sustain some standard of living. Precarious work seeks labor-cost concessions which undermine workers' ability to make money. This is certainly not a new or novel idea. The centuries prior to labor law legislation in the 1930s operated in a free-market economy in which corporate power reigned supreme and was backed by court decisions which favored employers. The New Deal era ushered in a short period of worker security backed by the National Labor Relations Act, the Fair Labor Standards Act, and the Social Security Act which provided protections to workers' wages, hours of work, rights to un-ionize, and a social safety net for workers who retired. Because of this legislation, a new middle-class arose which brought prosperity to many, but there soon followed a period, beginning in the 1970s, which brought macro-economic changes catapulting the United States into a global economy branded by worldwide competition. An influx of Asian imports in the auto and steel industries during the 1980s forced American workers to compete with workers worldwide and a race to the bottom for labor costs began.

This new neoliberal economy, characterized by privatization, deregula-tion, deunionization, and dehumanization encouraged corporate power based on property rights to expand while worker power and worker rights de-creased. Worker protections in the form of unions, labor laws, and National Labor Relations Board and court decisions were becoming inadequate to protect employees. As technology continued to displace human labor, precar-ious work gained a greater foothold in U.S. manufacturing, and productivity gains for workers eroded. The service sector emerged as the burgeoning arena for work opportunities yet provided lowered wages, few if any bene-fits, and little job security. Ideologies shifted from the collective as the arbi-ter of wage gains and good jobs to an individualistic approach focused on individual responsibility for one's own welfare. The market, driven by unfet-tered capitalism, shifted the balance of economic power to privatization and corporations and away from government intervention. Employers, taking ad-vantage of lax government regulations, easily adjusted the number of work-ers and their schedules to conform to supply and demand of their business models. As Kalleberg (2009) states, "precarious work has contributed to greater economic inequality, insecurity, and instability" (p. 8).

THE NATURE OF THE EMPLOYMENT RELATIONSHIP

The nature of the *employment relationship* has changed over the course of time. Marx posited this relationship to be based on the ability of a society to produce in a form beneficial to all citizens and is the basis for Marx's claim about the social relations of production. "Any system of production requires the deployment of a range of assets or resources or factors of production: tools, machines, land, raw materials, labor power, skills, information, and so forth" (Davis and Welton, 1991, p. 13). This means that at any time and place in history, all production functions (ways of producing goods and services from raw materials into salable products) are governed by the social relations that people have to the production process. Different people have different kinds of rights and powers over the use of the inputs and over the results of their use. The actual ways in which inputs are combined and used in produc-tion depends as much on the way these rights and powers are wielded as it does on the strictly technical features of a production function. The sum total of these rights and powers constitutes the "social relations of production" (Davis and Welton, 1991, p. 13).

When we talk about the rights and powers people have over the means of production, we are talking about the relationships people have with each other when using resources productively. So power relationships involve the ways in which individuals are "regulated and controlled" (Davis and Welton, 1991, p. 13) by other people, and the laws, rules, and policies those people make about how resources will be owned and allocated. When there exist unequal distributions of power over productive resources, there also exists unequal appropriation of the productive outputs. Marxism distinguishes three types of relationships which refer to the rights and powers individuals have in economic relationships: *feudalism, slavery*, and *capitalism*.

This then is the story of unequal economic power relationships between people who have a relationship to the means of production. When discussing economic power relationships in terms of employment relationships, we're talking about individuals who own the means of production and allocate the means of production (employers) as well as individuals who add value to the production process by turning raw materials into salable goods and services (employees).

From feudal times when lords ruled over serfs to times when masters ruled over slaves to times when employers paid wage earners to produce goods and services, the employment relationship has remained one of employer domination over worker servitude. Over the course of history, numerous associations between those who owned production and those who produced have existed but in all instances, this stark contrast between owners of production and workers has remained one of employer power over worker power. The employment relationship has always been guided by some overarching law, rule, principle, or policy. These guidelines have determined the nature of the employment relationship, its effect on owners of production and workers, and the resulting standard of living for workers, the ability of workers to respond in a meaningful way to the relationship, and the security/insecurity of workers within their positions. Looking at these relationships over time allows us to see the ebb and flow of power between employers and workers. Exploring early employment relationships such as those of feudal serfs and lords during the ninth through the sixteenth centuries prefaces a discussion of changes in the employment relationship under various labor market policies sanctioned by U.S. law.

EMPLOYMENT RELATIONSHIPS OVER TIME

Feudalism

During medieval times, the employment relationship in Europe was one of *feudalism*, a practice in which individual lords or barons administered estates, adjudicated disputes, dispensed justice, coined their own money, taxed their constituents, and conscripted military service from their *vassals*. The feudal system was based on security. According to Wright (2002), feudalism can be viewed as a society within which feudal lords and serfs have *joint ownership* rights in the labor of the serf. The conventional description of feudalism is a society within which the peasants or *serfs* are forced to work part of each week on the land owned by the lord and are free to work the rest of the week on the land to which they have some kind of customary title. This obligation to work part of the week on the lord's land means, in effect, that the lord has property rights in the serf which take the form of the right to use the labor of the serf a certain proportion of the time. This ownership is less absolute than that of the slave owner, thus the expression "joint ownership" of the serf by the lord and serf" (Wright, 2002, p. 15). This perspective of property rights is very different than the view of property rights we hold today in which we view property as a personal possession exchanged or traded in the market. Within the feudal system, property was commonly owned by all beings "conceived of as a 'Great Chain of Being,' a rigidly constructed hierarchy of responsibilities that ascended upward from the lowest creatures to the angels in heaven" (Rifkin, 2014, p. 30). Each individual within the chain inhabited a certain status as well as responsibilities. This theological conceptualization of property was based on the idea that God owned all property and entrusted various individuals, from lords to serfs, with it (Rifkin, 2014).

The elite wanted security in maintaining control over their vast land holdings, and the workers wanted security from marauders, invading armies, and barbarians. A feudal king was the chief feudal lord but was more of a figurehead and held his position by *divine right*, the idea that God granted to specific men the right to rule and passed that right on through heredity; in reality the estate lords held more power. Because the king's land holdings were so vast and communication was so poor, it was ineffective for the king to maintain control over his kingdom, so contracts were formed with *barons* or *lords* who were the ruling elite and provided *fiefs* or land to their vassals. Vassals swore allegiance or *homage* to their lord and upon the vassal's death, their heirs must also swear homage to the lord. The vassal and the lord shared a relationship of reciprocity. A vassal was obligated to provide military service, attend his lord's court, help administer justice, and provide money to support the lord's entourage when the lord visited his fief. The lord was obligated to provide protection and military aid and guard the vassal's children. The vassal lived on a *manor*, the economic and social equivalent of a village. On the manor were the manor house, one or more villages, and thousands of acres of land distributed to *peasants* and *serfs*, the workers of the fields. Peasants lived in the villages which consisted of ten to sixty families living in meager huts which they often shared with livestock. Serfs were bound to the lord for life, owned no property, and needed the lord's permission to marry or leave the land. The serf was technically not a slave because if the serf successfully left the land and stayed away for one year and one day, the serf was a free person. The serf was not required to fight, was entitled to the protection of the lord, and wasn't sold or displaced if the lord of the manor changed. So the serf actually had more rights than did the slaves living in American during the 1700s and 1800s. Each worker had an equal share of land, some good and some poor. The peasants lived a rather sparse existence which consisted of work and family life. Ninety percent of the population on the manor were peasants.

This feudal economy lasted until new economic forces in Tudor England and Europe began transitioning communal property into private property. Kings and governments began enclosing communal property from 1500–1800. Known as the Enclosure Movement, this economic reshaping displaced millions of peasants who then sought work as free agents, demanded a food supply no longer provided to them through the feudal system, and watched as the land they had tilled for centuries became pasture for the lucrative raising of sheep. Rivkin (2014) writes that many historians viewed The Enclosure Movement as "the revolution of the rich against the poor" (p. 31).

Slavery

Marx's central concept of slavery embraces the idea that "a slave owner 'owns' the slave . . . [and] specif[ies] a range of rights and powers that the slave owner has over one particular resource used in production—people. In the extreme case, the slave owner has virtually absolute property rights in the slave" (Wright, 2002, p. 15).

There is some distinction made between *slave labor* and *wage earners*. Slaves, those workers who have no ability to leave the employment relationship because of their servitude status, were prominent in the market-based policies of the United States for hundreds of years. The United States constitutionally and scripturally based a system of slavery on the inferiority of a race said to be incompetent to manage its own affairs and therefore found it necessary to keep this race under the bondage of servitude for their own protection, survival, and Christianization. In reality, the Southern system of agrarianism was dependent upon slave labor which fueled the planting and harvesting of King Cotton, the engine providing economic stability to the region. Other crops were also harvested such as rice, tobacco, and sugar, but cotton reigned supreme. Regardless, slavery was sanctioned in the United States for more than two centuries and was only outlawed in the 1860s with the *Emancipation Proclamation* and the passage of the Thirteenth Amendment. The concern of plantation owners at this time was their economic well-being. How would they manage to maintain a hold over their workers without the stranglehold of slavery? How could they conscript workers into fourteen- to sixteen-hour days without pay if slavery was abolished? Slave owners saw The Emancipation Proclamation as a document which destroyed their way of life because it unseated the foundation of their labor-market policies by stripping them of their ability to conscript free labor.

During the early days of the United States, there were two different labor markets operating which dictated the employment relationship. Owners of production reacted differently to these policies depending upon their geographic location. Because of different climates, land topography, and availability of workers, northern property owners gravitated toward the production of wheat while Southern land and plantation owners gravitated toward the production of cotton. During the 1700s and 1800s, the first global trade in the textile industry took hold in Britain and India.

The production of goods and services was moving from the home and craft industry in which families produced most of their own goods and clothing into a more industrialized arena in urban factory settings because of population growth and the expanding demand for more and more goods and clothing. The first real global trade in the textile industry between Britain and India resulted from the British demand for more clothing for their growing population because they could not produce enough cotton to supply that demand. India began producing cotton in large quantities and selling it to Britain; Britain then produced the clothing for their own population as well as selling clothing back to India. This first global export/import system soon was insufficient to supply the market needs of British and Indian customers, so other sources of cotton were necessary.

The South, with its warm climate, long growing seasons, and rich river valley soil, began producing cotton, and between 1815 and 1860, the South was producing one billion pounds of cotton per year. Seventy percent was exported to England; this surge in production was made possible not only by weather and soil conditions, but because southern land owners could evade competition in the labor markets by engaging in slavery. Slavery was an employment relationship in which slave owners conscripted workers into servitude; the institution of slavery was a scripturally and constitutionally sanctioned policy of the U.S. government which protected slave owners from operating in a competitive market. A scriptural foundation for slavery emerged because slave intellect was thought to be inferior to white intellect;

whites felt they had an obligation to "Christianize" blacks for their own salvation. The viewpoint held by many in the South was to save the black man's soul, colonize him, and send him back to Africa (Liberia or country of origin), so he would then in turn spread the gospel to others in his native land. Since blacks were thought to be an intellectually inferior race, a Constitutional amendment counted black men as 3/5 of human for Census purposes, so the idea of partial humanness became embedded in the law of the land.

The production of cotton is labor intensive. Workers must be available year round because the cotton planting and harvesting season is around eight months long. Cotton producers then need an available workforce most of the year, so it was important for plantation owners to be able to keep their workforce on the plantation throughout the year. The institution of slavery was necessary in order to maintain such a workforce. The life of the slave was grueling. Slave owners or masters had complete control over their slaves and used a system of patriarchy to control, reward, and/or punish. Masters could withhold food and engage in negative reinforcement such as whipping, binding, or selling nonconforming slaves who didn't respond to the master's requests. Slaves were always at a disadvantage because they lacked education and a cultural background. Nameless individuals with no history are easier to control, and masters used the slaves' loss of identity as a control tool. Slaves worked from sun up to sun down with little time for family bonding or leisure. Strong, healthy slaves could pick about 300 pounds of cotton per day, and child labor among slave children was rampant. As soon as children could carry the cotton picking bags, they were required to go into the fields. The benefits of slavery to the cotton industry developed with slave labor which enabled slave owners to avoid the competitive wage market, be assured of a constant labor force, cultivate greater acreage which allowed cotton production to increase, and create plantations which produced most of the world's cotton by 1860. Blacks were neither able to participate in wage labor nor purchase land, so they were relegated to slavery.

The institutionalization of slavery in the South allowed slave and plantation owners to circumvent the competitive labor market because wages were completely taken out of competition. A very different employment relationship emerged in the North, one of the land owner and wage earner.

Wage Earners

The North, with its cooler climate and shorter growing seasons, was not conducive to growing cotton, so the planters turned to wheat as the main production crop. Growing wheat is less intensive because workers are only needed a few weeks in planting and harvesting season. Northern land owners did not need an available workforce year round because the cost of feeding and housing that workforce would have been cost prohibitive to the production of wheat. Therefore, it made economic sense for northern land owners to simply pay wages to workers for short periods during the planting and harvesting season. The benefits of wage earners in the North rested on the premise that wage labor allowed whites to buy cheap land for family farms, hire laborers only when necessary, and have no responsibility for feeding/ housing entire worker populations year round. This practice of paying wages to workers instead of engaging in the institution of slavery allowed the North to express outrage at southern slave owners who conscripted humans into servitude. The employment relationship practiced by the North permitted northerners to engage in a *moral hazard* because they would not incur as much risk if slavery were abolished. In reality, the North could better afford to participate in the competitive market because the employment relationship of employer/wage earner was more profitable and beneficial to them whereas the South had to circumvent the competitive market in order to make a profit and remain viable.

The demand for cotton grew in China and India, but the demand shifted from course cotton to finer cotton from which to make more refined clothing and textiles. The South, able to produce only course cotton, became faced with a two-fold problem: how to diversify the cotton industry by not only growing cotton but deseeding cotton as well and the introduction of the boll weevil, an invasive insect which destroyed cotton plants. The South had become King Cotton because the supply and demand model was such that they could produce and supply enough rough cotton to fill the demand of India and Britain. Once the demand changed from rough cotton to finer cotton, the South was unable to fill the demand because they could not supply the product wanted by consumers. The climate and soil in Texas and Oklahoma, further to the west of the Deep South, was suited for the production of finer cotton, so the locus of cotton production moved westward. Ranchers, who initially had received land from the government as a result of the Homestead Act, filled the void and replaced southern plantation owners as the major global cotton suppliers.

As noted earlier, a healthy slave could pick about 300 pounds of cotton per day, but one slave could only deseed about one pound of cotton per day. The laborious and time-consuming process of taking the seeds out of the cotton was hampered by the sharp pointed stickers in which the cotton rested. A new way of deseeding cotton was necessary if the South was to continue supplying cotton in the global market. Eli Whitney, an inventor and entrepreneur, produced a mechanism by which seeds could be removed from cotton more easily and quickly; he called it the *cotton gin*. The cotton gin revolutionized the way cotton was deseeded and allowed cotton producers in the South and the West to increase profits by sending more deseeded cotton to Britain and India. The introduction of the cotton gin had two major effects on cotton production: the supply of workers for other jobs was increased because fewer workers were needed to deseed cotton so more workers could go back to the field to plant and harvest cotton or move to other jobs in other arenas and the institution of slavery was solidified because the South and West could continue to grow and deseed cotton and fill the global demand for the product. Slavery might very well have been dismantled earlier had it not been for the invention of the cotton gin, for without this new technology the process for cleaning cotton easily and quickly might not have materialized.

After the Civil War ended in 1865 and the institution of slavery was abolished, the employment relationship once again shifted from slavery to *sharecropping*; sharecropping still circumvented the labor market and took wages out of competition. Southern plantation owners had to devise a new way of retaining their workforce since they could not legally conscript slave labor. They moved to a Sharecropper model in which labor was exchanged for housing and food rather than cash. The sharecropper model was in reality little different than the slave model because of the passage of *Crop Lien laws* which shifted the legal definition of sharecropper in favor of the landowners. Plantation owners still needed to keep a year-round workforce, and one way of facilitating that was through sharecropping. Sharecropping circumvented *tenant farming*, which would mean landowners must pay cash for services. Crop Lien laws shifted the cash aspect to *script payments*, kept sharecroppers illiterate through opposition to public schooling, and kept them in perpetual debt. Scripts had to be exchanged through the landowners' store. Sharecropping, as a public policy, skirted the competitive market and was a way to solidify a non-competitive market.

The shift of cotton production from the Deep South to the West meant the new landowners were not wealthy plantation owners but ranchers, who had vast amounts of farm land. The ranches were vast and encompassed thousands of acres, so it was difficult to travel from one ranch to the next or even from one ranch to the nearest town to purchase food, medicine, or other necessities. This geographic isolation lent itself to the advent of *company towns*, more or less self-contained towns with a general store, bank, doctor's office, church, and bar. Since the ranchers owned the company towns, they controlled the goods sold, businesses that existed, and the currency used to purchase those goods. Script payments were given to workers instead of cash; workers lived in company houses because no other housing existed, bought goods from the company store because other stores were not accessable, and frequented the local church and bar. Ranchers kept a tight rein on the workers by controlling every aspect of their life. This ensured ranchers an available workforce dependent upon them for every need and did little to alter the employment relationship from sharecropping. Company towns were efficient, productive, and avoided wage competition in the labor market but kept workers in a state of dependency on the ranchers.

Capitalism and the Take-off

The Industrial revolution signaled a move from an agrarian society to an industrial society. Because of the changing nature of markets due to human behavior, decisions, and consumer demand for more products which made life somewhat easier, factories began producing more perishable and durable goods. When millions of consumers make purchasing decisions, manufacturing firms supply that demand with more and different products. So factory systems grew and employed more workers. Workers displaced from the cotton industry moved from the South to the Northeast for jobs and worked for subsistence wages in deplorable and inhumane conditions. Most factory workers lived in poverty. When workers were harmed or disabled on the job, there existed no social safety net to ease the transition from a paid to an unpaid existence. Because there was no government intervention in the market during this period, the burden of caring for the injured or disabled fell on family, church, and community members or organizations. These workers began demanding from their employer higher wages, benefits, and some compensation for injury or disability.

Operating under a *laissez-faire economic system*, *Common law*, law made by the courts, tended to favor owners of production and property rights over worker rights. So when workers tried to cooperatively band together and form alliances which would give them some collective strength to change the economic employment relationship, the courts always sided with employers; if workers went on strike, the courts issued injunctions against the strikers forcing them back into the factories or suffer the consequences of job loss. This abuse of economic power by the owners of production and the courts led to much worker unrest and dissatisfaction.

There was unprecedented strike activity and social unrest during the 1920s and 1930s under the administration of Herbert Hoover. Under the system of capitalism, the laissez-faire policies discouraged any kind of government intervention in the markets which were left to self-correct. High unemployment and rampant poverty increased public dissatisfaction which led to the presidency of Roosevelt in 1933, who made sweeping reforms in government policy affecting the employment relationship. In order for public policy changes to be successful, there must be public awareness and concern and legislators to marshal the changes in law. These conditions existed under Roosevelt, and pro-worker legislation in the form of the *National Labor Relations Act* was passed in 1935; this legislation ushered in a new economic order. The employment relationship had shifted from pro-management to pro-labor.

This new economic order was called the *Take-off*. Rostow (1956) defines this period as "an industrial revolution, tied directly to radical changes in methods of production, having their decisive consequences over a relatively short period of time" (p. 47). Certain economic conditions must exist and certain institutions must be in place for an economy to "take off" in a positive direction. These conditions are such that investment increases so that real output *per capita* rises. This initial increase carries with it radical changes in production techniques and the disposition of income flows which perpetuate the new scale of investment and thereby the rising trend in per capita output (Rostow, 1956, p. 22).

The Take-off required some pre-existing conditions to exist: a stable agrarian economy, well executed and enforced production methods, risk-taking entrepreneurs with capital backing willing to pursue profits in commerce, and institutions for mobilizing capital such as banks or financial institutions. As the economy grows, overall per capita income increases because more workers have income with which they consume goods and services. Also the flow of money must be controlled in order for wealth to accumulate in the hands of productive forces. In this case that money flow traveled from workers to owners of production who *plough-back* money into the economy via savings and investments in new businesses, especially those businesses favoring domestically produced manufacturing goods. This then is the crux of capitalism: the idea that wealthy individuals who earn great sums of money will reinvest that money in the U.S. economy and consequently grow that economy through the expansion of jobs. Rostow (1956) describes this phenomenon as "The notion of economic development occurring as a result of income shifts from those who will spend (hoard or lend) less productively to those who will spend (or lend) more productively [as] one of the oldest and most fundamental notions in economics" (p. 39). This shift in income flow must be accompanied not only by government's fiscal policy but by banks and capital markets.

A new business infrastructure in the areas of finance, insurance, transportation, and communication developed to meet the needs of new industrialists. The business powerhouses of this period, John Rockefeller, J. P. Morgan, and Andrew Carnegie, sometime referred to as the *robber barons*, needed resources to keep their business running; so we see the advent of a transportation system to take workers from home to work, a communication system so business could communicate with their workers, and the addition of departments into factories such as insurance and payroll departments. All these new departments came into the factory as a result of a new economic order taking place, a new business infrastructure. New urban populations of workers in the towns needed to purchase goods/services which brought about an increase in retail trade, so firms sprang up to provide those services in food, drink, medicine, and house wares.

The demographic shift of workers from the south to the northeast increased the supply of workers available to take factory positions in the industrialized north. A plentiful supply of workers means owners of production can be selective in their choice of employees and pay lower wages because there is always someone willing to work for less. In the Deep South when cotton production moved west, many cotton farmers moved to the northeast cities to take factory positions. We see women and young girls working in the factories as well children as young as five, some of whom were orphans who paid for their keep by working. Women and children were desperate for jobs which were few and far between, and factory owners wanted to hire women/children because they were hungry, docile, and plentiful. Unfortunately in many sectors of our current economy, this condition still exists today.

Another demographic shift of workers occurred by 1930 when manufacturing, once prominent in the northeast, began moving back to the south because of cheaper labor, fewer restrictions on hours of work, and fewer labor laws with which to comply. The Stock Market Crash of 1929 catapulted the United States into the *Great Depression*, and there were no government intervention programs available to correct the *market failures*. The free-market economy which expected the market to self-correct failed; 25 percent of the population found themselves out of work with no social safety net available to save them. This called for some type of government intervention to shore up the sagging economy and that came about in the form of New Deal legislation passed during the Roosevelt administration. Roosevelt instituted the *alphabet soup programs* to combat high unemployment, hunger, and economic reform; soup kitchens sprang up, the Social Security program began, and social programs which functioned as a social safety net for unemployed workers were put into place. The period from 1935–1947 became known as the *Golden Age of Labor* in which peace and prosperity grew; economic power shifted to workers during that time.

In 1941 the entry of America into WWII saw many American men sent to war and women and minorities manning the factories. Strike activity at this time increased, and the *War Labor Board* was resurrected to take care of the glut of unfair labor practices filed. The end of WWII brought changes to the employment relationship once again. Because Americans were tired of war and violence, the idea that unions and management had to get along in some better fashion grew in the court of public opinion. Corporations and the government claimed the increased strike activity and worker unrest were a disruption to interstate commerce and affected the economic stability of the United States. Consequently we see an era of civility to the labor-management discord emerge called the *post-war accord*. This shifted the balance of economic power from the workers back to management. Instead of worker discord and strike (sabotage of plants and riots), the civil resolution of the discord would move toward a more sophisticated grievance and arbitration processes, so the post-war accord moved the strife and discord to a paper solution. Sometimes called a softer, gentler militancy, this era brought civility to the labor-management relationship and ushered in the concept of a *business model of unionism*, an approach in which unions negotiate wages and benefits via a collective bargaining agreement and resolve disputes via a grievance and arbitration procedure.

The end of WWII also saw the creation of global institutions to stabilize economic and monetary policy. In 1944 at Bretton Woods, New Hampshire, Stalin, Churchill, and Roosevelt met to address the war's repartitions. As a result of this conference, the *International Monetary Fund* was established to stabilize global international economic policy, and the *World Bank* was established to help underdeveloped countries eradicate poverty.

In 1947, the Taft-Hartley Act was passed; this Act gave to employers the same rights given to unions during the NLRA. Firms could file an unfair labor practice (ULP) against unions, and the economic power shifted back to management. This act set the beginning stages of the weakening of unions; employers scored big in moving the discourse from violence to a paper resolution and the establishment of international tribunals to settle economic international discord.

Though there had been international trade in earlier centuries, the era of globalization is said to begin around 1970. One of the premier elements for truly global trade is the ability to quickly move money from one country to another. The United States became able to do this during the Nixon administration when Nixon moved the U.S. currency base from the gold standard to capital fluidity. The ability to infuse and extract money into and out of other country's financial systems gave the United States an edge in investment opportunities in countries that had cheap natural resources which could be exploited through *structural adjustment policies*, credit extended to developing and underdeveloped countries by the International Monetary Fund and the World Bank which helps them become economically self-sufficient. In reality, these policies allow developed nations like the United States to hold hostage the debtor nations by infusing money into their economy in exchange for products which exploit the developing country's natural resources because it is cheaper for the United States to buy cheap imported goods than to produce the goods. This puts the developing country in the position of not only producing cheap goods for developed nations but paying interest on the debt owned which leaves little or no money to infuse into their economies for infrastructure building and social programs.

Globalization

American workers have taken the brunt of globalization. Many people are unemployed or underemployed as a result of global competition in the global market place. Though American productivity continues to rise, wages are lower because of competition with global workers who earn little pay and work long hours. The move from an industrial economy to a high-tech and service-based economy means many American workers, skilled in industry or firm-specific jobs, are at a disadvantage because their current skill level isn't sufficient for high tech or green jobs. These workers need training, and the United States doesn't provide worker training to the needed level. The United States spends about 0.7 percent of Gross Domestic Product (GDP) on worker retraining which pales in comparison to other industrial democratized countries which spend 2–3 percent of GDP on training. Consequently the gap between employers' demands for skilled workers and the availably of skilled workers continues to grow. Firms interested in the profit motive move production offshore in order to secure skilled and cheaper labor.

The current employment relationship between employers and employees is a very unbalanced relationship with most of the economic power on the side of employers. Employee protections are at a minimum because of Supreme Court and NLRB decisions. The power of corporations to influence anti-worker legislation is well documented in the recent passage of right-to-work legislation in Indiana, Michigan, Ohio, and Wisconsin. One of the premier reasons worker's rights are so weak is known as the *conservative social welfare function*, a model of efficient distribution of income. The conservative social welfare function looks at aggregate income and says the most efficient way to distribute income is so that no one loses as a result of trade. In the promotion of free-trade policies, the United States uses the concept of a positive social net benefit of trade which means that even if some groups are harmed because of free-trade policies, the results of the policies are positive if the overall net benefits are positive. Currently U.S. trade policies are not primarily concerned with workers' rights but rather are concerned with free-trade policies which theoretically more cheaply produce worldwide benefits. This is the trade-off in globalization. American workers may be harmed at the expense of workers in third world countries being lifted from poverty. The idea is that free trade is a benefit to all people because the trade barriers that come down promote peace and prosperity for all workers, that benefit produces lower prices that all people can pay because of competition in the market.

Though the employment relationship has primarily remained one in which workers have little economic power to effect changes in their working wages, benefits, or conditions that does not mean that workers are without hope in changing the employment relationship. Currently new forms of organizing workers are taking place in response to the unbalanced economic labor-management relationship. New forms, strategies, tactics, and techniques are explored worldwide such as global unions rather than industry-specific unions or workers' associations which form outside of the umbrella of current labor law. New ways of challenging employer power will ebb and surge much like they have done for centuries. Workers will continue to struggle to make the employment relationship a more equitable one.

From the early days of the Industrial Revolution when Henry Ford was hiring forty thousand workers each year to man fourteen thousand jobs in his River Rouge Ford auto plant, the worker has remained expendable. The management credo has always been that decisions made at the top by owners of production were the wisest and best decisions to be made, and that workers at the bottom of the working relationship hierarchy were simply to carry out the directions of the "experts" at the top. From the early days of craft work when workers actually were the experts and carried the wisdom, knowledge, and how-to experience of their craft in their brains as well as their hands, management has tried to wrest from craft workers control of the work process. The advent of Fordism, mass production, and the incorporation of scientific management helped to move the knowledge of production processes from the skilled craft workers to the owners of production and rendered skilled craft workers as little more than interchangeable parts in a production system which continuously ground through workers much as it ground through raw material such as cotton and steel. Skilled craft jobs which previously provided security in the form of wages, benefits, and lifetime employment have been replaced with temporary, sub-contracted, and free-lance positions which provide insecurity, anxiety, and uncertainty for many workers.

JOB INSECURITY IN EMPLOYMENT RELATIONSHIPS

The use of Taylor's principles of scientific management, previously most prevalent in manual jobs and currently resurging in professional and managerial jobs, has increased job insecurity for professions previously immune from its reach. The post-Fordist era which began around 1970 saw the emergence of job insecurity for middle-management professions as the result of neo-Taylorism, a term coined to encapsulate the centrality of scientific management principles in "corporate strategy, its global scope, and its sweeping occupational purview" (Crowley, 2010). Under Fordism, workers were systematically deskilled, monitored, and constrained through a work organization system which controlled the speed at which workers produced, eliminated extraneous motion in the performance of segmented tasks, and logistically situated workers to discourage social interactions. Workers, the actual experts on the ground in the production of goods, had little incentive to provide suggestions about making the work more efficient or improving working conditions. Though short-term production quotas may have been met, the long-term consequences of reducing workers to automatons were reduced efficiency and neglected opportunities to capitalize on human creativity and ingenuity.

Under Fordism, the demand for standardized and mass-produced goods was met through a relatively rigid production system. The demand for more customizable goods and services during the 1970s necessitated a change in production procedures which required a more "flexible" approach to production. This meant changing the production systems to include less hierarchical and more lateral decision making, a team approach requiring participation and consent from all team members before the team moved forward, and the continuous movement of not only the product but the process through which the good is produced. Global competitors who could produce the goods more cheaply and quickly had adopted these "lean manufacturing" processes so American workers were pushed into adopting "lean" practices in order to stay competitive in the market.

The move toward more flexible production systems still had cost reduction and increased productivity and profits as the goal. Manual workers had always experienced a push for productivity and profits through increased line speeds, demanding shop floor bosses, and decreased break time, but professional and managerial workers had previously been insulated from job insecurity because they retained decision-making power. After 1970, these professions began to feel the pressure from globalization's relentless drive to increase shareholder profits and market shares, deregulate government policies requiring firms to conform to environmental policies, and international competition. The thrust to increase profits at all costs meant professional and managerial professions were now targets of layoffs, outsourcing, and contingent work. According to DiTomaso (2001), "This 'loose-coupling of jobs' has generated uncertainty and anxiety in the knowledge-based sectors" (p. 247).

The concept of neo-Taylorism suggests new aspects of scientific management have emerged, been reaffirmed, and somehow viewed differently in the post-Fordist era. To understand neo-Taylorism it is important to look at the four best practices suggested by Taylor in his treatise on scientific management. Taylor posited four key managerial responsibilities: (1) amass working knowledge traditionally possessed by workers; (2) reduce those techniques to a series of smaller tasks dictated by written procedures; (3) scientifically select workers, train them, and ensure they use established methods; and (4) separate from manual workers the decision-making components of work tasks, including all aspects of planning and coordination (Taylor, 1947, pp. 36–37).

Crowley (2010) suggests Henry Ford adopted some of Taylor's principles and abandoned others. Ford did incorporate into his manufacturing processes the idea of task segmentation and the separation of the actual production of the goods from the administrative execution of the goods. Clear lines of demarcation existed between manual workers and the "bosses." But Ford did not embrace the idea of worker selection on the basis of the best fit for the firm. Instead Ford hired and trained thousands of workers each year and disregarded worker attributes; he believed all workers could be taught simple repetitive tasks which required little or no thinking. Taylor, on the other hand, was very concerned with choosing the right worker for the job and repeated throughout his writings the necessity of filtering out "second-class" workers described as "lazy and uncompromising candidates" in favor of "first-class" workers described as having "mental caliber," "character," and "fit" (Taylor, 1947, p. 90). As globalization forced firms to increase output at lower costs, the resurrection of Taylor's best practice suggesting workers be selected through some sifting mechanism, weeding out undesirable workers, would bring into the firm only those top-notch employees who would conform to the firms' dictates, policies, and visions. Bringing only workers into the team or the firm's family who will comply with team requirements, adopt a team mentality, and embrace team behavioral expectations encourages a normative culture emphasizing "attitude[s], . . . and organizational history, values, and practices" (Crowley, 2010, p. 424). Should a renegade team member stray from the fold, peer and supervisory pressure and surveillance quickly sanction the member and force him or her into conformity. The catalyst for this technique is compensation tied to team performance. If one member of the team misbehaves, the entire team is harmed.

The increased use of outsourcing and temp work has infused into professional and managerial professions a structured insecurity among a group of workers who are generally educated and achievement oriented. Their drive to outperform others lends itself to the competitiveness fostered by firms who pit worker against worker in order to wring more effort from employees at lower costs to the firm. If a professional believes she can obtain a promotion, secure a bonus, and receive other compensation by outworking and outperforming her peers, then she will complete more tasks, put in extra hours, and volunteer for more work at no or little cost to the firm. This Darwinian approach to outperform others allows firms to terminate lower performance workers which places extreme pressure on those remaining workers. Though this is beneficial to the firm to lower production costs and maintain a market edge, it is extremely detrimental to most workers in terms of lowered compensation, physical and mental wellbeing, and social distress.

The post-Fordist work organization embracing neo-Taylorist principles has profound effects on contemporary work practices. Expanding Taylor's principles of scientific management, which emphasize profit and efficiency and discount human value, into the professional realm has introduced uncertainty into an employment relationship once shielded and protected from Taylor's principles. Negative consequences of flexibility in work organizations for workers include intensified scrutiny in hiring processes, stress associated with performance, conflict with superiors and peers, and a reduced commitment to the job. When workers, whether manual or professional, are devalued and considered easily replaceable, human creativity, an important component for the success of a firm, and communication, vital to the free flow of information, is harmed so the ability of the firm to grow and remain competitive is diminished. Sadly, the push for flexible innovative work arrangements appears to be firmly entrenched in current work organization structures at the expense of all workers.

There exist in the current new economy few remnants of the old economy's cradle-to-grave employment, industry-specific skills, or benefit packages assuring workers of retirement pensions, health insurance, or seniority in the workplace. Those features of the old economy which provided to workers the ability to make good wages, pay off a mortgage, send their children to college, and put money back for retirement have been subsumed by short-term, low-wage employment which gives to employers all the power to control every aspect of a worker's work life: wages, hours of work, and benefits such as health insurance, retirement packages, holidays and vacations, and duration of service. There are severe direct and indirect consequences for workers and the firm as a result of these practices.

The changing nature of the employment relationship over time is mediated by social, cultural, and economic forces which shift the balance of power and control between labor and management. Traditionally management has successfully controlled workers through joint ownership as in feudal times, by circumventing labor markets as in the case of slavery, sharecropping, and company towns, or through court decisions and legislation which generally favor property rights over worker rights. In competitive labor markets under capitalism, corporations and government have reduced workers to little more than interchangeable parts or commodities in a production system which cranks out goods and services for consumption. In the rush to increase short-term profits, few if any incentives are given to workers to be creative. Creativity is the engine of innovation, and without incentives to try new things or be creative, workers simply do their jobs and leave the innovation to management. This is a huge waste of human capital. When workers in any employment relationship are devalued and simply treated as inputs in a system, the long-term profits of the firm are compromised, and the lop-sided future of the labor-management relationship remains in place.

GLOBALIZATION'S EFFECT ON WORKERS

Globalization is a term that has been around for centuries, but its use has greatly increased since the 1980s. On newscasts, in classrooms, and over conversation in the cafe, we hear about globalization. Globalization is the broadening of regional and local economies into a broader arena, the world. Opponents of globalization believe it negatively affects our economy while proponents trust it has some messianic quality which will eventually save the world. Terms like free trade, *laissez-faire,* neoliberalization, and economic, monetary, and fiscal policies are used in conjunction with globalization. Spirited debates suggest the United States should either embrace globalization and adopt a totally free-market approach to the economy or should allow the government to step in to control some or all of the market.

There have been efforts toward a globalized economy throughout history. Each time there was growth in an ancient civilization, a form of globalization was taking place. New trade routes carved throughout the world by ancient traders and governments created conduits through which goods could more easily flow from one country to another. So globalization has been slowly taking place for hundreds of years. The acceleration of globalization has more recently been effective because of speedier communication and transportation systems. The introduction of the Internet in the late 1980s absolutely changed the way the world does business. A new knowledge-based economy has replaced the industrial economy of the twentieth century. Information, as the new product, has replaced manufacturing, which produced tangible goods. Changes in product require new delivery modes and methods of transportation. The instantaneous transfer of information has revolutionized our financial, political, and social world. No longer can we think within the old pre-Internet paradigm. Globalization has turned our world on its head.

The decisions concerning our approach to globalization in the United States have consequences for every American citizen. Decisions made on Capitol Hill about free trade agreements, increases and/or decreases in our taxes, and the federal budget filter down through the fabric of society and affect the monetary decisions made in our households. The approach our nation, our state, and our local government take concerning globalization is extremely important.

Modern globalization is the result of the aftermath of World War II. Our nation had, within thirty years, fought two world wars and been through the Great Depression. Politicians, economists, and business leaders wanted to create an environment in which those conditions would never exist again. They believed the United States should take the lead in helping design policies which would foster good trade relations with other countries and counter the idea that *protectionism,* an economic policy which restrains trade, discourages imports, and prevents foreign take-over of local markets, was in the best interest of the country. Toward that end, in July, 1944, the United Nations Monetary and Financial Conference was held in Bretton Woods, New Hampshire; in attendance were 730 delegates from forty-four Allied nations who established rules for commercial and financial relations among the world's major industrial states.

One of the most prominent figures at the conference was John Maynard Keynes, an economist from Britain and author of *The General Theory of Employment, Interest, and Money* (1936). Keynes promoted the idea that the free market, *(laissez-faire)* was not the best way to approach economic policy, and that sometimes the state or government had to intervene with economic policies and regulations. This approach became known as *Keynesian Economics*. Franklin Roosevelt, president of the United States at that time, adopted Keynes's ideas. Keynes had enormous influence at the conference and shaped the results of the conference. The conference's goal was to stabilize and regulate the international monetary system. Those present created two major agencies: The *International Monetary Fund*, which was to monitor exchange rates between countries and bridge temporary imbalances, and the *World Bank*, which initially was to finance reconstruction of nations torn apart by WWII, but whose focus now is on the eradication of world poverty.

These agencies have a global mission: to facilitate stability in the world's financial markets through the international exchange of free trade. To facilitate this exchange of free trade, the IMF and the World Bank promote a reduction or elimination of tariffs and the creation of free-trade zones, reduced transportation costs, reduction/elimination of capital controls, and reduction/elimination/harmonization of subsidies for local businesses. This exchange of free trade can only happen if there exist no barriers to trade between countries. For instance, *tariffs*, taxes charged to other countries who import goods into the United States, are barriers to free trade. Tariffs increase the cost of imports to buyers in the United States, thus discouraging American buyers from purchasing foreign goods. The higher the tariff, the less imports sold. With the creation of free-trade zones which require reduced/eliminated tariffs, countries participating within the zone can import goods into the United States at low tariff or no tariff. These goods are cheaper, thus purchases by American citizens rise. This logic is used to promote free-trade agreements around the world and was prominent in the discussion to promote the North American Free Trade Agreement (NAFTA), a free trade agreement between Canada, the United States, and Mexico.

During the second half of the twentieth century, the economic system of the United States began to shift away from Keynesian economics and move back toward free-market enterprise. This evolution of our economic system back toward free-market capitalism started at the University of Chicago with a philosopher-economist named Friedrich von Hayek. Hayek favored what is known as *classical liberalism* which favors letting the market decide the winners and losers and disfavors any kind of government intervention or socialism. Hayek's student was Milton Friedman, a leader in the Chicago School of Economics, who had much influence on the administrations of President Reagan, Canada's Brian Mulroney, Britain's Margaret Thatcher, New Zealand's Roger Douglas, and Chile's Augusto Pinochet. This influence helped shape policies favorable to privatization, deregulation, deunion-ization, and dehumanization and thus a move back to free-market capitalism.

Though there are many barriers to globalization such as government regu-lation, environmental regulation, government stability, and so forth, within different global arenas such as world-wide environmentalism, world-wide poverty, or world-wide governance, our focus here is on the economic aspect of globalization or the realization of a global common market based on the freedom to exchange capital and goods. So, within an economic context, globalization means to extend the market world-wide. Economics, simply put, is the study of scarce resources and unlimited wants. Each individual reading this has something she or he wants and cannot have because of scarce resources—not enough time to see a movie or not enough money to buy that new car. Unless one has a very wealthy uncle somewhere or has recently won the lottery, one can relate to scarce resources and unlimited wants or the study of economics. When we focus on economic globalization, we're looking at four components: (1) goods and services, (2) labor/people, (3) capital, and (4) technology.

Proponents of globalization use terms like "leveling the playing field" or creating choice for consumers as arguments for economic globalization. What they mean by "leveling the playing field" is the creation of opportu-nities in all countries in a free-trade zone to participate more fully in the competitive process. Theoretically, all individuals within the free-trade zone would have similar opportunities for jobs, education, and career advance-ments. This way, employers would be able to choose the best and the bright-est from among a huge talent pool in many countries, not just one local region. For instance, an employer in the United States who is looking for information technology workers could also look to India, China, or England for these workers through a virtual system made available by Internet tech-nology. Because the wage structure of other countries is often lower than that of the United States, the employer is likely to find cheaper labor abroad, and since the information technology job can be performed anywhere in the world, the employer has found "cheaper" labor, thus diminishing his labor costs and increasing his or her profit margin.

Some employers *outsource* part of their work to other countries to save labor costs as in the above example. Outsourcing means that a firm moves part of its production to another country. Other firms offshore their produc-tion abroad for the same reason. *Offshoring* means the firm has moved its entire operation to another country and no longer produces goods in the United States. For instance, Nike, the maker of athletic shoes, offshored its production to Indonesia and paid its workers around eighty cents per hour. Apparently this labor cost is also too high, and Nike may move its production to other third world countries where labor costs run about fifteen cents per hour. The problem with corporate offshoring to save labor costs lies partly in the devastation left behind when a mill or factory moves out of an area. When Nike offshored production to Indonesia, thousands of American workers lost relatively good-paying jobs. Often a large manufacturing firm is the primary source of income for thousands of workers in a city. When the plant shuts down, there is little other available work to be found. Therefore, these workers will draw unemployment benefits, if they are eligible, take other lower-paying jobs, move to another area to find other work, or remain unemployed. Manufacturing jobs infuse enough money into the economy which supports four to five secondary jobs in the community such as dry-cleaning workers, fast-food workers, and auto mechanics. When one good manufacturing job leaves a city or a state, four to five other jobs are unsupported and leave the area as well. When good paying union jobs leave the area, seven to eight others jobs leave as well. There are consequences to the outsourcing and offshoring decisions corporations make, and corporations must assume some responsibility for the public good.

The policies of privatization, deregulation, deunionization, and dehumanization associated with globalism are more appropriately termed *neoliberalism*. Neoliberalism is a political movement which began in the 1960s during a decade of social unrest. The 1960s saw many tragic and destabilizing events: the assassination of President John F. Kennedy in 1963; the assassination of Robert Kennedy and Martin Luther King in 1968, the riots at the Democratic National Convention in Chicago in 1968 when Mayor Daly called out the National Guard Troops, the underpinnings of the Vietnam War, and in 1971, the shooting of four Kent State students by the National Guard. Individuals and groups dissatisfied with the status quo use their power of dissent to create a space in which old paradigms are questioned. This was the case in the sixties when Keynes's dominant philosophy of state intervention hampered those who believed that competition within the free market provided all the answers. Competition separated the wheat from the shaft, the men from the boys, and the competent from the incompetent. This social Darwinism approach (survival of the fittest) supposedly allocated natural physical, human, and financial resources more efficiently.

The neoliberal approach has particularly gained momentum during the last thirty years. Pundits of free-market capitalism promote deregulation in industry, which means that corporations do not have to abide by rules other than their own; privatization, which means that firms and individuals compete for available resources and the stronger always wins; deunionization, which discounts workers and jobs as being expendable; and dehumanization, which cares not about human dignity or respect. Neoliberalism has been embraced by those on the political and religious far right as a mechanism to move forward their own agendas in the name of competition such as vouchers for public schools, private health insurance with a move away from Medicaid and Medicare, privatized social security, fewer environmental controls, tax cuts for the wealthy and corporations, fewer social welfare benefits for the poorest of our citizens, and a host of others.

Competition has somehow been elevated to a virtue, so the results of its implementation and continuation are less likely to be questioned. In a world where the dominant paradigm of competition embraces the notion that only the strongest survive, the value and worth of the weak is easy to dismiss as unimportant or not worth the effort. In a government peopled by politicians who promote competition, free trade, and the neoliberal agenda, there is little qualm about voting for legislation which cuts unemployment benefits, food-stamp programs, Women's, Infant's and Children's Nutritional Programs, health benefits, and educational and training programs. The argument for not taking care of the weakest members of our society is that everything that has happened to them (job loss, little education, poor skills) is their own fault, and that the government owes those individuals nothing.

The U.S. economy is currently clawing its way back from the results of free unfettered market capitalism after the October 2008 crash of the financial market, the sky-high compensation packages for CEOs, the entrance into a manufactured war, the rise in unemployment, the increase in poverty levels, and the mortgage meltdown. According to free-market capitalism, these entire phenomena are the result of individuals making bad choices. There is no inference that the system under which we function is at fault. Currently there are policies in place which begin to correct these injustices to workers and all citizens. Just as workers in unions sometimes use militant tactics in the labor-management relationship to achieve gains with employers, it is time for all American citizens to take seriously the idea that policies at the top do make a difference in our daily lives. American workers have a great deal to lose if they remain complacent.

Chapter Seven

Compensation for American Workers

TIME-ORIENTED LABOR VERSUS TASK-ORIENTED LABOR

Most workers would agree they should be compensated adequately for a fair day's worth of work with a fair wage, and many workers believe they are inadequately compensated for their work. How does this mismatch between workers' perceptions of what workers should receive in compensation and what workers actually receive in compensation occur? How does this compensation affect leisure time or time away from work? Have technological and organizational advances made work easier or are workers simply expected to do more work, thus increasing their work burden? Has the intensity with which workers are expected to produce diminished or increased since the Industrial Revolution? How do American workers define a good job? A bad job? What determinants are included in good and bad jobs? An exploration of the evolution of American worker *agency* under changing economic conditions, institutions, and structures will help answer these questions.

The original work day of the eighteenth and early nineteenth centuries was based on an agrarian schedule of farming in which workers rose at sunrise to begin their work day and quit at sunset when they could no longer see to perform plowing, planting, and harvesting functions. The *task-oriented labor* of the agrarian work force revolved around seasonal planting and harvesting seasons so there was, depending upon the geographic location of the land, down time between seasons and during winter months when crops were dormant; family life could be strengthened during these down times through increased time together. Tasks dictated the work schedule, and workers adjusted their work and life schedules around the farming schedule. Agrarian work and family life were not mutually exclusive; they reinforced each other.

As factory systems replaced agrarian life during the Industrial Revolution from the late nineteenth century through the early twentieth century, workers found work in different locations at different jobs but continued working long and laborious hours. That agrarian work schedule was still the model for early factory schedules during the Industrial Revolution when factory workers journeyed to the mills, primarily on foot, to put in a twelve- to fourteen-hour work day before walking home. Workers adjusted their life and work schedules to the needs of production which forced workers to adjust their agenda to conform to the ever increasing demands of the factories and mills. The accommodation workers made to the task in their work/life balance prior to the Industrial Revolution was eliminated with the introduction of technology in production processes which altered the length of working hours and the speed at which workers performed. A new system of *time-oriented labor* fueled by Taylor's theory of scientific management, the division of labor, and processes of specialization led to round-the-clock continuation of work and the necessity of various shifts and hours to accommodate continuing operations. As workers necessarily altered their family lives to conform to various evening, weekend, or non-traditional work schedules, family traditions and customs followed suit. Families spent less time together and more time at work.

American workers, among the most productive in the world, spend more hours at work that do workers in other countries (Sweet, 2013, p. 8). The individualist mindset on which Americans base their belief in the free market and the traditional beliefs that work has value and integrity undergird the conviction that individuals who spend long hours working are virtuous, honest, and trustworthy. From American revolutionary days when men and women worked long hours just to provide enough food and shelter to survive to the present when workers work through their breaks and sell vacations back to employers to meet monthly mortgage payments and put food on the table, hard work has been exalted to a god-like quality. The compensation workers receive for their labor is often not commensurate with the importance or difficulty of the work performed. Take for instance the example of a professional such as a doctor or attorney and a service worker such as a garbage collector or housekeeper. The professional spends many years and much money in being credentialed or licensed for his or her career and commands a high salary in the workforce. The garbage collector or the housekeeper moves into entry level jobs which do not require much training or education and are paid low wages. But if we look at the importance of these two trajectories, we see that garbage collectors' and housekeepers' duties are extremely important in a society which values sanitation to prevent the spread of diseases, rodents, and other maladies. We only have to look at historical pandemics to see that cholera, bubonic plague, and infestations of flies, rodents, and vermin result when garbage isn't collected and properly disposed of and homes and workplaces are not sanitized and kept clean. So the importance of a particular job doesn't seem to be particularly tied to the wages paid to the worker who performs the job. This is not to say that doctors and attorneys do not have important jobs; most of us rely on professionals for any number of services, but it is to make note that when talking about the importance of specific work in relationship to earned wages, our society doesn't seem to reward the importance of a job in any measurable way.

Perhaps American workers are compensated for their work based on the difficulty of the task. Again, we can take a look at professionals and general laborers. Certainly doctors and attorneys spend countless hours in hospitals and operating rooms or judges' chambers and court settings. Their work is intellectual, cerebral, and analytical. They must solve intricate problems concerning physical and mental health and law and policy. Their schedules are dictated by how many clients they have, the institution which hires them, and their dedication to their jobs. Most of us would agree many doctors and attorneys often work long hours usually inside some type of climate-controlled environment. These professionals are usually well compensated for their work. On the other hand, general laborers, such as the garbage collector or the ditch digger, also work long hours in less than perfect conditions. Their work is often back-breaking and requires muscle and brawn. Inclement weather is no excuse for not working because their jobs require working outside all the time in all conditions. Their schedules are primarily dictated by the demands of the firm for which they work. As the firm's client base grows, the worker often works harder and faster to keep up with client demand. The compensation for laborers is usually low, especially if the worker is an *employee-at-will*, a worker who can be hired and fired for good reason or no reason. The distinction between compensation for the professional and the laborer then is not entirely based on the difficulty of the task.

How then are wages determined for American workers? The general idea is that workers are compensated for their work based on the education and training they incur prior to and during their work. If we once again take a look at the professional worker and the general laborer, we find some sort of credentialing that must take place prior to entry into professional work and little or no training necessary to enter into the general labor workforce. The credentialing can take the form of licenses, certifications, or professional and academic degrees. The cost and time involved in acquiring credentialing is often very robust and can act as a sorting mechanism by which some individuals enter into educational and training programs and then must leave the program because the costs in money and time become prohibitive. This often leads to outcomes suggesting only those who have resources initially can finish the credentialing process and move into professional careers. Though the United States has some policies in place which try to provide assistance to individuals who are economically challenged through *Pell Grants*, the *Workforce Investment Act*, and other training programs, the problem is far from alleviated. This division between highly paid workers and poorly paid workers contributes to the inequality in income in the United States more so than in any other country in the world.

HUMAN, SOCIAL, AND CULTURAL CAPITAL

Human Capital

If investments in education and training or *human capital* were the sole determinant of compensation for workers, then all workers would try to receive as much education as possible in order to command higher wages. We know there are other factors, though, which help determine how much wage an individual can command: gender, race, ethnicity, abilities, talents, and so on. Weiss (1995) explains that in "standard human capital models, wages rise with the length of time spent on a job because workers learn on the job" (147). Weiss (1995) separates on the job learning into two different types of human capital: general and firm-specific. "*General human capital* includes skills that are valued by many firms" (Weiss, 1995, p. 147). That means these skills are portable, and workers can take these skills with them when they change jobs. Such skills might include soft skills such as critical thinking, problem solving, or conflict resolution or hard skills such as welding, plumbing, neurosurgery, customer service, or computer programming. *Firm-specific human capital* includes skills "applicable only at a worker's current employer" (Weiss, 1995, p. 147) and would include industry-specific skills such as running Kidder printing presses for a specific firm or utilizing software designed to run programs for specific accounting firms. A worker's productivity may be tied to his or her wage. When workers acquire firm-specific skills, their tenure at that firm usually lengthens, wages rise, and turnover is diminished. In these cases, experience is valued, and training costs are lowered because workers stay with one employer. When workers acquire general human capital, the wages they command are usually similar among various employers.

Social Capital

In our currently networked world, we are bombarded with *social media* like Facebook, Twitter, Linkedin, and other social networking tools which allow us to share important (and some not so important) information with friends and acquaintances. The ability to have social connections is known as *social capital*, a bank of resources filled with human contacts. Social networking is vital for today's workers in securing employment because most job opportunities are advertised via the Internet and applications are online; social networking requires resources such as computers and Internet accessibility which may be limited to low-wage earners who have fewer resources. Social networks tend to be *homogamous networks* (Sweet, 2013, p. 175) in which participants share similar attributes such as race, social or economic status, or educational level. The relationships formed within these groups are intra-networks often limited by geography or language. Sweet (2013) writes that minorities use these social networks in different ways to find jobs, help/not help co-ethnics, acquire references, or access "resource-rich networks" (p. 176).

Cultural Capital

Cultural capital is also an important asset for workers integrating or reintegrating into the workforce. Cultural capital is a bank of resources which allows one to "fit in" to a group or organization. Cultural capital is necessary for success in moving up the economic and social ladders in most cultures and might involve proper language skills, the ability to be a member of the team, the skills to problem solve, critically think, or resolve conflict, and the capacity to adapt to changing situations within the workplace. These soft skills are often taught as stand-alone classes in educational institutions, or specific soft skills are embedded in already existing classes. Employers in all work genres complain they cannot find enough workers who have these valuable soft skills and are turning to private firms who produce and disseminate via the Internet courses in everything from critical thinking to team development. This *spray and pray approach* entails exposing (spraying) workers with online content in specific subject areas, sending them back into the job, and praying that some of the substance of the course will translate (stick) into cultural capital for the worker. This approach is costly to employers and seems to be producing few results. Adult learning theory suggests that adult learners need continued support when acquiring new knowledge, so some type of course follow-up would seem to be in order for virtual exposure to new content to "stick."

WORK VERSUS LEISURE

American workers have a tenuous relationship with *leisure* which has been defined and redefined over the course of time. The changing nature of work and discretionary time has contributed to the difficulty in pinpointing a universal definition which fits all disciplines. Leisure has been subjectively defined as a state of mind irrespective of time (Pieper, 1952; Russell, 2009;

Woody, 1957), objectively defined as a time constraint (Boulding, 1941), or some hybrid definition of leisure which further divides time away from work into sections such as non-work and discretionary time (Brightbill, 1961; Neulinger, 1981; Soul, 1957; Voss, 1967). Voss (1967) defined leisure as

> that period of time when an individual feels no sense of economic, legal, moral or social compulsion or obligation nor of physiological necessity. The choice of how to utilize this time period is solely his. In leisure time, an individual feels he does not "have to" do anything, where *have* refers to the various states of constraint described above. (p. 101)

Voss (1967) writes the work/leisure dichotomy suggested work was associated with pain and exertion which led to some future good, so leisure meant engaging in activities which didn't produce pain and exertion or "freedom from the disutility of work" (p. 92). This definition lends itself to the idea that leisure is time away from paid work which contributes to "economic purchasing power" (Voss, 1967, p. 100), and the only way to increase leisure is to work fewer hours. Economic theory would explain this phenomenon in terms of *normal goods*. Leisure would be treated as any other good or service one might purchase. As one's income rises, so does the price of leisure because to choose not to work one hour in exchange for one hour of leisure means giving up one hour of wages. The price of that lost hour of work is the same as the price of one hour of leisure.

Neulinger (1981) developed a concept of leisure activities in which an individual perceives she or he has the freedom to engage in an activity, and non-leisure activities in which an individual perceives she or he is constrained from engaging in an activity. Neulinger developed a continuum ranging from pure leisure, an activity in which one engages for the pure satisfaction or joy of the activity (such as a walk in the park) to pure job, an activity in which one engages only because of external rewards. The motivation correlated to this continuum moves from intrinsic (purely for personal satisfaction with no extrinsic reward) on the left to extrinsic (purely under constraint with no intrinsic reward) on the right. Categorizing work/leisure activities on this continuum allows individuals to see which of their activities can be considered work and which can be considered leisure.

Other definitions of leisure exist. They include leisure as a "social instrument in which leisure is seen as a means of promoting self-growth and helping others" (Leitner, 2012, p. 10); leisure as transformation or an opportunity to acquire new knowledge and skills in order to handle new situations and environments (Edginton, 2008), and leisure as a symbol of social status or social class in which the wealthy have free time not available to the working class (Leitner, 2012). Edginton and Chin (2008) define leisure as a non-work activity but this definition requires further delineation of the term work. Since work can mean paid work and non-paid work, the term leisure then becomes conditional on the definition of work. Finally a holistic definition of leisure embraces the notion of leisure as non-work but further complicates the concept of leisure as interconnected with the concept of work to the point they are fused and cannot be separated because leisure can be embedded in all aspects of our work and social life (Edginton, 2002; Leitner, 2012).

As we can see, the term leisure can have different meanings. A current and useful definition of leisure is posited by Leitner (2012) who proposes leisure be defined "as time that does not involve work or performing other life sustaining functions" (p. 3). Further explanation reveals work as time which is obligated to earning money to purchase food, housing, health care, and so forth (sustaining functions) while leisure is non-obligated time devoted to personal care and recreation.

Many low-wage workers in the present economy might take exception to the idea that leisure has increased; in fact, most low-wage workers are experiencing quite the opposite in their lives. Workers, particularly those in the service industries, are often working two part-time jobs for less money to make ends meet and sacrifice time with family, time for rest, and time for other activities. In fact, work often consumes the life of many workers. The idea of filling one's day with work fits into the idea of the American work ethic as discussed earlier. Hard work, long work hours, and a drive for success take a toll on the American worker who often thinks less of him- or herself when work is relegated to lesser status than leisure. When leisure is valued more than work, the visibility of the rugged individualist spirit in workers is supplanted by the picture of lazy and slothful workers and undermines an image of the American worker as less dedicated, less driven, and less committed.

Americans tend to identify themselves with their work. When introduced to another person, most Americans give their name and their job or career. Work is closely tied to one's identity, and those who overwork are often praised. Praise and pride in one's work translates into increased self-esteem. Other reasons Americans overwork might include the benefits associated with working long hours such as accruing hours toward personal time off, holiday, or vacation time or line of progression upgrades in pay, economic need, policies in state and federal law which encourage more work, and the idea that work life is more rewarding than home life. Some workers might work more hours because they receive premium pay, and stressors at home, children, marital problems, housework, and so forth, often make work a more relaxed and rewarding environment than home.

Lines between work and home are blurred. Capitalism has shifted the burden of training, commuting, preparations for work such as packing lunch, laundering uniforms, and gassing up the car to the worker; employers do not share in this expense. Virtual work can be done from home, while traveling, and on vacation. The Bureau of Labor Statistics reports 21 percent of employed persons, men and women, did some or all of their work at home, and 85 percent did some or all of their work at their workplace. Fifty-six percent of self-employed workers were three times more likely to work at home than 18 percent of their wage and salary counterparts. Thirty-six percent of employed workers with at least a bachelor's degree did some work from home while only 11 percent of employed workers with less than a high school education worked from home (Labor, 2012b).

AMERICAN WORKERS AND LEAVE TIME

Often, American workers faced with work or time away from work choose work. According to the Bureau of Labor Statistics, "90 percent of workers had access to paid or unpaid leave," and "men and women were about equally likely to have access to paid or unpaid leave at their main jobs in 2011" (Labor, 2012a). Fifty-seven percent of private sector workers have access to paid leave while 76 percent of public sector workers have access to paid leave. Seventy-one percent of full-time wage and salary workers have access to paid leave while only 21 percent of their part-time counterparts have access to paid leave. Full-time workers in the highest earning range, those with at least a bachelor's degree or those in management, business, and financial operations jobs, were more likely to have access to paid leave than in the lower earning range or those with less than a high school education. According to the American Time Use Survey (ATUS), a continuous household survey providing estimates on how people spend their time, 59 percent of wage and salary workers had access to paid leave while 77 percent of wage and salary workers had access to unpaid leave, and an additional 7 percent of workers were unsure whether they had access to unpaid leave. This data represents only workers' knowledge because some workers do not know whether they can use leave time or adjust their schedules or location.

About 21 percent of wage and salary workers took paid or unpaid leave averaging about 15.6 hours per week during the average work week in 2011. Another 56 percent of this workforce adjusted their work schedules (*flextime*) or locations or worked away from their place of employment (*flexplace*) because they didn't have access to leave or instead of taking paid or unpaid leave (Labor, 2012a). If leave time is available for the vast majority of wage and salary workers, why then do American workers not take advantage of leave time?

According to Ray (2008), the United States ranks twentieth out of twenty-one high-income economies in "offering job-protected leave and by offering financial support during that leave" (p. 2) and is one of two countries which offers no paid *parental leave*. Parental leave is defined as taking time away from work for the care of a newborn or adoption of a child. Some workers in the United States have access to unpaid parental leave through the *Family Medical Leave Act* (FLMA) which was passed during the Clinton Administration. FMLA provides up to twelve weeks of unpaid leave per year for qualifying workers. Only about 60 percent of workers are eligible for leave under FMLA which means 40 percent of workers are ineligible because they do not meet the threshold for eligibility; to be eligible workers must be

> employed by a covered employer and work at a worksite within seventy-five miles of which that employer employs at least fifty people; have worked at least twelve months (which do have to be consecutive) for the employer; and have worked at least 1250 hours during the 12 months immediately before the date FMLA leave begins. (Labor, 2012c)

U.S. employers are free to offer more leave time, paid or unpaid, but most choose not to do so. Only about "7 percent" of U.S. firms offer paid family leave which is separate from vacation, holiday, personal, or disability leave while "68 percent offered unpaid 'family leave'"(Ray, 2008, p. 9).

WAGE THEFT

Wage theft is an important issue which indirectly affects all workers and has a great deal to do with changing employment relationships. Though there exist various forms of wage theft which deal with stealing by employees, this discussion focuses on wage theft by employers (Sieh, 1987). Wage theft occurs when

> employees are not paid all of their wages, workers are denied overtime when they should be paid it, or workers aren't paid at all for work they have performed. Wage theft is when an employer violates the law and deprives a workers of legally mandated wages. (Bobo, 2011, p. 7)

In other words, wage theft is defined as employers stealing legally earned wages from employees. Rogers (2010) surmises since wage and hour laws are on the books, the laws "reflect a social consensus that they are desirable even if inefficient" (p. 9). Bobo (2011) argues wage theft is at epidemic proportions and that "as a nation we are facing a crisis of wage theft" (p. 8). "A conservative estimate would be that 10 million workers [are] victimized in this way each year—or about 10 percent of the US workforce" (Lynch, 2011, p. 256).

Wage theft by employers was prevalent in many industries such as garments and textiles in the late eighteenth century and the early nineteenth century and continues today. One method employers use to steal wages from their employees is *subcontracting*. Subcontracting shifts the burden of liability for paying workers correct wages in exchange for their labor from the owner of production or employer to some intermediary charged with the minutia of operating the firm such as hiring and firing, discipline, and payroll. This handing off of duties insulates the owners of production from court actions which might impinge on their profits and create bad public relations for their firms.

Instances of employers subcontracting work is documented in one well-known case, the *Triangle Waist Fire* of 1911, in which 146 young immigrant workers died in one of the worst industrial disasters since the beginning of the Industrial Revolution. Working in inhumane conditions in a sweatshop in Manhattan, New York, on a wintery Saturday March afternoon in 1911, 500 primarily female, Italian and European Jewish immigrant seamstresses were trapped in the Asch Building in the Triangle Waist Company. Some of the female workers were as young as fourteen years old and had come to America with their families to find a better life. Instead, they found poverty conditions in their home and work life. The workers worked twelve- to fourteen-hour days making cotton shirts in a non-union factory which paid low wages. The owners of the building, Max Blanck and Isaac Harris, subcontracted work to other individuals who hired and fired workers and pocketed some of the firm's profits for themselves. This system led to the exploitation of workers who had little choice but to continue working at the factory or face starvation.

A fire broke out on the top floors of the building, and many workers on the ninth floor were trapped in the building by exit doors which were locked because management said workers were stealing product. The fire escapes on lower floors collapsed under the weight of fleeing workers, and the fire department's ladders were too short to reach the upper floor. Many women jumped to their deaths in lieu of being burned to death. Witnesses and the city of Manhattan, horrified by the tragedy, mourned the dead and demanded justice and restitution which would prevent further such tragedies. Calls for improvements in safety and working conditions, stronger unions, and punishments for the company's owners ensued.

The owners of the Triangle Waist Company, Blanck and Harris, were unscrupulous owners who paid no attention to basic workers' rights and forced workers to endure unsafe and dangerous working conditions. After the fire, the owners were interviewed and declared the Asch Building was fire-proof because it had been inspected and approved by the New York Department of Buildings. Regardless, charges were brought against Blanck and Harris by the District Attorney of Manhattan, and a grand jury indicted them on April 27, 1911, on seven counts of manslaughter in the second degree under section 80 of the Labor code which mandates that exit doors cannot be locked during working hours. The trial lasted twenty-three days; a jury acquitted Blanck and Harris of any wrongdoing because Max Steuer, their attorney, convinced them his clients were not onsite that day and had no way of knowing the exit doors were locked. Individual civil suits filed later resulted in Blanck and Harris paying 75 dollars for each lost life. Restitution took three years. Defiant attitudes from Blanck and Harris continued even though the Asch building was found not to be fireproof, littered with trash and flammable material, and locked exit doors. Fines rendered for these violations were minimal, and judges apologized to Blanck for the imposition of his court appearance.

History is littered with such tragedies in which subcontracting leads to inhumane working conditions and wage theft. In 1938, the Fair Labor Standards Act was passed in order to provide some stability in the free exchange of commerce by introducing some standards in labor conditions which had been determined detrimental to the long-term best interest of workers and their well-being. Section 206 of the act requires payment of minimum wages, and Section 207 requires time-and-a-half for hours worked in excess of forty per week ("The Fair Labor Standards Act (FLSA)," 1938). The act provided for a minimum wage of $0.25 per hour, a guaranteed 150 percent per hour wage for hours worked in excess of forty hours per week with one employer, established record-keeping and reporting requirements, and prohibited some forms of child labor. The mechanism to adjudicate violations of the act was to sue in federal court; aggrieved workers individually or through class-action suits or the Secretary of Labor could kick start the adjudication process. The crux of the act is as follows:

> (a) The Congress finds that the existence, in industries engaged in commerce or in the production of goods for commerce, of labor conditions detrimental to the maintenance of the minimum standard of living necessary for health, efficiency, and general well-being of workers (1) causes commerce and the channels and instrumentalities of commerce to be used to spread and perpetuate such labor conditions among the workers of the several States; (2) burdens commerce and the free flow of goods in commerce; (3) constitutes an unfair method of competition in commerce; (4) leads to labor disputes burdening and obstructing commerce and the free flow of goods in commerce; and (5) interferes with the orderly and fair marketing of goods in commerce. That Congress further finds that the employment of persons in domestic service in households affects commerce.
> (b) It is declared to be the policy of this chapter, through the exercise by Congress of its power to regulate commerce among the several States and with foreign nations, to correct and as rapidly as practicable to eliminate the conditions above referred to in such industries without substantially curtailing employment or earning power. ("Fair Labor Standards Act," 1938)

Unfortunately wage theft continues to be a major problem particularly in "an unskilled workforce, a common or even dominant practice within agriculture, building services, garment manufacturing, and warehouse work" (Rogers,

2010, p. 10). The changing nature of the employment relationship, which began morphing from one of *vertical integration* in the 1970s to one of globalized *just-in-time production*, lends itself to continual subcontracting and *outsourcing*. The acquisition of human, social, or cultural capital can somewhat mediate the position of some skilled workers who are able to move from firm to firm with their general skills, acquire new experience and training, add to their skill's tool box, and command high wages from a firm's owner for whom they specifically work. Unskilled and semi-skilled workers face a different challenge, though, because there may be several intermediaries between the worker and the firm's owner, each of whom have some control over the worker's wages, hours of work, or working conditions.

Such is the case with sixteen housekeepers, mostly Latino, in downtown Indianapolis, Indiana, hotel chains who filed a class-action law suit against the Embassy Suites, Marriott, Westin, Hyatt, Holiday Inn and Omni properties in 2011 for wage theft. A group of housekeepers charged these corporate hotel chains knowingly forced them to work off the clock and during their breaks for no pay which effectively drove down their minimum wage jobs to below the current $7.25 per hour minimum wage. The management of the housekeeping staff was subcontracted by the corporate hotel chains to Hospitality Staffing Solutions (HSS), an agency which provides temporary service workers to hotel chains. HSS labels itself as an agency that can reduce employer costs by 12 percent annually on average. Often low-paid temporary workers hired by HSS work beside better compensated workers hired directly by the hotel chains. Forced to perform backbreaking and laborious task which include lifting mattresses and pushing heavy amenities carts, these primarily minority and immigrant workers are often required to come in two hours early, work through their breaks, and stay past their shifts to complete their assigned duties. They are forced to clock in and out for an eight-hour shift, so this extra work is uncompensated and not counted in overtime calculations. Many of these workers were terminated for speaking out against these illegal practices.

The suit was settled in favor of the housekeepers in December 2012 and they were awarded their back pay. One of the plaintiffs, Eva Sanchez, reported she was satisfied with the outcome of the lawsuit which allows some workers to more easily work directly for the hotel chain and grants some benefits in the form of holidays, sick days, vacation benefits, and higher wages.

A report published in 2009 by the University of California Los Angeles (UCLA) Institute for Research on Labor and Employment exposes a world of work in which the core protections many Americans take for granted—the right to be paid at least the minimum wage, the right to be paid for overtime hours, the right to take meal breaks, access to workers' compensation when injured, and the right to advocate for better working conditions—are failing significant numbers of workers. The sheer breadth of the problem, spanning key industries in the economy, as well as its profound impact on workers, entailing significant economic hardship, demands urgent attention (Bernhardt, 2009, p. 2). This study looked at 4,387 low-wage workers in Chicago, Los Angeles, and New York City (Bernhardt, 2009). Findings from the study include:

- Minimum wage violations: 26 percent of survey workers were paid less than minimum wage in the previous work week and 60 percent were underpaid by more than $1 per hour.
- Overtime violations: 76 percent of participants were not paid for work over 40 hours as required by law, and the average worker had 11 hours of overtime for which they were not paid.
- "Off the clock" violations: 25 percent of participants worked outside of their scheduled shifts, and 70 percent of those workers did not receive compensation for that work.
- Meal break violations: 69 percent of participants eligible to receive meal breaks during their working hours received no break, a shortened break, were interrupted by their employer, or worked through their break.
- Pay stub violations and illegal deductions: 57 percent of participants did not receive documentation required in CA, IL, and NY noting their earning and deductions, and 41 percent of participants had illegal deductions taken from their checks for work-related tools, material, or transportation.
- Tipped job violations: 30 percent of tipped participants were not paid state minimum wages, and 12 percent of tipped participants experienced stealing of their tips by supervisors or employers.
- Illegal employer retaliation: 20 percent of participants complained to their employers about working conditions or tried to unionize, and 43 percent of those participants experienced some form of employer retaliation such as termination, suspension, or threats to call immigration authorities, cut pay, or cut hours of work. Another 20 percent reported being afraid to complain for fear of employer retaliation.
- Workers' compensation violations: of the participants who experienced serious injury, only 8 percent filed a workers' compensation claim; 50 percent experienced illegal employer retaliation in the form of termination, calling immigration authorities, or instructing worker not to report claim, and 50 percent of participants paid their own medical bills for injuries out of pocket or used their own health care coverage to pay the bills. Only 6 percent of participants had claims paid by workers' compensation. (Bernhardt, 2009)

Wage theft obviously continues to be a serious problem for workers, particularly low-wage workers. Deterring wage theft can be pursued through the courts but court battles are expensive and time consuming. Another avenue to deter wage theft is to provide resources to the Department of Labor so they can better enforce wage and hour laws and punish perpetrators of wage theft.

Chapter Eight

Race and Ethnicity in the Employment Relationship

DEFINITIONS OF RACE AND ETHNICITY

Historically, race and ethnicity have directly affected the employment relationship. To discuss how race and ethnicity affect the employment relationship, we need to define and clarify the terms *race* and *ethnicity*. Since all living human beings belong to the same species, I view race as a social construct and adopt the meaning of race as utilized by Miles (1987) in which humans are categorized into "races" by reference to real or imagined phenotypical or genetic differences (p. 7). These social constructions are developed through "processes of racialization embedded in daily interactions, ideologies, policies and practices" (Fuller, 2008, p. 32). This conceptualization of race is consistent with Fredrickson (1988) who defines race as a "consciousness of status and identity based on ancestry and color" (p. 3) and Ramirez (2004) who writes,

> Racism is a fundamentally social convention. In a neoclassical market-based economic system, the social construct of race is complex and is not simply a function of the market. It is driven by infirmities in human cognition, widespread imperfections in information, the desperate need for those at the bottom rungs of society to achieve some semblance of status, and destructive human impulses. It is driven also by social convention, societal inertia, and racial stigma. . . . Race causes suppressed and distorted market action. (p. 371)

Race has historically been used to categorize humans into classifications and grew from eighteenth-century social mechanisms which referred to populations in colonial America. The classification system embodied an inequality of status to rationalize European "attitudes and treatment of the conquered and enslaved peoples" (Association, 1998). This ideology emphasized differences and was used as a rationale for colonialism of those with physical traits different than white European males. The ideology spread worldwide and was used to justify slavery in the United States (Fredrickson, 1988) and the eradication of Jews in Nazi Germany. Fredrickson (1988) contends

> the "rise of neo-Marxian 'class analysis' has clearly provided a deeper understanding of the social context of black-white relations . . . and has "demonstrated convincingly that one cannot fully understand racial oppression and discrimination without considering the formation of social classes arising from the growth of merchant capitalism in the sixteenth, seventeenth, and eighteenth centuries and of industrial capitalism in the nineteenth." (p. 3)

As a worldview, race prejudges the differences of human groups. Our social, cultural, economic, and political perceptions and policies are influenced by our racial attitudes.

"Ethnicity is a complex phenomenon" (Isajiw, 1992, p. 1). According to Isajiw (1992), ethnicity is continually "negotiated and constructed" (p. 4) as a way of survival. Isajiw (1992) sees ethnicity as both individually and collectively constructed. The social construction of ethnicity involves the internal perceptions and connections individuals have with their culture, their total way of life, or their historical experiences as a group (Bourdieu, 1997; Foucault, 1967; Isajiw, 1992; Miles, 1987; Miles, 2003) as well as external boundaries established by "power-holding, policy-making and influence-exerting bodies" (Isajiw, 1992, p. 6). The perceptions exerted by external parameters such as government bodies influence the rationale behind economic, social, and immigration policies which directly affect individual lives. Isajiw (1992) and Spickard (2007) posit ethnicity as the progenitor of race because the differences within groups are featured as reasons to categorize and exclude for political, economic, and social purposes. Fredrickson (1988), on the other hand, suggests that ethnicity is defined as deleting the "color criterion" (p. 7) from the concept of race. This is also a socially constructed perception of ethnicity in that removing any reference to color necessarily relegates the definition of ethnicity to internal and external cultural, social, economic, and political determinants. For the purposes of this discussion, I'll adopt the definition of ethnicity as defined by Isajiw (1992).

RACIAL AND ETHNIC IMMIGRATION FLOWS

Because race and ethnicity are bound in cultural, social, economic, and political perceptions which make distinctions between groups of individuals through internal and external referents, this exploration necessitates a discussion about the different racial and ethnic collectives in the United States and how their arrival histories, work opportunities, and employment impacts the U.S. employment relationship. Race and ethnicity are directly tied to the stream of human immigrants in and out of the United States, so we must look at the way past and present immigration flows have affected U.S. workers and how the assumptions about these various groups have altered the way employers view employees and employees respond to employers. Although all host countries are affected by *emigration*, leaving one country for another, and *immigration*, settling in a non-native country, the United States is a particularly attractive region for those seeking better lives. "America is a country of immigrants" (Spickard, 2007, p. 4). Spickard (2007) contends that "99 percent of the current U.S. population can at least theoretically trace its ancestry back to people who came here from somewhere else" (p. 4). Histories of American immigration originally focused on Northwestern European immigrants (Adamic, 1945; Wittke, 1940) with little attention given to South or East Europeans, Asians, Mexicans, Africans, or Native Americans. English immigrants are assumed to be "native to the American landscape" (Spickard, 2007, p. 5) or "natural Americans" (Spickard, 2007, p. 6) and, therefore, become the standard bearers for behavior, religion, and politics. Spickard (2007) calls this "Anglo-conformity" or "Anglo-normativity" (6) and suggests that adherence to the standard meant all other non-English immigrants should be willing to subsume their own culture and heritage in favor of the English standard.

These immigrants to the United States around the turn of the twentieth century were primarily Northwestern Europeans (Lee, 2004), and this period of immigration from around the nineteenth century is known as "The Old Immigration." A second wave of immigration, "The New Immigration," began around 1880 and ended around 1924 and included Southern and Eastern European immigrants. Some English, Scottish, Italian, German, Scandinavian, and Austro-Hungarian immigrants came to the United States through Ellis Island in New York "attracted by the higher wages and abundant jobs in their specialties that were to be found in the world's most extensive and dynamic national economy" (Asher, 1990, p. 4), while others found their way to America because of poor job opportunities in their country of origin (Spickard, 2007). Asian immigrants from India, China, Korea, Japan, and the Philippines came for higher paying jobs. Irish, Italian, Sicilian, Mexican, and Caribbean immigrants sought relief from starvation and poverty; German dissidents sought political asylum after the Revolution of 1848 while "Jewish and Armenian immigrants hoped to find refuge from genocidal assaults endorsed and executed by the Russian and Turkish government" (Asher, 1990, p. 4). Many of these immigrants were greeted by the Statue of Liberty and an inscription which read "Give me your tired, your poor, your huddled masses." These words must have been soothing to the many poor, weak, and downtrodden souls who suffered mightily to come to U.S. shores. Yet, their experiences after arrival were anything but soothing and comforting. Not all immigrants came to American through Ellis Island though (Spickard, 2007). African-Americans, brought to the United States through forced immigration in slave ships, found only centuries of sorrow and despair through chattel slavery. Mexican immigrants who came as contract laborers found no comfort in the American Dream or America as the land of opportunity. Native Americas, who one could argue were part of the natural landscape and not immigrants at all, were conquered, displaced, and almost eradicated as a people. Outcomes then, for most immigrants, were very different than expectations.

Whatever the compunction for immigration, ethnic groups gravitate to the United States because of freedom and opportunity. They move into a multicultural country which requires them to blend in, take on the attitudes, beliefs, customs, and lifestyle of "White" Americans. The ability of immigrants to assimilate into U.S. culture means they must discard through "choice or compulsion" (Spickard, 2007, p. 7) their country of origin culture and accept the Anglo-American norm. This European assimilation model discounts the struggles (or at least views the struggles differently) of African Americans, Native Americans, Mexican Americans, Asians and their descendants. The Ellis Island immigration model, sometimes called the Melting Pot model, assumes immigrants are Europeans and therefore places non-European immigrants into "other" category. The model assumes that all immigrants, over the course of generations, will shed their original culture and morph into New Americans, a multicultural composite of all ethnicities. The idealized idea of the Melting Pot, though, is predicated on the assumption there exists an Anglo model to which all should strive. This *assimilation* into some dominant European-Anglo model structurally necessitates blending through intermarriages. This model presupposes a one-way transmission of culture in that immigrants willingly (or not so willingly) conform to an idealized model of a new American. The model does not consider *acculturation*, the idea that immigrants can or should "adopt the cultural skills of the dominant Anglo-American group" (Gordon, 1964, p. 12) while maintaining their own cultural identity through connections with their immigrant group.

What immigrants often found when coming to America was an unforgiving land which actually exploited and demonized immigrants based on their skin color. Asher (1990) writes, "Immigrants and their offspring, especially if they were nonwhite, also suffered grievously as they were psychologically traumatized and physically mangled because of prejudice and the drive of business owners to produce for profit" (p. 25). A hierarchy of status developed which favored some immigrants more than others depending on their country of origin and their "whiteness." Spickard (2007) terms this *normative whiteness* (p. 27), the assumption that normal people are white. Equating whiteness with normalcy suggests that non-whiteness is abnormal and thus requires some explanation. It is interesting to note most "publications also assume a normative maleness and a normative heterosexuality" (Spickard, 2007, p. 27). U.S. policies, American literature, and the media identify people when they are "other" than white. For instance, news reports may identify Blacks or Latinos as suspects, but refer to White suspects simply as suspects. Whiteness begets privilege internally and externally. Internally, Whites have historically assumed genetic and intellectual superiority and relegated non-whites to positions of genetic and intellectual inferiority. Externally, social, economic, and political structures emerged based on the privileged position of Whites. Our U.S. Constitution, written by privileged Whites, reflects those assumptions. Though constitutional amendments, Supreme Court decisions, and policies such as affirmative action, civil rights, and voting rights have somewhat ameliorated those structures in favor of non-whites, the playing field still slants toward normative whiteness. It is with the assumptions of normative whiteness in place that we turn to the exploration of racial and ethnic diversity and how it affects the employment relationship of employers and workers in the United States.

When we talk about racial and ethnic diversity within the workplace, we are acknowledging recognition of differences and distinctions among members of racial and ethnic groups. Diversity only resides in groups and not in individuals (Ditomaso, 2007; Tilly, 1998), so racial and ethnic diversity within the workplace is based on embedded "structural or institutional bases" (Ditomaso, 2007, p. 475) which are reinforced through workplace policies and interactions. Continued reification of the strutural and institutional bases adds a stability to status ranking and differentiation and disadvantages those considered "other." This built-in bias against "other" consequently tilts the playing field on which immigrants complete against the dominant white group.

The existence of inequality in the employment relationship did not appear out of nowhere. The long history of discrimination toward "other," the focus on human differences as compared to normative whiteness, and the assignment of status and hierarchies in the working environment have been developed and codified into "routines, policies, and practices that organizations employ to recruit, evaluate, hire, and retain employees" (Stainback, 2010, p. 230). Though a move toward a formalization of human resource management within some workplaces with stronger formal rules and procedures has somewhat ameliorated the effects of inequality by committing to equal opportunity for all workers, thus attempting to remove bias from the hiring, promotion, evaluation, and firing process, there still exists inequality in many work environments with formalized policies because internal divisions of labor "codify workplace inequality" (Stainback, 2010, p. 229), original beliefs and values associated with status and hierarchy are embedded in the firms' cultures (Baron, 2007; Sorensen, 2004), and internal workplace dominant and subordinate constituencies fight to retain control over allocation of resources (Stainback, 2010; Tomaskovic-Devey, 1993).

It would be naïve to believe that simply formalizing the administrative processes and procedures associated with human resource management would eliminate bias and prejudice in the employment relationship. After all, human behavior guides and sometimes dictates the way employers and employees make decisions, so simply codifying rules and policies may provide some guidelines for hiring, firing, promotion, and evaluation processes and mitigate some inequality but will not completely objectify the process. Weber (1968) believed objectification of the administrative processes would encourage formal rationality and mitigate inequality in employer/employee transactions. Though formalized rules "may reduce the basic social psychological mechanisms" (Stainback, 2010, p. 230) associated with personnel decisions, personal characteristics and loyalties to in-groups and out-groups continue to contribute to decisions "based on stereotypical views"(Stainback, 2010, p. 230) thus reinforcing status hierarchies based on differences. This approach assumes that employers, the decision-makers, have motivation to discriminate against "other" and therefore intent in discrimination exists. Known as *disparate treatment analysis*, this approach assumes employers will act objectively unless there is some motivational intent not to do so. Anti-discrimination laws are designed to mitigate the bias in the employer-employee relationship if employer intent can be proven. This is a very difficult task because intent assumes motivation to discriminate against a worker because of protected status, one of which is race and/or ethnicity. In essence, the law would have to recognize that an employer was intentionally providing false information about a worker before the worker could receive justice. Under Section 7.3 of Title VII and 42 U.S.C. sections 1981 and 1983, a plaintiff bringing forward a claim of discrimination against an employer must prove she or he was not only treated differently, but that such treatment resulted from purposeful or intentional discrimination (Krieger, 1995). To prove intent, the aggrieved worker must prove the "employer's conscious state of mind at the moment a decision was made . . . holds stereotyped views of the plaintiff's group" (Krieger, 1995, p. 1172) so that stereotyping and intent are connected.

According to Roscigno, Garcia, and Bobbit-Zeher (2007), much of the racial and ethnic inequality experienced by workers in the U.S. employment relationship results from employers' "arbitrary and subjective decision making within firms" (p. 20), discrimination and bias in hiring and firing decisions (Kirschenman, 1991; Moss, 2001; Pager, 2003; Roscigno, 2007), and race and wage disparities (Huffman, 2004; Peterson, 2004; Stainback, 2010). These tenets of inequality presuppose disparate treatment analysis and cognitive bias. *Cognitive bias*, defined as socially constructed categories based on memory, experience, and inferences resulting in stereotypes, may be both unintentional and unconscious (Krieger, 1995). Cognitive bias assumes decision makers are information processing machines making rational decisions based on objective criteria. But because employers as decision makers are an amalgam of their past experiences and education, their socially constructed perceptions may be anything but rational and objective. *Social cognition theory*, which says decision making is a composite of "perception, interpretation, attribution, memory, and judgment" undermines the idea that employers are "systematic information processors" (Krieger, 1995, p. 1213) and lends itself to the idea that employers can make subjective administrative decisions based on their own preconceptions about race and ethnicity. This comports with the literature on cognitive bias processes (Stainback, 2010), which include stereotyping (Ridgeway, 2004) and in-group typing (Ditomaso, 2007), and helps us understand the "reproduction of inequality (Stainback, 2010, p. 227).

It isn't difficult to find quantitative evidence which suggests racial and ethnic workplace disparities exist. One only has to look at the differences in the number of foreign-born or non-white workers holding service sector or blue-collar jobs which tend to pay less versus native-born or white workers holding managerial or professional jobs which tend to pay more. According to the Bureau of Labor Statistics (2013), 25.2 percent of foreign-born workers have service sector jobs while 16.5 percent of native-born workers have service sector jobs, and within service sector employment, 66 percent of foreign-born workers are employed in food preparation, serving industries, construction, and building maintenance while 50 percent of native-born workers are employed in these industries. About 15.5 percent of foreign-born workers are employed in production, transportation, and material moving while 11.2 percent of native-born workers are employed in those industries (Statistics, 2013). Foreign-born workers make up 12.7 percent of the natural resources, construction, and maintenance employees while 8.3 percent of native-born workers are employed in these occupations (Statistics, 2013). See table 8.1.

The median weekly earnings of foreign-born workers who are full-time wage and salary workers are $625 or 78.4 percent of their native-born counterparts who earn $797 per week. Educational attainment, occupation, industry, and geographic region have an influence on earnings of both foreign-born and native-born workers (Statistics, 2013).

CAUSES AND CONTINUATIONS OF RACIAL AND ETHNIC DISPARITIES

Understanding the causes and continuations of these disparities necessitates an understanding of racial and ethnic stratification within the employment

Table 8.1.   Comparison of Foreign-born and Native-born Workers' Disparities in Industries.

Industry	Foreign-born	Native-born workers
Service	25.2	16.5
Production, transportation, material moving	15.5	11.2
Natural resources, construction, and maintenance	12.7	8.3
Management, professional, related occupations	30	39.5
Sales and office occupations	16.5	24.6

Source: Bureau of Labor Statistics.

relationship which acknowledges how the structure of the employment relationship and the actions taken by employers reinforce and maintain inequality through "institutional exclusion and dominant group positioning" (Roscigno, 2007, p. 21). Whether the inequalities are a result of deliberate, unconscious, or some combination of decision making, this posturing by employers is a form of *social closure* (Parkin, 1974, 1979; Reskin, 2003; Weber, 1978), a process whereby internal organizational structures such as workplace policies and procedures are reified or closed by external forces such as labor markets (Roscigno, 2007), discrimination laws (Feagin, 2003), and in more subtle forms of workplace interactions through "language, symbolic acts, and/or physical control or force" (Roscigno, 2007, p. 21). This suggests that even though external policies exist which are designed to prevent blatant discrimination by employers concerning workplace practices and policies, employer assumptions about race and ethnicity color their administrative and personnel decisions (Stainback, 2010).

Situated within the employment relationship, social closure is a mechanism used by the collective to maintain economic advantages resulting in the reproduction of inequality (Ditomaso, 2007; Parkin, 1979; Tilly, 1998; Weber, 1978). The concept of social closure helps us understand how and why groups which function as a collective maintain their position, economic power, and privilege; the maintenance of status by the collective is achieved by developing and reinforcing racial and ethnic hierarchies. Employers, the dominant group in the employment relationship, act as a collective to maintain their higher status through the use of power, control of resources, and control of work processes (Ditomaso, 2007). Reskin (2003) conceptualizes this macro-level process which includes exploitation, economic hoarding, and social closure as the "why" (Ditomaso, 2007, p. 479) dominant groups sustain their privilege and conceptualizes the micro-level process which includes the nuts and bolts of "how" (Ditomaso, 2007, p. 479) privilege is maintained through workplace policies and job requirements. The decline in diminished union power and worker power in the United States is linked to lowered wages and income inequality (Kim, 2008). Employees, as individual workers, have little or no power to mediate the employment relationship. Unless employees can work as a group, such as a union, they remain subordinate to the dominant group.

Roscigno (2009) gives some examples of dominant group maintenance which reinforce status hierarchies in a study exploring social closure and workplace incivilities within the context of organizational chaos. He defines *organizational chaos* as "poor organization and coordination of the labour process," suggesting it is a cause of managerial bullying which "captures physical and/or psychological abuse aimed at harming, tormenting, or intimidating subordinates in a manner that causes discomfort, distress, or public embarrassment" (Roscigno 2009, 749). Roscigno (2009) posits "minority workers and those with insecure positions are most likely to be bullied by supervisors" (p. 757) as evidenced by examples from a Midwest meatpacking plant [in which] Asian American, Latino, and black workers were routinely bullied by managers in ways that white workers were not (Fink, 1998). Fink (1998) notes one Hispanic worker, who spoke minimal English, was disciplined for not keeping up with his line work and was publically sent to the cafeteria (the equivalent of the woodshed) for disciplining. The supervisor yelled at the worker and called him Pedro, the name given to all Hispanic men on the shop floor. This exemplifies social closure as supervision disregards the dignity and civility which should be afforded to all workers. Roscigno (2009) concludes minority status is a significant determinant of managerial bullying.

Stainback (2008) studies the mechanisms and social processes which perpetuate inequality in the workplace by examining racial/ethnic networking in job searches within the framework of social closure theory. Conclusions from this quantitative analysis suggest racial and ethnic workplace inequities are reproduced through in-group conscious and unconscious motives such as "mutual obligation to in-group members, ties to race/ethnic identity, or even feelings of trust based on social similarity" (Stainback, 2008, p. 879) which exclude out-group members and have the effect of maintaining racial and ethnic categories within the workplace.

Ethnic and racial diversity in the current working environment actually undermines the ability of workers to secure better paying jobs, work under humane conditions, and improve their standard of living because their relational status to white, European males, the standard bearers of the American economy, is considered inferior or substandard and, in the case of African Americans, subhuman. Though racial and ethnic diversity could be used to further economic improvements in workers' lives, long-standing prejudices and biases against the 'other' are embedded in our work practices, our pre-conceived notions of work and workers, and our employment relationships.

The markers between whiteness and "other" began to blur around 1920, when large-scale European immigration of Italians, Irish, and Jews ended. As these ethnic minorities assimilated into the U.S. social and market structures, their ability to claim "whiteness" increased as did their distance from African Americans. African Americans, as a race, were still considered different. Lee (2004) suggests this widening gap between whites and blacks reinforced a color line which it was taboo to cross. This barrier was further exacerbated by the legal discrimination in place against African Americans, a barrier which other immigrants did not face. Other ethnic groups, once considered non-white, also changed their status by "achieving economic mobility, emu-lating the cultural practices of whites, intentionally distancing themselves from blacks, and rejecting fellow ethnics who married blacks" (Lee, 2004, p. 225). Lee (2004) denotes that for ethnic groups who change from non-white to white "race is a cultural rather than a biological category that has ex-panded over time to incorporate new immigrant groups (p. 225–226). As immigrants are Anglicized, they are subsumed into American culture and the distinction between Whites and "other" becomes more blurred.

When discussing the immigration effect on the employment relationship, we need to look at the supply side of the equation as well as the demand side of the equation. "Immigrants affect both the supply side and the demand of the local economy from the day of arrival" (Longhi, 2010, p. 358). Whether immigrants gravitate toward urban areas for factory or service work or to-ward rural areas as seasonal agricultural workers, they impact the regional or local economy through production and consumption. The American work-force, the most diverse workforce in any industrialized economy, expands and constricts based on the laws of supply and demand. So an economic system of capitalism has historically both welcomed and shunned immigrant workers based on the need for workers. Based on a fluid business model, the free market lives and dies through the consumption of goods and services. In good economic times, consumption increases and more workers are needed to produce; in bad economic times, consumption decreases and fewer work-ers are necessary. Both skilled and unskilled laborers are necessary to fill the growing needs of consumers. A system of capitalism works best when there exists an oversupply of workers. When employers have a large pool of work-ers from which to choose, the wage rate for workers falls. Conversely, when the labor supply pool is diminished and workers are scarce, wage rates for workers rise. Therefore, it is beneficial to employers to have a worker surplus because their overall labor costs decrease. Longhi, Nijkamp, and Poot (2010) conducted a meta-analysis of immigration's impact on labor markets at a regional level. They conclude "the wage and employment effects of an immi-gration shock are very small" (p. 383). Longhi, Nijkamp, and Poot (2010) used weighted averages that a 1 percent increase in immigrants into a local labor market decreases the wages of the native born by 0.029 percent and decreases employment of the native born by 0.011 percent. They estimate these averages for localized markets are smaller than those of national averages (p. 383).

A capitalist economic system has complicated the ability of immigrants to achieve the American Dream by pitting worker against worker in a competitive framework which seeks to lower labor costs. The justification for relegating immigrant workers to the bottom rungs of the social, economic, cultural, and political hierarchy is blamed on their immigration status, skill, country of origin, or their "whiteness." Because immigrants into the United States since the eighteenth century have received different levels of support and because U.S. policies affecting immigration, discrimination, and civil rights for racial and ethnic groups have morphed with the changing economic conditions, immigrants to the United States have changed and been changed by internal and external pressures. When exploring immigration's history, causes, consequences, absorption ability, laws and policies, and tensions on the U.S. employment relationship, we acknowledge workplace hierarchies are continually reconstructed through built-in employer assumptions regarding immigrants' status as a subordinate group, and dominant group positioning is reinforced by the collective attempting to maintain control over ownership and allocation of resources.

Chapter Nine

Gender and the Employment Relationship

The term *gender* is often confused with the term *sex* when trying to delineate between male and female roles in the workplace. Often used synonymously, the two terms carry distinctively different meanings. The term gender is a social construct and describes the behaviors, attributes, roles, and activities appropriate for males and females within a society. Sex is defined as the biological and physiological characteristics of men and women. Our definition of the roles men and women have occupied within the workplace changes as our culture and society become more aware of the similarities and differences associated with those roles. Unfortunately, the policies which govern those work roles often do not keep up with changing attitudes. This chapter explores the changing roles of men and women in the employment relationship and some of the economic and social policies which undermine or deter workplace equality.

BRIEF HISTORY OF WOMEN'S DEVALUED STATUS

For centuries, women have taken a secondary spot to men in the social hierarchy. Women's placement in American society is the result of many cultural influences and values having to do with *"democratic egalitarianism* and *individualism*, the *Protestant work ethic, patriarchy, marriage and family values,* and the *American ideal"* (Day, 1989, p. 141). Democratic egalitarianism is the concept "that all citizens are equal before the law, and no one has privileges above the law based on class, heritage, wealth, or any factors irrelevant to citizens" (Day, 1989, p. 5). Despite this ideal, the founding fathers adopted a Constitution which gave unequal property rights to white men who "owned" their wives, children, and minorities. This situation didn't change until after the Civil War and the passage of the Thirteenth Amendment eradicating slavery and the passage of the Twentieth Amendment in 1921 giving women the right to vote. Minorities and women continued to be exploited until the passage of the Civil Rights Act in 1964. Even then, cultural restrictions and inadequate policies prevented women and minorities from equal participation in the political process, and social conventions continue to repress women, minorities, the poor, the *Lesbian, Bisexual, Gay, and Transgendered (LBGT) community*, and the *differently abled*.

Individualism is the idea that personal responsibility and motivation will lead to success. It is a hold-over from America's frontier days when there was ample land available for exploration, and rugged individualism was necessary to forge new frontiers. The term now means explorations of education, technology, and other unexplored horizons like space and oceans. Individualism suggests that the absence of hard work results in poverty, so those individuals in poverty or the working poor are considered unsuccessful because they didn't work hard enough. There is no credence given to the idea that macro systems like the *polity*, which is the exercise of power in a society, and the economy, a system of capitalism which by its nature fosters inequality, or micro systems such as the social institutions of *religion, family*, or *social welfare*, all of which derive from puritanical and patriarchal traditions, are skewed against the powerless, the voiceless, women, minorities, and the poor.

The Protestant work ethic places a high value on individuals who work hard and achieve personal and economic success. The idea that wealth is a result of moral self-worth hails from the "mercantilist movement of the Middle Ages, the many new technologies of the fourteenth century, and the Protestant Reformation" (Day, 1989, p. 7). "Martin Luther's belief in work as a 'calling' and John Calvin's teachings on predestination were interpreted to mean that those predestined to salvation in this life could be identified by evidences of their wealth" (Day, 1989, p. 7). The Protestant work ethic valued effort, efficiency, and morality as the key to wealth, success, and salvation. Those less successful or poor were thought to be lazy, inferior, and undeserving of assistance. Because religion and the law were synonymous during this period, patriarchal influences as gleaned from Biblical scriptures were taken literally. The masculine flavor of scriptures was interpreted to mean men were superior in God's eyes, and therefore men were favored to rule, make all decisions, and own all resources. This *Puritan morality* or *puritanism* continues to permeate American ideas and polity. Within the system of Puritanism, patriarchy, a governmental or societal system in which men have ultimate authority and power, controlled every institution, the government, church, school, and the family. The combination of Puritanism and patriarchy gave legitimacy to a society dominated by men and birthed our present-day Western system of *sexism, classism, racism*, and *colonialism* or *imperialism*.

Patriarchy underlies the values associated with marriage and family. The institution of marriage is a social, sexual, and economic relationship forming the nuclear family unit traditionally consisting of mother, father, and children. For centuries women were subservient to men and had two choices in life: to marry or give their life to God. Charlotte Perkins Gilman (1900) wrote:

> And when the woman, left alone with no man to "support" her, tries to meet her own economic necessities, the difficulties which confront her prove conclusively what the general economic status of women is. None can deny these patent facts—that the economic status of women generally depends upon that of men generally, and that the economic status of women individually depends upon that of men individually, those men to whom they are related. (26)

"Monogamy was both law and custom" (Day, 1989, p. 10) within the sanctity of marriage, and females who practiced sexuality outside the bonds of marriage were considered promiscuous while men were considered macho. If females became pregnant outside the bonds of marriage, they were blamed for risqué behavior while men often remained non-culpable. In traditional families, the male husband was the primary wage earner while the female mother was responsible for home and child care. Men made economic and social decisions concerning the family's welfare while women were expected to acquiesce to their husband's wishes. Women seldom trained for careers because the expectation was they would marry and have children. Consequently if the family unit dissolved for some reason, women found themselves ill prepared for the work world and gravitated toward low-paying service or clerical work. Even after WWII when women took over factory and mill work replacing men called to military service, females were expected to abdicate those jobs when the men returned from war. Soaring divorce rates in the 1950s did little to alter the patriarchal and puritanical viewpoint toward the traditional family. Females did not train in significant numbers to become wage earners until the feminist movement in the 1970s. So the disadvantages associated with low-wage, low-status jobs are rooted in historic perspectives about the way society views the role of women.

The American ideal has evolved from the Anglo-Saxon Protestant ideal which says that white, tall, handsome, virile, and male is good and anything else is bad. When we characterize some set of perfection as the standard by which all others are gauged, then we create a false sense of attainability which most of us will never reach. Our history books and religious texts are steeped in Anglo-Saxon Protestant idealism which features strong and courageous men who conquered peoples, battled nature's elements, and forged a new nation. Conspicuous by its absence is the contribution of women, immigrants, and minorities in the building and fortifying of this country. Written passages about the frontier mothers or the immigrants who supplied skills and labor in building our country's infrastructure are given short shrift in historical chronicles. The terminology in our textbooks and religious writings used to describe those other than white men of European descent suggest inferiority or deviance. Native Americans are referred to as heathen and savages while black men are called slaves and counted as three-fifths human in our Constitution. Women who express their sexuality outside the realm of marriage are called harlots and prostitutes, and children born outside of wedlock are deemed bastards. The branding of individuals as dissimilar from the American ideal labels them as "other" and sanctions different, discriminatory, and often hurtful treatment and policies in government and economic institutions and in religious and family social units. Women's position within the economic and cultural system has been and continues to be influenced by the historical dictates of democratic egalitarianism and individualism, the Protestant work ethic, patriarchy, marriage and family values, and the American ideal.

Gender differences attributable to Protestantism and patriarchy in the workplace often influence wage disparities between men and women and are reinforced through the structural dimensions of job classifications and valuation of women's work. Job classifications have historically been designed based on some male standard of performance as the ideal standard. *Ideal workers* are identified as those who work long hours, never complain, are available 24/7, can work late anytime, and are not tethered to familial or community obligations (Sweet, 2013; Williams, 2000). These conditions tend to be better suited to men more so than women who often have many obligations to family and community. Job designs also include structural biases. Physical tests of strength for such jobs as police and fire protection should be considered, but their relevancy to the job should be considered as well. Sweet (2013) suggests the use of technology such as Tasers, the use of teams to subdue criminals, and often mundane daily activities or report writing and filing suggest physical tests of strength are used to "determine who can *enter* into police jobs, but not who can *keep* [the jobs]" (p. 150). These tests also likely ignore skills attributable to women such as the interpersonal skills of negotiation and mediation which are important when dealing with the public. This structural application design favors less qualified males over highly qualified females and limits a female's career path into higher levels of law enforcement which progress through entry-level law enforcement positions.

The devaluation of women in the paid labor force also creates wage disparities. Entire professions devoted to nurturing such as education, childcare, and nursing, tend to pay lower wages than do jobs in engineering and science. The idea of a job's *comparable worth* is tied to women's and men's roles (Feldberg, 1984). Nurturing jobs typically pay about 5–10 percent less than jobs in manufacturing, finance, or construction even when controlling for factors such as education, seniority, or responsibilities (England, 2002).

WOMEN'S PARTICIPATION IN THE LABOR FORCE

We can divide women's participation in the labor force into non-paid participation and paid participation, though this distinction is often blurred. During the mid-nineteenth century, from around 1820 to 1865, the idea of two spheres developed: the public sphere in which men were king, owned all property, had voting rights, and made all decisions, and the private sphere in which women ruled as "domestic goddesses," responsible for the home and child rearing. This *cult of domesticity* or the *cult of true womanhood* resulted from the ideology that family and work were changing because men were entering the rough world of work away from the home and leaving their weak and delicate wives at home to care for hearth, home, and children. A woman's place, therefore, was in the private sphere where she would be protected from the vile outside world. Popular culture, in the form of "women's magazines, advice books, religious journals, newspapers, [and] fiction" (Lavender, 1999) reinforced the idea that women's roles revolved around "piety, purity, domesticity, and submissiveness" (Lavender, 1999). Cott (2002) writes:

> The cult dictated that True women were the moral guardians of the family. . . [and] they were particularly appropriate for that role because they were spiritually pure—and therefore closer to God. They remained pure because they stayed away from the degrading environment of the outside world, which ruined innocence; moral purity could not withstand the brutality of a world dominated by the unrestrained competition of the free enterprise system.

The idealized work of women during this period suggested women's roles were peripheral to the subsistence of the family. Though this viewpoint was applicable for wealthier households in which husbands were doctors, lawyers, and merchants, it was fiction for most households in which women's work was mostly toil and drudgery. Nevertheless, the fiction of the cult of domesticity was used in the "courts and the churches [to] reinforce women's seclusion in the home through legal decisions and sermons that emphasized women's frailty by dwelling on women's moral purity" (Cott, 2002). Interestingly, the cult also provided women a way to enter the public sphere through their writings which extolled the necessity of "being in the world" in order to educate their future sons as community and national leaders (Cott, 2002).

Prior to the Industrial Revolution, most work was performed at home, and women made a significant contribution to that work. The nineteenth century woman writer, Charlotte Perkins Gilman (1900), recognized the secondary economic status of women to men but made the argument that women "earn their share of it [wealth] as wives" (p. 10). She wrote, "This assumes either that the husband is in the position of employer and the wife as employee, or that marriage is a 'partnership,' and the wife an equal factor with the husband in producing wealth" (Gilman, 1900, p. 10). Gilman (1900) continues, "The labor of women in the house, certainly, enables men to produce more wealth than they otherwise could; and in this way women are economic factors in society" (13) and says that horses are also economic factors in production because they are not economically independent. She argues both horses and women are dependent on men for their survival because if the "property of the man, is obliged to perform this service, and is not paid for it, he is not economically independent" (13).

Mingling care for the home and children with work that provided the family a living, women workers were "visible and socially recognized" (Sweet, 2013, p. 127). We can still find remnants of this type of *household economy*, also known as *household production*, in society. The household economy "describes the collective economic activities of households" (Iron-monger, 2001, p. 5) in which production and consumption take place outside of the market economy. In the household economy, family members produce their own goods and services for their own consumption using their own capital and unpaid labor. This would include growing, harvesting, preparing, and eating their own food, building and living in their own shelter, or con-cocting and administering their own medicines. Much of this work was done by women as unpaid labor, and this traditional gender rendition of household production was relatively unquestioned until the beginning of the Industrial Revolution (Gilman, 1900). Current examples of household economies still in existence would be some Amish communities or family farms in which women often share the same responsibilities for their livelihoods as do their husbands, and most economic activities take place outside the market.

The blending and merging of household economies and market econo-mies began in earnest around the 1890s when the shift in production moved out of the household into the factory. This arrangement was significant be-cause it not only moved men from the farm to the mill but women and children as well. The invention of household appliances such as vacuum cleaners and washing machines during the early twentieth century made household work easier for women, housewives, and mothers, but then fe-males were expected to do more such as work outside the home. Day (1989) writes,

Freed by new homemaking technologies—washing machines, nonfire cookers, vacuum cleaners—and new amenities that freed them from food preparation—canned food, bread cheaper to buy than to bake—middle class women aspired to paid work, social reform, and college. . . .

More and more married women and mothers worked outside the home because of a stagnating economy which made extra income a necessity to maintain some standard of living. Puritan upbringings and Protestant belief still dominated American thought, and a moral outcry was raised against women, who, by working outside the home, flaunted the natural order. Part of this was economic because women now controlled their own money and undercut men's wages in the marketplace (Day, pp. 214–15)

According to Day (1989), 18 percent of the labor force in 1890 was women.

Women's roles within the family and the workplace are historically influenced by cultural attitudes as well as external economic forces. As the family unit changes so does the family's place in the economic structure. Women respond to these changes by adapting their family and work life roles as nurturers and wage earners. Current examples of household economies merging with market economies exist in the form of moving food production from the kitchen into restaurants and fast-food establishments, staying in motels instead of staying at home, putting children in outside-the-home day care instead of providing home childcare, and using public transportation versus using one's own vehicle.

WOMEN AS PRIMARY CARE-GIVERS

Primary care responsibility for children, the frail elderly, and people experiencing sickness or disability has traditionally been assigned to women, reinforcing economic significance of genders (Blau, 2013; Folbre, 2012, p. xi). According to the Bureau of Labor Statistics, married women "employed full time were more likely to do household activities and provide childcare on an average day than were married fathers employed full time" (Labor, 2008). The American Time Use Survey (ATUS) focuses on married parents who live in the same household as do their children under eighteen years of age. An average day in this survey is defined as an "average distribution of time across all seven days of the week" (Labor, 2008).

The Department of Labor defines full-time workers as those working thirty-five hours or more each week, and reflects that "43 percent of married mothers and 88 percent of married fathers were employed full time" (Labor, 2008). Women still carry the greater burden of child and household care. Seventy-one percent of full-time working married mothers spent 1.2 hours per day caring for children under the age of eighteen in the household while 54 percent of full-time working married fathers spent forty-nine minutes per day caring for children under the age of eighteen in the household. Eighty-four percent of full-time working married mothers in households with children under eighteen spent 2.6 hours each day doing housework, cooking, and lawn care while 64 percent of full-time working married fathers in households with children under eighteen spent 1.2 hours engaging in household activities (Labor, 2008). In contrast, full-time working married mothers spent 2.9 hours engaging in leisure activities while full-time working married fathers spent 3.7 hours engaging in leisure activities. In households with children under eighteen, part-time working mothers spent 3.4 hours daily engaging in leisure activities while part-time working fathers spent 3.6 hours daily engaging in leisure activities (Labor, 2008).

Women are also the primary caregivers to the elderly. Eldercare in America is increasing because the baby-boomer generation is aging and moving toward retirement. The Bureau of Labor Statistics defines eldercare providers as "those who provide[d] unpaid care to someone over the age of 65 who need[s] help because of a condition related to aging" (Labor, 2012b). There are currently 16 percent or 39.8 million of the U.S. civilian non-institutional population age fifteen and over who are eldercare providers. The majority of these eldercare providers, 56 percent, are women.

Today's women face a "double bind" (Hill, 1990, p. 2) because of their work load and child rearing and eldercare responsibilities. Even when women are able to drop out of the workforce for caregiving responsibilities, they sacrifice present and future earnings, time accrued toward promotion, and loss of currency in their fields. Because women are disproportionately affected by care giving, their labor-market participation is diminished and this has an effect on the economy in terms of lower productivity and less efficiency. According to Hill (2009), to move the care giving dynamic to reflect more male participation would require creating social policy which pays women for care giving responsibilities much like the GI Bill awarded service-men the opportunity for higher education in return for their military service and encouraging firms to provide flexible work schedules for care giving females.

Currently female wage earners, faced with caring for children and the elderly, are dubbed "the sandwich generation," because these females engage in "*informal care*" (italics mine) (He, 2013, p. 2), defined as unpaid care provided by family members. Increasing mortality rates for humans because of better health care and cleaner environments mean rising longevity for baby boomers. Anticipated long-term care for an aging population suggests a greater demand for more informal care. Rising health care costs and a preference by the elderly to stay in their homes as long as possible means informal care givers make a choice between labor-market participation and care giving.

WAGE DISPARITIES RESULTING FROM GENDER

Women make less money than men in almost all arenas. Let's explore why this continues to be true even today with policies which dictate equal pay for equal work (Congress, 1963), anti-discrimination laws (Congress, 1964), and adjustments to wage discrimination (Congress, 2009). Beginning in 1947, the Census Bureau tracked wage data for wage earners. Figure 9.1 reflects trends in wage data for female wage earners from 1947 to 2012.

Men and women are socialized from birth to aspire to different careers. Girls are often steered toward nurturing jobs such as teachers, nurses, or social workers while boys are directed toward engineering, construction, and mechanics. *Agents of socialization,* influences which guide/direct young minds toward a certain career, lifestyle, or way of thinking, often impact choices made in education and training, associations with various groups, and worldviews (Sweet, 2013). Young men often move into the sciences because they believe they are better suited to math-oriented careers than do young women who gravitate toward care work because they believe they are better suited to nurturing careers (Cici, 2009). Care work contributes to the development and maintenance of human capabilities that represent a public good. Human capabilities have intrinsic values and also yield important positive spillovers for living standards, quality of life, and sustainable economic policies (Folbre, 2012, p. 183). These firmly rooted gender expectations are

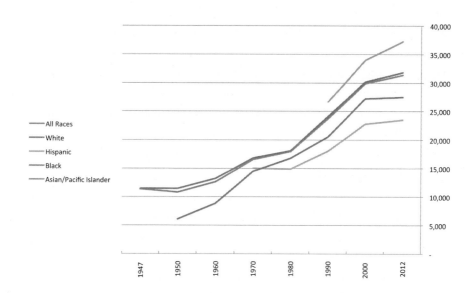

Figure 9.1. Female Earning by Race: 1947–2012. Source: Author's Analysis: U.S. Census Bureau.

self-fulfilling prophesies which result in gendered divisions with males prominent in medicine, engineering, and construction, and females dominating in the teaching, nursing, and social work professions. Distinct gender roles also exist within fields such as education and medicine. Women tend to be teachers and nurses, while administrators and doctors tend to be men. The nurturing professions filled with women tend to pay less money, have fewer opportunities for advancement, and are less prestigious than are the analytical professions such as engineering and computer technology which are filled with men. These factors contribute to a gendered wage disparity in almost all fields.

GENDER DISCRIMINATION IN THE WORKPLACE

Gender discrimination in the workplace takes several forms, some overt and some hidden. *Overt discrimination* occurs when visible and conscious decisions are made to enjoin an individual from entering an occupation based on his or her sex. One's sex is usually apparent by one's appearance, so we are primarily talking about women being prohibited from entering into male-dominated professions because they are women. This form of sexual discrimination, once a huge problem in manufacturing, construction, and logging, was legally condemned with the passage of the Civil Rights Act of 1964. Most workplace discrimination currently takes the form of subdued or hidden discrimination or *covert discrimination*. Though not necessarily difficult to detect, its existence is more difficult to prove. Take the issue of *hostile sexism*, "the belief that [women] are inferior to men at specific tasks" (Sweet, 2013, p. 142). This discriminatory position contributes to workplace stratification which gives men more opportunities for advancement than it gives to women. *Benevolent sexism* suggests that women are better at "women's work" such as nurturing and socializing so employment opportunities are often geared toward less difficult tasks which do not subject women to danger or risk, thus limiting women's prospects for learning new skills. *Statistical discrimination* means an individual is targeted because of aggregate data suggesting generalities about a group. For instance, young women are often categorized as potential child bearers and may not receive jobs or promotions because the employer believes they will divert time away from the job to care for their child. This *stereotype* of young women then lessens their chances of a successful career (Sweet, 2013).

By the same token, women often experience the *glass ceiling*, a level within upper management above which they cannot rise because of structural and institutional barriers within a firm. Sometimes a *hostile work environment*, a caustic work setting sexually charged with explicit artifacts or unwanted sexual advances, makes women's or racial or sexual minorities' competent work performance impossible. A hostile work environment must rise to the level of legal classification before any court actions can be pursued. Harassment in the work setting must involve some protected status as defined by the Civil Rights Act of 1964. Protected status involves race, gender, sexual orientation, military status, pregnancy, political affiliation, disabilities, age (over forty), and certain health statutes (AIDS or HIV). It is unlikely that cases not involving some protected status will ever be able to establish a court claim.

According to Day (1989), there were over five million women or 20 percent of the total workforce employed in 1900. Within one decade, that number rose to 25 percent. Most women worked for economic reasons and about 25 percent were the primary wage earners for their families. Prior to WWI, most women in industry were employed in the manufacture of clothing, food, or tobacco products. As the United States became embroiled in WWI, women were recruited into a broader array of manufacturing occupations, and "by 1920, 25.6 percent of working women were in white-collar jobs; 23.8 percent in manufacturing; 8.2 percent in domestic service; and 12.9 percent in agriculture" (Day, 1989, p. 248). The labor force during this time was extremely segregated so white workers made more than their black counterparts. Day (1989) writes:

> In the 1920s, less than two million of the eight million wage-earning women were married, but by 1930 more than three million were married. Employers often refused to hire married women and frequently fired them when they married. Twenty-six states had laws prohibiting the hiring of married women."
> (249)

In response to women's entry into factory work resulting from the U.S. entrance into WWI, the *Women in Industry Service (WIS)* was organized by the Department of Labor in 1918. Faced with the wartime production of munitions, rations, and military clothing, women became the

> sole reserve force of labor to be called upon to measure up to the demands of an augmented program of production for the war in the face of the withdrawal of men for military service at the rate of a quarter of a million a month.
> (Service, 1919, p. 3)

As wider public recognition of the necessity of women entering industry became entrenched in the minds of Americans, it became clear the federal government must not only recruit and retain women in production but also safeguard their health while promoting efficiency as they entered into jobs to which they were unaccustomed. Since the long-standing purpose of the Department of Labor is to "foster, promote, and develop the welfare of the wage earners of the United States, to improve their working conditions, and to advance their opportunities for profitable employment" (Service, 1919, p. 3), and though public sentiment toward women in industry was sharpened during war time, it became apparent that during times of war, adjustment, and peace there should be a program on behalf of women in industry to shape policy determining their conditions of employment. One important facet of the WIS was to prevent employers from using the war as an excuse to pay lower wages to women for the same work done by men, determine localities in which the greatest production needs existed, and present educational materials about women's work to serve as recruitment tools. The WIS was active for four months prior to the WWI armistice being signed and eight months after its signing. During this time, field investigations concerning women's readjustment from war production to domestic production resulted in "Standards for the Employment of Women," a publication for standards and recommendations of employment conditions which were used to craft state legislation. Versions of this publication were reprinted until 1965. The WIS was then incorporated by the Women's Bureau.

In 1920, Congress enacted Public Law No. 259 which established *The Women's Bureau*, a federal agency in the Department of Labor charged with the duty to "formulate standards and policies which shall promote the welfare of wage-earning women, improve their working conditions, increase their efficiency, and advance their opportunities for profitable employment" (Bureau, Women's, 2012). During the 1920s and 1930s, the Bureau focused on working conditions for women in the retail, textile, food, tobacco, clerical, and laundry industries and was at the forefront of legislation which eventually resulted in the *Civil Service Commission* issuance of a ruling which allowed women and men to take the *Civil Service Exam* and the *Fair Labor Standards Act of 1938* which set minimum wages and hours of work. In the 1940s, the Bureau turned its attention to wartime production once again and focused on women in the production of aircrafts, munitions, shipyards, foundries, and wartime modifications of state labor laws for women. By the 1950s, the Bureau was focusing on women college graduates by examining women's employment in medical and health sciences, social work, legal services, and mathematics and the sciences. Their major legislative contributions during this period were the passage of the *Equal Pay Act of 1963* and the *Civil Rights Act of 1964* (Bureau, Women's, 2012).

During the 1970s, the focus of the Bureau turned to issues of protection versus discrimination which required a reassessment of standing policies since new opportunities were now open to women. This led to the identification of sexually discriminatory provisions within state laws; the Bureau also supported the passage of the *Equal Rights Amendment* (ERA), new job training models as a result of the *Comprehensive Employment and Training Act* (CETA), and new programs to help low-income and domestic workers (Bureau, Women's, 2012). During the 1980s and the 1990s, new initiatives concerned employer-sponsored childcare, career pathways, training in the *Job Training Partnership Act* (JTPA), which replaced CETA, contingent and temporary work, work-life balance, and non-traditional employment for women. Currently the Worker's Bureau is promoting women in *Science, Technology, Engineering, and Math* (STEM) education, flexible work options such as flex-time and job sharing, and helping women veterans reintegrate into the workforce.

GENDER DISPARITIES IN UNIONS

The American labor movement's rhetoric, press, and ideology also served to relegate women to secondary status and contributed to the "conventional social attitudes concerning women's role[s]" (Schofield, 1983, p. 337). All women, and especially working women, were curbed to the private sphere and controlled by cultural and structural pressures which "reinforced a sexual division of labor both at home and in the workplace" (p. 337). By the early 1900s, the dominant trade union was the AFL which practiced the exclusion of everyone other than white, skilled males. *Samuel Gompers*, founder and first president of the AFL, adamantly decried the inclusion of working married women in trade unions because "the wife or mother, attending to the duties of the home, makes the greatest contribution to the support of the family" (Schofield, 1983, p. 343). His viewpoint on single women was different in that they should be organized and imbued with the principles of unionism because as future wives and mothers they would provide support to their husbands and his union efforts. Some years later, Gompers's attitude was softened because of his entanglement with the political polemic of the time which was that women should have the right of suffrage.

Ann Schofield (1983) writes:

> Women's relationship to the American labor movement has been historically problematic. Following the Civil War, the cigar makers, printers, and the National Labor Union accepted female members. During the 1880s the Knights of Labor made an active effort to recruit women from all walks of life, and throughout the nineteenth century women workers organized themselves into alliances and working women's associations. Despite this activity, though, until the turn of the century women workers were a negligible portion of the American wage force and were generally not welcome participants in the mainstream labor movement. Even with the growth of the female wage labor force to 20 percent of the adult female population by 1910, women continued to hold a marginal position in the industrial world. Their work was located in areas of low-skill and poorly paid employment, and trade unions viewed them with either indifference or hostility. (p. 336)

Women tended to have low-paying jobs and work in less than perfect conditions; factories and mills were rife with "industry-bred diseases . . . and
women workers had a mortality rate more than double that of nonworking
women and a third more than working men" (Day, 1989, p. 249). Women of
color were often segregated from white women workers and suffered indignities such as lack of clean drinking water and no bathrooms. These horrible
working conditions and low wages led women to become active union affili-
ates who saw the union as a way to improve their lives and provide some
protections from overzealous bosses. The impetus of organized labor during
this period was the concept of a *family wage*, more specifically a man's wage
which could solely support a family. The AFL, largely unsupportive of wom-
en joining their ranks, believed women would drive down men's wages, so
women orchestrated the formation of their own unions.

Working-class women, who made up one-fifth of the total work force,
founded the *National Women's Trade Union League of America* (NWTUL)
in 1903. Aided by professional reformers and wealthy women sympathetic to
the plight of oppressed working women, this coalition "assist[ed] in the
organization of women wage workers into trade unions and thereby [helped]
them to secure conditions necessary for healthful and efficient work and to
obtain a just reward for such work" (Cooper and Essrow, 2013). The
NWTUL arranged for legal representation, picketed, and engaged with the
press in matters involving the betterment of working women. The issue of
women's health in industry was regularly defined in the labor press through
the dominant cultural ideal that women were the mothers of future generations and "should not be employed at jobs injurious to their health which
might jeopardize the 'future of the race'" (Schofield, 1983, p. 342). In 1909,
the NWTUL, along with the International Ladies' Garment Workers Union
(ILGWU), "which by 1914 was the third largest unit in the AFL" (Day, 1989,
p. 249), called a strike against the Triangle Waist Factory in Manhattan, New
York (Day, 1989).

The factory employed primarily young immigrant women of Italian and
Jewish descent who worked in sweatshop conditions for very low wages.
This strike coupled with other strikes in the shirtwaist industry led to the
Uprising of the 20,000 in 1909–1910, a strike notable for its "size, duration,
and support from middle-class women" (Cooper and Hall, 2013). In 1910,
the *Great Revolt*, a strike by male cloak makers in New York City resulted in
the *Protocol of Peace*, a contract limiting work by gender in which only men
could be hired in certain higher paying positions while women, even those
performing the same work, could legally be paid a lower wage (Cooper, D.,
and Hall, D., 2013; Day, 1989). Though the Protocol provided for the "establishment of the Joint Board of Sanitary Control, [a] Committee on Grievances, and a Board of Arbitration, many health and safety protections were
omitted. Consequently, a fire, the worst industrial disaster in U.S. history at

that time, occurred at the Triangle Waist Factory in 1911 which killed 146 young workers, primarily women. The owners of the firm were indicted by the attorney general of Manhattan but were exonerated by the courts. Three years later resulting civil suits brought by the families of the dead required restitution of $75 for each life lost. For a fuller discussion of the Triangle Waist Fire, see chapter 5.

The AFL's interest in only unionizing skilled workers created a space in which the unskilled, the semi-skilled, women, and minorities could form bonds of solidarity to upgrade their pay and working conditions. In 1905 the *Industrial Workers of the World* (IWW), also known as the Wobblies, filled this void. This Chicago-born radical organization advocated the overthrow of capitalism, which they viewed "as the root cause of evil" (Schofield, 1983, p. 349), and the installation of a socialist system. Advocates of direct action, the IWW engaged in strikes, lockouts, boycotts, and propaganda and shunned collective bargaining, political interventions, and sabotage. This revolutionary, industrial union was attractive to women who saw it as a vehicle for reform. But the IWW saw working women's plight as a class issue and not a gender issue. Though the IWW believed women should be organized at the point of production, they believed that the new economic order of socialism they envisioned would alleviate the oppression of all workers, not just women (Schofield, 1983). During the remainder of the twentieth century, the ideology of patriarchy consigning women to secondary status overshadowed capitalist ideology as the oppressor of women.

After WWII, there was a marked period of growth and prosperity. Legislation protecting workers' rights in the form of minimum wage laws, the ability to collectively bargain, and unemployment insurance helped workers feel more secure in their jobs. A capitalist economic system embracing Fordist production techniques dominated manufacturing, and career ladders for *organization man*, a career man who gives his all for his organization and company, epitomized the upward ladders of mobility. Whyte (1956) made popular the term organization man, referring to a career-driven male who sacrificed his life for the organization or company. His book, *The Organization Man*, refuted the idea that the collective was a more powerful and effective way to run a company or a country (Whyte, 1956). Women during this period were moving from the economic fringes of the market into the public sphere. Korpi (2010) notes that though "women have traditionally been more or less marginal participants" (p. 20) in Western labor markets, women now moved into more paid labor than unpaid care work. This inequality in gendered work is known as *Wollstonecraft's Dilemma*, referring to Mary Wollstonecraft, an eighteenth-century feminist writer who posited that women should have rights equal to men. *A Vindication of the Rights of Woman* (1792) argued since women have equal powers of reason, they should be afforded equal rights and that a society which violated women's rights was wasting women's skills and abilities (Wollstonecraft, 1792).

Though the effect of declining unionization on worker's wages is greater for men, declining unionization accounts for "a fifth of the inequality increase for women and a third for men" (Western, 2011, p. 514). Declining unionization has contributed to wage inequality as a result of an erosion of distributional norms (Western, 2011). Unionization has an effect on wages for union workers because it standardizes wages for skilled workers, thus taking wages out of competition within unionized workforces. But unionization also has an effect on nonunion workers in two ways. Some firms will pay their workers comparable union wages to influence their employees not to unionize; this is known as the *spillover effect*. Sometimes firms will also pay their employees union wages if the employees threaten to form a union. This is known as the *threat effect*. Unions raise wages for low-paid or blue collar workers who may have less education than their managerial counterparts. Unions not only raise wages for all workers, they "contribute to a moral economy that institutionalizes norms for fair pay, even for nonunion workers" (Western, 2011, p. 514).

Union membership for women is historically lower than union membership for men, but that trend is changing. According to Bronfenbrenner and Hickey (2004), "women make up the majority of new workers organized at least since the mid-1980s" (p. 443). Though the number of women participating in the labor force continues to increase, the number of women affiliated with unions is disproportionately small. Several reasons account for this discrepancy. Women's participation in labor unions differs according to region, industry, occupation, union, and race and ethnicity (Bronfenbrenner, 2005). Most successful organizing initiatives take place in industries dominated by women such as education, service, and caregiving industries which, in general, pay lower wages, offer few opportunities for advancement, and provide scant benefits. Primarily more women than men currently unionize because men tend to dominate heavy industry such as manufacturing, construction, and mining in which organizing losses occur. Targeted efforts to unionize service, caregiving, and educational industries which primarily employee women suggest the majority of new workers organized each year will be female. The trend toward women organizing means that future union membership will reflect a female majority which may not be reflected in leadership positions.

Organizing efforts to include women in labor unions has met with limited success even though women who earn union wages make 31 percent more than their non-union counterparts (Bronfenbrenner, 2005; Spalter-Roth, 1994). Figure 9.2 reflects women's participation in labor unions in comparison to the total number of employed workers in labor unions. In 2012, women made up 48 percent of the workforce and 45 percent of the unionized workforce (author's analysis). According to Bronfenbrenner (2005), "It has become increasingly clear that labor unions are the only major U.S institution equipped to help women overcome these [gender discrimination] barriers in the workplace" (p. 3).

The lower numbers of women participating in the labor movement is often denoted as a lack of interest in unionizing, yet research has shown that women maintain positive attitudes about unionization and join unions when they feel it is in their best interest to do so. Structural and cultural forces such as gender and workplace discrimination often complicate the issue of women organizing into labor unions and this exacerbates the gendered wage gap often connected to workplace discrimination. Win rates in organizing women are higher when the unit being organized is predominately one gender or one race. In her research on organizing women workers, Bronfenbrenner (2005) found public industries which have greater female density such as social services and healthcare also have higher densities of women of color, and industries within private industries such as manufacturing and construction have lower densities of female workers and female workers of color. Because women tend to vote for unionization more than their male counterparts, win rates for unionization tends to be higher in public industries. Also public industry is less susceptible to the flight of capital mobility often dictated by competition and market forces, so jobs in public industry tend to be more stable. The higher win rates in industries dominated by women suggest wom-

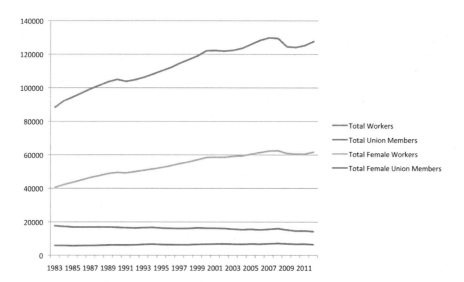

Figure 9.2. Women's Participation in Labor Unions 1983–2012. Source: Author's Analysis, Current Population Survey.

en believe labor unions are beneficial because they promote women's economic empowerment (Akchurin, 2013), equal pay, leave policies, and daycare support (Hunt, 2002), and leverage connections between the labor movement and external market, social, and cultural policies which promote opportunities for women. Figure 9.3 reflects the proportion of employed women by race to their union membership.

The social construct of female gender influences economic and social policies which impact the employment relationship by undermining or deterring workplace equality. The historic undervaluing of the female role in the social hierarchy results from the historical cultural influences of "democratic egalitarianism and individualism, the Protestant work ethic, patriarchy, marriage and family values, and the American ideal" (Day, 1989, p. 141) which have a profound impact on women in the workforce seeking equity and equality in the workplace. External market forces and internal societal pressures create a playing field slanted against women's full and equal participation in the labor force which legislation and polity have yet to correct. The cultural mores which see women primarily as caregivers and "keepers of the hearth" has profound effects on women's wages and opportunities for career advancement through covert discrimination, sexism, and stereotyping. The necessity of women in the workplace because of military action, household necessity, or global competition forces society to reconsider the role of women in the workplace and their status as contributors to a local, national, and

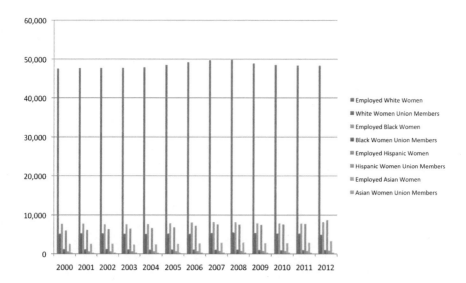

Figure 9.3.   Women's Participation in Labor Unions by Race: 2000–2012.
Source: Author's Analysis, Current Population Survey.

global economy. Government and corporate polity must reflect equality in the workplace and the employment relationship for women workers. Labor unions are currently seen as one mechanism by which women can increase their efficacy in the employment relationship.

Glossary

Ability to pay: the economic ability of the employer to provide an increase in wages.

Accretion: adding employees to an existing bargaining unit.

Acculturation: the idea that immigrants should or can "adopt the cultural skills of the dominant Anglo-American group"(Gordon, 1964) while maintaining their own cultural identity through connections with their immigrant group.

Across-the-board increase: an increase of equal cents-per-hour for all bargaining unit jobs.

Ad hoc arbitrator: an arbitrator who is appointed to hear a certain case(s).

Administrative law judge: a judge charged with interpreting the application of federal labor law in unfair labor-practice cases not settled between the parties.

Agency: the capacity of an individual to affect some change in some structure.

Agency fee: a union security clause that requires employees who are not union members to pay a service fee to the bargaining agent.

Agents of socialization: influences which guide/direct humans toward certain careers, lifestyles, or ways of thinking.

Ally doctrine: the employees of a secondary employer do not commit an unfair labor practice by refusing to perform struck work.

Alphabet soup programs: a series of New Deal economic programs instituted by Roosevelt to infuse money into the economy and create jobs.

Ambivalent sexism: a theoretical concept which furthers the understanding of gender-based prejudice.

American Federation of Government Employees (AFGE): an industrial-type union which asserts jurisdiction over federal employees.

American Federation of Labor (AFL): the first permanent national labor organization which housed craft unions and took a business-union approach toward gaining benefits for its members and influencing public policy.

American Federation of Labor-Congress of Industrial Organization (AFL-CIO): the primary labor federation for international and national unions in the United States which coordinates national public policy initiatives for the labor movement.

American Federation of State, County, and Municipal Employees (AFSCME): an industrial-type union which organizes nonfederal public-sector employees.

American ideal: a standard of perfection based on the Anglo-Saxon Protestant male.

American Plan: a strategy designed in the 1920s to discredit organized labor's influence on the public, promote company unions, and oppose union organizing.

Appropriate bargaining union: an appropriate group of employees with similar interests who can be represented by a bargaining unit as determined by the National Labor Relations Board.

Arbitrability: the state of a grievance which alleges a contractual violation if the contract terms allow for arbitration.

Arbitration: a dispute resolution procedure in which a neutral third party (arbitrator chosen by both parties) renders a binding decision by which both parties agree to abide.

Assimilation: melting or blending into another culture so differences are minimized.

Associate member: a status bestowed on nonunion members who wish to participate in union group benefits.

Associational unionism: a group of professionals who join together to put pressure on employers.

Attitudinal structuring: techniques and processes designed to alter a party's position at the bargaining table.

Authorization card: an employee-signed card authorizing a union to act as a representative bargaining agent which is necessary for the establishment of interest in requesting an NLRB election.

Bacon-Davis Act: a federal law requiring employers to pay prevailing area union wages to workers on federal construction projects.

Bad-faith bargaining: a refusal by a union or a company to bargain or to discuss mandatory or permissive issues to impasse.

Bargaining book: a collection of historical contracts, their interpretations, and settlements used in determining past bargaining issues at contract time.

Bargaining convention: a meeting of union delegates prior to contract negotiations to determine the union's position on mandatory bargaining issues.

Bargaining power: the capacity of one party to dominate the other due to influence, economic power, size, status, or some combination of the above.

Bargaining structure: the organizational relationship between unions and companies legally bound by terms of an agreement (formal bargaining) or unions and companies affected by the result of negotiated settlements through pattern bargaining or other non-binding processes (informal bargaining).

Bargaining unit: a group of employees represented by a representative bargaining agent.

Barons: a lower title of nobility acquired through heredity in the European nobility system; also known as lords.

Benefit-status seniority: the precedence of position over others within a specific environment by reason of length of service which entitles an employee to certain benefits during reductions in workforce, and so forth.

Benevolent sexism: a theoretical concept which stereotypes women as superior to men in "women's work" such as caregiving, social planning, and nurturing.

Boycott: to abstain from purchasing a good/service as a means of intimidation or coercion in order to influence the firm's policies.

Bumping: the contractual right of a senior employee to replace a junior employee in work reassignments.

Business agent: an elected or appointed union member in a paid position who is responsible for the business affairs and representation of the union.

Business unionism: a particular type of trade union philosophy and activity concentrating on collective bargaining and raising the living standards of workers.

By-product theory: the concept of providing a good as a result of membership in an organization.

C charge cases: NLRB cases involving allegations of unfair labor practices against an employer or union.

Capital gains: the increase in the value of an asset between the time it is purchased and the time it is sold.

Capital: a factor of production that has been produced for use in the production of other goods and services (Rittenberg, 2011).

Capitalism: an economic system in which the private market owns and allocates all goods and services.

Capital-labor accord: a time from 1950-1960 "in which employers conceded the legitimacy of unions and negotiated wage increases closely tracked to productivity growth" (Fossum, 2005, p. 561).

Cease and desist orders: a remedy issued by the NLRB to stop activities violating labor law.

Central bodies: the local arms of the AFL-CIO which conduct union and political affairs.

Central labor councils (CLC): local arms of the AFL-CIO which help coordinate national union interests on a local level. CLCs report to the federation and engage in political lobbying and politics on the state level.

Centrally planned capitalism: an economic system in which resources are owned by private individuals and allocated by the state.

Centrally planned socialism: an economic system in which resources are owned and allocated by the state.

Certification election: an NLRB sanctioned election in order to determine the initial representation of a union for collective bargaining representation.

Certification: an NLRB determination concerning the results of a representative election.

Check off: an automatic dues deduction from an employee's paycheck as part of a collective bargaining agreement.

Chilling effect: the fear of penalization inhibits the use of speech/conduct in the willingness of parties to negotiate an agreement.

Citizenship: "A bundle of rights and duties associated with different aspects of citizens' lives" (Korpi, 2010, p. 14).

Civil Reform Act: a federal act passed in 1978 which reformed the civil service of the U.S. federal government, attempted to replace incompetent officials through merit assessments, abolished the U.S. Civil Service Commission and created three new agencies to administer and enforce human resources in the federal government. The act created the U.S. Office of personnel Management (OMP) to provide guidance to executive branch agencies, the Federal Labor Relations Authority (FLRA) to oversee the rights of federal employees to collectively bargain, and the U.S. Merit Systems Protection Board (MSPB) to conduct studies of the federal civil service and hear federal employees' disciplinary appeals.

Civil Rights Act of 1964: landmark legislation signed into law by President Johnson which outlawed discrimination against race, ethnicity, religion, and sex in public facilities, accommodations, and employment.

Civil Service Commission: an organization appointed by the U.S. president which controls appointments and advancements to members of the civil service.

Civil service system: a public sector employment for appointing government employees on the basis of competitive examinations instead of political patronage.

Class: a social construct which groups or categorizes humans by common attributes, such as income, wealth, characteristics, qualities, traits, education, abilities, talents, and so on.

Class divisions: hierarchical arrangements of individuals divided by social stratification due to wealth, income, education, race, ascribed and achieved status, or other defining characteristics.

Classical liberalism: a political ideology which emphasizes freedom from government interference in religion, speech, assembly, and press.

Class structure: socioeconomic divisions between groups of individuals. Individuals are placed in political, religious, racial, ethnic, educational, economic, and/or gendered groups based on some inherent or perceived feature.

Classism: belief, doctrine, prejudice, discrimination, behavior, attitudes, or conditions which foster stereotypes of social roles based on distinctions made between social or economic differences in groups or categories of people.

Classless society: a society in which no economic or cultural arrangement of groups (classes) exist.

Clayton Act: a federal law limiting court injunctions against unions in labor disputes and sanctioning picketing and other union activities.

Closed shop: a firm in which an employee is required to join and financially support a labor union as a condition of employment.

Coalition bargaining: a process in which more than one employer negotiates with the union or in which more than one union negotiates with one employer; it is different than collective bargaining.

Cognitive bias: a pattern or tendency of socially constructed categories based on memory, experience, and inferences resulting in stereotypes.

Cognitive bias process: a subjective social reality created by an individual's perceptions of input which influences behaviors in a judgmental fashion.

Coherence: the succession of superstructures such as politics, laws, customs, culture, morality, and ways of thinking created by the relationship of workers to the means of production.

Collective action: the ability of an organization to further the interests of its members.

Collective bargaining: the negotiation of a labor agreement between management and the labor union which has exclusive rights to bargain for and administer the contract for the collective.

Collective bargaining agreement: a contract between labor and management which stipulates the terms and conditions under which they will work for some specified period of time.

Collective goods: a class of goods beneficial to all individuals and from which no individual can be excluded because of ability to pay. Examples include the military, clean air, and a scenic view.

Collyer doctrine: the principle under which the NLRB refers unfair labor practices (charges) to arbitration if the issues are arbitrable under the collective bargaining agreement.

Colonialism: the domination, influence, and control of one country, territory, or people by another.

Command socialist economy: economic system in which the government owns and allocates all resources.

Committee on political education (COPE): a union's voluntary political action fund used for political purposes.

Common law: the development of law on a case by case basis via the court system.

Common situs picketing: picketing an employer's entire facility as a result of a grievance against a single subcontractor on the site (especially a construction site).

Communism: a revolutionary socialist movement which advocates for a classless, moneyless, and stateless social order in which private property is eliminated and all goods are owned in common.

Communist Manifesto: a socialist political pamphlet written by Marx and Engels in 1848 which describes the history of the working-class movement and outlines the principle of communism.

Communist Party: a political party which advocates for the resources ownership and allocation of all goods and services via the state.

Community action: a tactic which seeks to link the interest of a local union with the broader community to gain support for its positions.

Community of interest: NLRB criteria to determine the commonalities within a potential bargaining unit.

Community organizations: a collection of community groups with a similar goal who join together to further some interest through collective action.

Community organizing: the formation of alliances and coalitions between labor unions and other community organizations who share some goal.

Company town: a geographic location in which inhabitants are primarily dependent on one firm for necessities such as housing, food, transportation, education, recreation, and so forth.

Company union: a labor organization which is organized, financed, and dominated by an employer and is illegal under federal law.

Comparative advantage: a situation in which the opportunity cost of producing one good/service is lower for that economy than for any other (Rittenberg, 2011).

Comparable worth: the idea that equal pay for equal work of "comparable worth" to an employer. Also known as pay equity.

Compensating wage differentials: the additional amount of money that a worker must be offered in order to motivate the worker to accept a risky or undesirable job relative to other jobs that worker could perform.

Competitive status seniority: employees' seniority which allows them to hold, bid, bump, and/or avoid certain jobs/layoffs and is calculated from date of hire or entry into a department.

Comprehensive Employment and Training Act: Public law: 93-203 enacted in 1973 and provided training in the form of marketable skills to low-income workers. It was designed to decentralize control of federal job training programs and give more power to individual states. It was replaced in 1982 by the Job Training Partnership Act.

Concession bargaining: giving back previous gains such as wages or benefits.

Congress of Industrial Organization (CIO): founded in 1935 by John Lewis, the CIO organized unskilled and semiskilled factory workers and provided an organizational framework for their mobilization and unionization in response to the exclusionary practices of the American Federation of Labor (AFL). www.encyclopedia.chicagohistory.org/pages/326.html.

Consent election: a union election to determine a bargaining agent held at the request of the employer and the union.

Conservative social welfare function: an economic strategy which favors welfare reductions rather than increases.

Conspiracy doctrine: the doctrine that any group of employees who band together to secure favorable wages or benefits, working conditions, better hours, or resolve grievances against their employers is conspiring to fix wages; it was outlawed in the 1840s.

Conspiracy theory: a theory which holds that collective measures to coerce an employer to pay higher wages was considered a conspiracy against the employer and therefore an effort to restrain trade through wage fixing.

Constitutional conventions: gatherings of union members required by a union's constitution to change policy, elect officers, and/or amend constitutions.

Contract administration: a function of interpreting and enforcing the contract between the union and the company.

Contract campaign: a planning document in preparation for contract negotiations which outlines the strategies necessary to establish proposals, benchmarks, and timetables necessary to secure the union's goals.

Convention: the governing body of a national/international union which meets periodically to set policies, elect officers, and amend the constitution.

Coordinated bargaining: bargaining by multiple unions with one employer to settle on similar contractual terms.

Corporate campaign: a strategy in which an organized effort by unions pressure a firm's board of directors or governance committee deemed to be engaged in objectionable activities with a public relations campaign, protests, and media assaults in order to inform the public of the connections between the targeted company, stakeholder companies, and the buying public.

Corporatist policy: an approach to labor-management policy in which firms and unions agree to maintain stable relationships overseen by the government.

Cost-benefit analysis: a type of economics that seeks to quantify the costs and benefits of an activity (Rittenberg, 2011).

Cost-of-living adjustment (COLA): an annual wage adjustment tied to the consumer price index intended to offset a change in purchasing power.

Cotton gin: a machine invented by Eli Whitney which efficiently separates cotton fibers from their seeds.

Countervailing Theory of Labor and Capital: a theory which states that collective forces such as labor are necessary to combat the prevailing forces of capital.

Covert discrimination: subdued or hidden discrimination.

Craft severance: splitting a craft bargaining unit from a larger bargaining unit because of a dissimilar community of interests.

Craft union: a national union which represents employees in one occupation, trade, or skill.

Craft: a skilled trade or occupation.

Creative destruction: the tendency for old methods of production to be replaced by newer, more efficient approaches (Schumpeter, 1989).

Crop Lien Laws: a credit system instituted by southern land owners after the Civil War which allowed farmers to borrow against their crops.

Payment due at harvest time was often insufficient to pay back the debt.

The cult of domesticity: an ideology from the mid-nineteenth century or Victorian era which suggested a woman's nature was particularly suited to care-giving and homemaking roles because women were the natural conduits for cultural values such as piety and republican virtues passed on to successive generations. Also known as the Cult of True Womanhood.

Cult of true womanhood: an ideology from the mid-nineteenth century or Victorian era which suggested a women's nature was particularly suited to care-giving and homemaking roles because women were the natural conduits for cultural values such as piety and republican virtues passed on to successive generations. Also known as the Cult of Domesticity.

Cultural capital: a resource bank of intellectual, educational, and social knowledge which allows one to "fit in" to a group or organization.

Danbury Hatter Case: a 1908 Supreme Court ruling upholding a firm's right to engage unimpeded by union boycotts in interstate commerce.

Davis, Rebecca Harding: nineteenth-century author of *Life in the Iron Mills* (1865), a book of industrial fiction.

Decertification election: an election held to see whether a bargaining unit majority wishes to still be represented by a bargaining agent.

Defined benefit pension plan: an employer-sponsored retirement plan in which employee benefits are based on a formula using average pay and length of service.

Defined contribution pension plan: a retirement option based on a formula for calculating employer contributions toward retirement.

Democracy: government by the people in which supreme power is vested in the people or by representatives of their choosing.

Democratic egalitarianism: the social philosophy that no person is above the law with respect to social, political, civil, or economic affairs.

Democrats: a U.S. political party which promotes social liberalism and a progressive platform.

Demography: the quantitative and qualitative components of a population including composition, density, growth, movement, size, distribution, education, crime, wealth, social class, race, nutrition, diet, development, well-being, quality of life, and structure.

Depression: a severe decline in business activity in a national/international economy characterized by high unemployment and falling wages/prices (See panic and recession).

Differently abled: a term first coined in the 1980s as an alternative to describe individuals who were disabled or physically challenged. The term was thought to lend a more positive tone or message.

Discrimination: disadvantageous treatment or consideration of individuals or groups.

Disparate treatment analysis: an approach in the employment relationship which assumes employers will act objectively in the performance of their administrative duties unless there is some motivational intent not to do so.

Distributive bargaining: contractual bargaining in which one party gains while another party loses.

Divine right: the doctrine that a king, lord, baron, and such, holds power given directly or through heredity from God.

Doctrinaire organization: an employer who implements a pseudo-like unionization approach to labor relations in order to discourage unionization.

Dominant group maintenance: the process in which a collective such as employers develop and maintain status through the reinforcement of racial and ethnic hierarchies.

Drive system: "a production system in which supervisors have a great deal of power in rewarding and punishing subordinates" (Fossum, 2005, p. 563).

Dual commitment: the division of loyalty a worker feels between his or her employer and his or her union.

Dual governance: the idea that a bargaining agent can represent multiple locals and the members of each local can vote on separate contracts as well as select the bargaining agent.

Due process: a constitutional guarantee that no individual is deprived of life, liberty or property without the right to a fair and objective hearing.

Duplex Printing Case: a Supreme Court decision which reaffirmed the illegality of secondary boycotts because it interfered with interstate commerce.

Duty of Fair Representation: a legal duty of a union to equally and in good faith represent all employees in a bargaining unit regardless of their union membership.

Duty to bargain: the mutual obligation under federal law of labor and management to meet and discuss mandatory bargaining issues.

Earned income tax credit: a benefit for working people with low to moderate incomes.

Earned income: income from wages and salaries earned through paid employment.

Economics: the study of resource allocation in the production, distribution, and consumption of goods and services.

Economic strike: a work stoppage as a result of conflict over the impasse of mandatory bargaining issues.

Economy: an organized system for managing resources. An economy can be local, regional, national, or global.

Election bar: a time restriction (usually one year) in which another certification election cannot be held.

Electoral College: an institution made up of a set of electors selected by each state based on the state's population who indirectly elect the president and vice president of the United States.

Elitism: an attitude or behavior of an individual who believes himself to belong to a superior group by virtue of some attribute such as heritage, wealth, expertise, and so on.

Emigrant: an individual who leaves their native country to permanently live in another country.

Emigration: to leave one country and settle in another. The focus in on the original country.

Employee: an individual not involved in a labor dispute or not a supervisor, employer, agricultural or domestic worker, family laborer, or subject to the Railway Labor Act ("NLRA," 1935).

Employee-at-will: a contractual relationship (often unwritten) in which the employer can terminate an employee's work at any time for any reason, and the employee can quit at any time for any reason.

Employee relations: the activities between employers and employees which address workplace issues.

Employee stock ownership plan: a qualified defined contribution employee benefit (ERISA) plan which allows employees to invest in the stocks of their employers.

Employer: an individual representing and speaking on behalf of an organization who does not have the right to join a union nor actively participate in a union organizing campaign, having the authority to hire, transfer, suspend, lay off, recall, promote, discharge, assign, reward or discipline other employees, or the responsibility to direct them or adjust their grievances, or effectively recommend such actions which requires the use of independent judgment ("NLRA," 1935).

Employment relationship: the relationship between those who own or control the means of production and those who add value to the product; a legal link between employers and employees.

Equal Pay Act of 1963: a continuation of the Fair Labor Standards Act which prohibits sex-based wage discrimination between men and women in the same establishment who perform jobs that require substantially equal skill, effort, and responsibility under similar working conditions.

Equal Rights Amendment (ERA): an amendment to the U.S. Constitution which would guarantee equal rights for women. Ratified by both houses of Congress in 1972, the ERA failed to be ratified by the required thirty-six states within the ten-year period required by Congress.

Equality: the state, quality, or ideal of being equal in number, amount, degree, value, rank, ability, character, status, rights, and/or opportunities.

Equity: the quality, state, or ideal of being fair, just, and impartial.

Erdman Act: an 1898 federal law providing for mediation and arbitration in railroad disputes and outlawing yellow dog contracts.

Ethnicity: a subset of a race who belong to or derive from the cultural, ethnic, geographical, historical, linguistic, religious, and/or social traditions of a people or a country.

Excelsior list: a list of employees' correct names and addresses which must be produced by management seven days after the NLRB has authorized a representative election.

Exclusive representation: the right of a union to be the sole representative bargaining agent for a group of employees in a plant, craft, industry, or department whether or not those employees voted for the representation or are union members.

Executive board: the elected or appointed union members who serve as officers of a local union and are responsible for setting financial and governance policies.

Executive committee: elective/appointed officials of a union charged with financial and policy oversight.

Executive Order 10988: an order issued by President Kennedy in 1962 which recognized the rights of federal employees to bargain with management.

Expedited arbitration: an option for parties involved in resolving grievance disputes which speeds the process for resolution.

Fact-finding: "A third party method used to develop information about the issues in dispute and recommend a potential settlement" (Fossum, 2005, p. 563).

Factors of production: the resources available to the economy for the production of goods and services (Rittenberg, 2011).

Fair Labor Standards Act: federal law passed in 1938 requiring employers to pay overtime after 40 hours per week and the requirement of minimum wage for covered employees.

Fair representation: the legal obligation of a union to represent all workers in the unit whether or not they are union members.

Fairness: a concept which can mean equal treatment, opportunity, or outcome.

Family: "an economic and social unit in which people live within a society, and within which socially legitimated sexual relationships occur" (Day, 1989, p. 34).

Family Medical and Leave Act (FMLA): legislation passed during the Clinton administration which gives to covered employees 12 weeks of unpaid medical leave for themselves or to care for a family member.

Family wage: a concept held by the AFL that men's wages should be high enough to solely support a family without the help of a working wife.

Federal Labor Relations Authority: a federal law covering federal employees which oversees representation elections and the adjudication of unfair labor practices.

Federal Mediation and Conciliation Service (FMCS): a federal agency created by the Taft-Hartley Act in 1947 to assist labor unions and management in mediations if they have reached an impasse in negotiations.

Federal Mediation and Conciliation Service: A federal independent agency created by Taft-Hartley which seeks to prevent or settle labor-management disputes that affect interstate commerce.

Federal Reserve: the U.S. central banking system created in 1913 by the Federal Reserve Act in response to financial panics. The objectives of the Federal Reserve are to maximize employment, stabilize prices, and manage interest rates. www.federalreserve.gov/.

Federal service labor-management relations statue: a statue protecting the right of federal employees to organize which was created in 1978 by Title VII of the Civil Service Reform Act.

Federation: an organization made up of other organizations which retain control of their internal affairs and which provides to its members some benefits.

Feudalism: an employment relationship based on security in which lords or barons force peasants or serfs to work a certain proportion of the time for them in exchange for protection.

Fiefs: land holdings, a central element of feudalism, which were inheritable and given to vassals.

Field representative: paid, full-time international/national union employees who help local unions with negotiations and grievance processing.

Final-offer arbitration: dispute resolution method which refers to arbitration in which both parties are required to submit a final offer to an arbitrator.

Financial wealth: an economic concept which reflects one's net worth minus one's net equity in one's home or owner-occupied dwelling.

Firm-specific human capital: skills only applicable to specific workplaces.

Flexible work arrangement: a work design which allows/requires employees/employers to shift work hours, reconfigure job designs, and shift work schedules (Sweet, 2013).

Flexplace: non-traditional work locations which allow employees to work from sites other than the traditional workplace.

Flextime: non-traditional work scheduling which allows employees to alter their hours of work within some specified calendar of time, negotiate break lengths, and bank hours toward time away from work.

Fordism: a theory of manufacturing based on scientific management focusing on achieving efficiency through standardizing inputs, deskilling work and workers, and maintaining speed through the use of assembly lines. Fordism, named after Henry Ford, an auto magnet in the early 1900s, seeks to lower costs and maximize profits. Adjective: Fordist.

Fractional bargaining: bargaining taking place at a departmental level which might lead to an unwritten consensus to ignore certain contract provisions.

Fraternal Order of Police: a trade union of law enforcement officers which began as a benevolent organization.

Free good: a good for which the choice of one use doesn't require that another good by given up.

Free-rider: a union member who elects not to pay dues which is possible in an open shop.

Full employment: utilization of all production factors under current market conditions.

Functional democracy: the ability of union members to vote for contracts and officials.

Gainsharing: an employment arrangement in which flexible compensation is given to employees for improved performance resulting in cost savings.

Gender: a social construct referring to the roles, behaviors, attributes, and activities considered appropriate for men and women.

General human capital: skills which are portable between employers.

Gender schemas: "Stereotyped assumptions about women's behaviors and desires" (Sweet, 2013, p. 141).

General Motors: U.S. auto manufacturer headquartered in Detroit, Michigan.

General Motors Acceptance Corporation (GMAC): a firm created by Alfred Sloan which specialized in the credit market, a novel idea prior to the 1930s in which credit was taboo.

Gini ratio: a statistical measure of income equality ranging from 0-1 when 1 indicates perfect inequality (one person has all the income and all others have no income) and 0 indicates perfect equality (all people have equal shares of income).

Glass ceiling: an intangible level above which women cannot rise in management positions.

Global supply chain: worldwide networks of supplies, manufactures, warehouses, distribution centers, and retailers through which raw materials are acquired, transformed, and delivered to customers ("Guidelines for multinational enterprises: Responsible supply chain management—OCED—2002-Annual report on the OECD guildlines for multinational enterprises," 2002).

Golden Age of Labor: a period of time from 1935-1947 in which economic power in the labor-management relationship shifted to labor.

Gompers, Samuel: founder and first president of the AFL-CIO.

Good faith bargaining: the idea that labor and management will meet at reasonable times and places to discuss mandatory issues of bargaining.

Gorz, Andre: a French and Austrian social philosopher who promoted the New Left Labor Movement theory which says a guaranteed basic income should be a central component of wages.

Great Chain of Being: a rigid hierarchy of responsibilities in which all individuals had certain roles which corresponded to their station in the chain.

Great Depression: a severe decade-long economic depression prior to WWII in which 15 million workers were unemployed and half of all American banks failed.

Great Revolt: a largely Jewish cloakmakers' strike in 1910 backed by the International Ladies' Garment Workers' Union which resulted in a settlement establishing sanitation standards for factory workers.

Grievance: an employee complaint about a contractual violation.

Grievance proceedings: steps outlined in a contract which led to a resolution of a grievance.

Gross Domestic Product (GDP): the total value of all goods/services produced in a country.

Gross household product (GHP): the total economic value added by households in household production (Ironmonger, 2001).

Haymarket riots: a conflict in Chicago's Haymarket Square on May 4, 1886, between police and striking workers from the McCormick Reaper factory which turned violent when police tried to disperse the crowd. Rioters were blamed and punished, but later evidence suggests that a bomb was probably thrown by police and certainly the bullets fired were from police guns.

Hiring hall: a union office in the building trades from which union members are assigned available jobs.

Historical Materialism: a Marxist theory which maintains social structures such as politics and culture derive from economic structures such as capitalism and each class reproduces those structures from one generation to the next.

Homage: a medieval oath of allegiance used in feudalism in which the vassal swore loyalty to the lord in exchange for protection.

Homestead Strike: the second largest U.S. labor dispute beginning in June 30, 1892, when Andrew Carnegie, owner, and Henry Frick, general manager of the Homestead Steel Works in Homestead, Pennsylvania, locked out the Amalgamated Association of Iron and Steel workers who struck the plant when wages were reduced 18 percent and yellow dog contracts were required from all workers. The strike ended when the union was defeated.

Homogenous network: "a set of social relations with others who are similar in race and economic position" (Sweet, 2013).

Hostile sexism: a theoretical concept which stereotypes and devalues women as incompetent and inferior to men.

Hostile work environment: a caustic work setting in which harassment is documented as so objectively offensive as to alter the conditions of the individual's employment such as a tangible employment action.

Hot cargo: goods produced by nonunion labor which union members refuse to transport.

Household economy: the collective economic activities of households. Often called the household sector, the household economy is distinct from the business, government, or foreign sectors of the economy (Ironmonger, 2001).

Household production: the production of goods and services by the members of a household for their own consumption, using their own capital and their own unpaid labor. Goods and services produced by households for their own use include accommodation, meals, clean clothes, and child care (Ironmonger, 2001).

Human capital: the skills, abilities, knowledge, and experience an individual gains from training, education, and life experiences.

Human resource manager: an individual in an organization responsible for developing and implementing employment policies and practices, hiring, terminating, and disciplining employees, and advising managers on contractual issues.

Ideal worker: individuals who put work above all else, work long hours without complaint, are available 24/7, have no other obligations, and are insensitive to their other roles in life.

Illegal bargaining issue: issues over which the parties cannot bargain because they are illegal (discrimination, hot cargo, closed shop clauses).

Immigrant: an individual who comes to another country to permanently live.

Immigration: to enter and settle in a non-native country. The focus in on the new country.

Impasse: the inability to reach a decision over mandatory bargaining issues.

Imperialism: the practice or policy of territorial expansion, acquisition, domination, influence, and control either directly or indirectly over the political or economic life of a territory, country, or people.

Implied contract: an assumption by employees arising from past conduct that employers will continue to treat them in the usual fashion.

Impro-Share: a gainsharing program tied to worker productivity as determined by formula.

Income surplus: the difference in dollars between the income of a family or unrelated individual above the poverty level and its poverty threshold.

Individualism: a social theory emphasizing the rights, liberties, freedoms, and independence of the individual above that of the collective.

Industrial organizing: organizing around a specific industry. Also known as occupational organizing.

Industrial relations manager: the individual in a unionized environment responsible for developing and implementing employment policies and practices consistent with a collective bargaining agreement.

Industrial union: a national union which represents employees in a single industry.

Industrial unionism: the organization of all workers' skill levels under one union.

Industrial Workers of the World: a radical labor union of industrialists who embraced social justice and were led by Eugene Debs and Big Bill Haywood. Known as the Wobblies, they promoted the abolition of the wage system which they believed kept workers in a state of poverty and hunger, condemned free markets and corporations, and did not favor political action.

Industry-wide bargaining: a bargaining structure in which industry employers simultaneously bargain with a single union.

Inequality: an income distribution in which one or more population quintiles accounts for less or more than 20 percent of aggregate income.

Informal care: unpaid care for children or the elderly provided by family members.

Informal economy: a secondary or sub economy of unregulated and unprotected jobs resulting from lack of jobs in the primary economy.

Injunction: a court order requiring certain activities/actions cease.

Integrative bargaining: bargaining over issues in which labor and management are not in direct conflict (also called interest-based bargaining).

Intentional tort: an intentional civil wrong which causes an individual harm or injury and for which restitution can be sought in court.

Interchangeable part: a standardized unit which requires little or no skill in assembling or replacing.

Interest-based arbitration: a negotiating strategy in which labor and management declare their interests upfront and agree on certain perimeters for the bargaining.

Internal labor market: an administrative unit within an organization from which promotions and transfers are made according to rules and practices of the firm.

International Brotherhood of Teamsters: an international labor union which represents a diverse membership of blue collar and professional workers in public and private sector unions. Originally known as the Team Drivers' International Union (TDIU), the organization morphed into the Teamsters National Union which represented drivers of single teams (horses). www.teamster.org/.

International Monetary Fund: an international financial institution created after WWII which fosters monetary cooperation and makes loans to developing countries in order to create financial stability in the global market.

International union: union having affiliations in more than one country.

International Workers of the World (IWW): a Chicago-born radical union which advocated the overthrow of capitalism through revolutionary means.

Intraorganizational bargaining: the negotiations taking place within one bargaining unit (either labor or management) which lead to agreements.

Invisible hand of the market: an idea posited by Adam Smith in the Wealth of Nations (1776) that the free market will eventually take care of any imperfections in the market, making government intervention in the market unnecessary.

Iron law of oligarchy: a political theory in which the few rule the many through dominion of elected/represented officials; posited by Michels (1911) in his book, *Political Parties*, he claims the elections/appointments of representatives only legitimize a ruling elite, and oligarchy is inevitable.

Job evaluation: an assessment of the relative worth of a job which measures personal and job qualifications.

Job posting: a notice publicizing a job vacancy and its requirements.

Job security: assurance of continuity of gainful employment based on length of service.

Job Training Partnership Act (JTPA): Public law 97-300 enacted in 1982 that reestablished control at the federal level of job training for low-income and young workers. The JTPA was repealed in 1998 by the Workforce Investment Act.

John Lewis: born in 1880 to Welsh immigrants in Lucas, Iowa, Lewis became president of the United Mine Workers of America (UMWA) from 1920-1960 and is credited with helping form several national/ international unions as well as the Congress of Industrial Organization (CIO). www.umwa.org/?q=content/john-l-lewis.

Joint labor-management committee: a group from labor and management who deal with industry-wide problems.

Joint ownership: a perspective of property rights during feudalism in which lords "owned" part of the serf's labor while serfs retained the remainder of their labor.

Journeyman: a status reflecting a skilled worker who has completed an apprenticeship but is not yet a master craftsman.

Just cause: a common standard in labor arbitration and contractual language which provided a form of job security in the discipline and discharge of employees. Employers have the burden of proof or standard for discipline/discharge based on a 1966 arbitration decision which laid out seven tests for discipline/discharge and its application.

Just-in-time production: an inventory and delivery strategy which decreases inventory costs by producing goods for shipment when the goods are ordered and not storing them in inventory.

Knights of Labor: led by Terence Powderly and Uriah Stephens, the Knights, also known as the "Noble and Holy Order of the Knights of Labor," promoted the eight-hour work day, social and cultural advancement of workers, opposed strikes, and rejected socialism. Never well organized, the Knights membership expanded and decreased from 1869 to 1949 when it disbanded.

Labor force: the total number of people working, seeking work, or unemployed.

Laboratory conditions: ideal conditions for a union election in which employees are free to make a choice regarding representation.

Labor-management committee: a group of labor and management representatives who discuss non-contractual production and employment problems.

Labor-Management Reporting and Disclosure Act: passed in 1959, this major labor law provides standards for reporting and disclosure of financial dealings and administrative practices of labor unions and employers, the election of labor union officers, and guarantees certain rights to all union members. www.dol.gov/compliance/laws/comp-lmrda.htm.

Labor relations: dealings between labor and management over employment conditions.

Laissez-faire economic system: an economic environment free from government intervention in which the market corrects itself.

Landrum-Griffin Act: also known as the Labor-Management Reporting and Disclosure Act, this major labor law legislation passed in 1959 and requires labor unions to periodically submit internal affairs and financial dealings to the federal government. See Labor-Management Reporting and Disclosure Act. www.dol.gov/compliance/laws/comp-lmrda.htm.

Last chance agreement: a one-time opportunity in termination cases for the aggrieved employee to continue employment.

Leisure: "free or unobligated time that does not involve work or performing other life-sustaining functions" (Leitner, 2012).

Lesbian, Gay, Bisexual, and Transgendered community: distinct subcultures within a community who have sexual orientations other than heterosexual.

Liabilities: debt owed or obligations to pay.

Line manager: a supervisor over a process of production or delivery of an organization's goods or services.

Local union: the union body, the basic unit of the organization, in one locale which represents one employer, geographic area, or industry in which officers are usually elected/appointed full time.

Logrolling: the bargaining practice of packaging dissimilar issues together for trading.

Lord: a title of nobility bestowed on those in the lower ranks of a European nobility system; also known as baron.

The Lorenz Curve: a graphic representation of income or wealth inequality.

Mackay Radio Decision: a 1938 Supreme Court decision which said that striking workers could be replaced with strikebreakers. The employer is not required to discharge the strikebreakers if/when the strike ends. caselaw.lp.findlaw.com/cgi-bin/getcase.pl?court=us&vol=304&invol=333.

Macroeconomics: the branch of economics that focuses on the impact of choices on the totality or aggregate economic activity.

Maintenance of membership clause: a contractual clause which requires union members to pay dues if employment continues at a firm even when they are no longer union members.

Make-whole orders: an NLRB demand to restore employment/back pay to workers found innocent of unfair labor practices.

Management rights clause: a contractual clause in a collective bargaining agreement which specifics that management has the right to direct the workforce and establish policies except as specifically otherwise defined by the contract. This clause provides a basis for issues relating to discipline and discharge.

Mandatory bargaining issue: issues dealing with wages or conditions of employment.

Manor: feudalism's equivalent of a village on which the vassal and his family lived and worked.

Marginal revenue product: a change in revenue resulting from the addition of one extra unit (usually a worker) when other factors remain constant.

Marginal supply curve: "the functional representation of the additional costs associated with hiring each additional unit of labor" (Fossum, 2005, p. 566).

Marketable assets: the value of stocks, bonds, and real estate minus debts and liabilities to derive one's net worth.

Market capitalism: an economic system in which resources are owned and allocated by the private market.

Market failure: the failure of private decision in the marketplace to achieve an efficient allocation of scarce resources (Rittenberg, 2011).

Market socialism: an economic system in which resources are owned by the state and allocated by the market.

Market: a local, regional, national, or international arena in which buyers and sellers facilitate transactions.

Marriage and family values: attitudes about marriage, family, sex, divorce, cohabitation, and childbearing based on the traditional definitions of the family union and marriage.

Marxism: a political and economic theory crafted by Karl Marx and Friedrich Engels in which a classless society will eventually emerge when the working class overthrows the ownership class or bourgeois.

Meany, George: U.S. labor leader and the first president of the AFL-CIO.

Median voter: a voter in a bargaining unit or a political spectrum whose views are equidistant from extreme alternatives and who votes for the winning alternative.

Mediation: a procedure for dispute resolution in which a neutral third party maintains communication between the disputing parties in hopes of resolving an issue.

Mediators: neutral individuals who help settle disputes by keeping communication between parties open; they have no power to settle the dispute though.

Microeconomics: the branch of economics that focuses on the choices made by consumers and firms and the impacts those choices have on individual markets.

Militant action: direct, confrontational, disruptive action which alters the current landscape and may be violent or passive, but it must somehow attempt to alter, disrupt, or change existing conditions.

Minimum wage: a codified wage level below which employers cannot pay certain employees.

Modified union shop: a union security clause stating employees hired after a specific date must join the union.

Mohawk Valley Formula: a plan devised by anti-union businesses which presented a guide for breaking strikes. The plan described a formula which moved from violence to a more "scientific approach" based on discrediting labor organizations through propaganda.

Molly Maguires: a group of radical, activist Irish coal miners from Pennsylvania who were sentenced and hanged for alleged violence against industrialist Frank Gowen, owner of anthracite coal fields/mines and his mining operation.

Money income: earned or unearned income excluding social transfer payments.

Monopoly power: "the ability of a union to increase wages as a result of controlling the labor supply to the firm" (Fossum, 2005, p. 566).

Moral hazard: a situation in which a party is protected from incurring costs because of risks in which it engages.

Move work arrangement: a type of flexible work arrangement which allows the same amount of work to be done at different times/places (Sweet, 2013).

Multiemployer bargaining: multiple employers in the same industry agree with the union to bargain for all employers (also called association bargaining).

Multilateral bargaining: shared involvement among employers, unions, and public officials in reaching an agreement in public-sector labor negotiations.

Mutual gains bargaining: a bargaining approach in which both parties enter negotiations with the objective of improving outcomes.

Narcotic effect: an assumption that interest arbitration will continue to be used in the future because of its lasting effect on participants.

National Industrial Recovery Act: a federal statute passed in 1933 to relieve the serious depression and unemployment following the 1929 Stock Market Crash. The act regulates industry and permits cartels and monopolies in an attempt to stimulate economic recovery, establishes a public works program, and gives to the president authority to regulate industry.

National/international union: a union which establishes jurisdiction over workers in specific crafts, industries, or territories. They have two goals: increase membership and provide representative services to improve the wellbeing of their members.

National Labor Relations Board: an agency of the federal government created in 1935 to administer and enforce the National Labor Relations Act. The Board has two responsibilities: to adjudicate unfair labor practices and to certify representative elections. It is governed by five judges appointed by the president.

National Labor Union: the first national federation of labor organizations, 1866-1873, which actively promoted shorter working hours, arbitration over strikes, and called for the creation of a national labor party. It was led by William Sylvis.

National Mediation Board: an independently run governmental organization consisting of a three-person board created in 1934 to settle disputes within the transportation industry.

National Railroad Board of Adjustment: a grievance arbitration tribunal authorized under the Railway Labor Act to settle minor disputes in the railroad industry.

National Recovery Administration: an administrative bureau established under the National Industrial Recovery Act of 1933 as an emergency measure designed to encourage industrial recovery and combat unemployment.

The National War Labor Board (NWLB): created in 1918 by President Wilson to stem to tide of strikes, the NWLB acted as an arbitration tribunal in labor-management dispute cases to prevent work stoppages which might hinder the war effort; it was disbanded in 1919. It was resurrected in 1942 during the Roosevelt administration for the same purpose and disbanded in 1946 by Truman.

National Women's Trade Union League of America (NWTUL): a union of working-class women, reformers, and wealthy women sympathetic to working women's causes formed in 1903 to organize women wage earners into trade unions, secure healthy and efficient working conditions, and receive fair wages.

Negative tax: a government payment based on an individual's or family's income and regarded as a form of social welfare.

Negotiating/bargaining committee: a select group of union members who represent areas of expertise in their workplace and are responsible for contract negotiations and decisions on grievance handling.

Negotiation committee: an elected or appointed group charged with negotiating a contract.

Neoliberalism: an economic approach which favors no or limited barriers to capitalism and features privatization, deunionization, deregulation, and dehumanization.

Net worth: the value of an individual's wealth minus all debts and liabilities.

New Deal: a progressive set of programs and policies instituted during the Roosevelt Administration to promote economic recovery and social reform as a result of the Great Depression.

New economy: an organized system for managing resources which reflects digitized technologies, upgraded skill levels, flexible work arrangements, globalized markets, new managerial controls, lateral workflows, and an emphasis on service work rather than manufacturing work.

Noncollective good: a good provided by the government because private enterprise doesn't deem the enterprise profitable.

Non-income wealth: see financial wealth.

Non-labor income: see unearned income.

Non-standard employment relationship: a socially constructed relationship of part-time or contingent employees whose employers provide less employment security and often avoid legal obligations by engaging an intermediary to hire, fire, pay, and control work processes.

Normal goods: an economic term which describes the number (quantity) demanded for a good or service as a result of a change in income level.

Normative economics: a values judgment about economic fairness or what "ought" to be which is not proven true or false. For instance, a values judgment might be "All people need more help" or "Corporations make too much money." Neither of these statements can definitively be proven or disproven (Rittenberg, 2011).

Normative whiteness: the assumption that normal people are white so non-white people must be abnormal. From normative whiteness a hierarchy of status evolved which favors individuals based on their "whiteness."

Norris-LaGuardia Act: the second major piece of labor law legislation, passed in 1932, which prohibited some injunctions against striking workers.

Occupational organizing: organizing around a specific organization or trade. Sometimes known as industrial organizing.

Off-shoring: moving the production of goods/services to another country to take advantage of lower labor costs, economics of scale, or to evade environmental, taxable, or regulatory policies.

Old economy: an organized system for managing resources which reflects mass production in manufacturing goods, hierarchal workflows, scientific and bureaucratic management systems, interchangeable parts, local or regional markets, and rigid job definitions.

Ombudsman: an individual designated to investigate complaints and mediate fair settlements within an organization.

Open-door policy: an employer policy which allows workers to bring problems to higher-level management personnel in order to resolve issues.

Open shop: a firm in which one is not required to join or financially support a labor union as a condition of employment.

Opportunity cost: the value of the best alternative forgone in making any choice.

Organization: a group of individuals who join together for some purpose, for some period of time, and have some set of resources.

Organizational chaos: the poor organization and coordination of the labor process in which workers lose a sense of mutual commitment.

Organization man: a term made popular by Whyte (1956) which epitomized a man who gave his all for his organization or company.

Organizing campaign: activities which attempt to gain recognition for employee representation through a union.

Outsourcing: contracting work to an external organization which provides the goods or services back to a firm more efficiently.

Overt discrimination: intentional, visible, and conscious prohibition of a person's activity due to race, class, gender, age, sexual orientation, religion, and so forth.

Panic: a sudden onset of declining business activity (see recession and depression).

Parental leave: an employee benefit offered by some firms so parents can care for a biological or adopted infant.

Past practice: a traditional and accepted practice, which has some history, recognized by labor and management.

Patriarchy: a government or societal system in which male authority permeates every institution.

Pause work arrangement: a type of flexible work arrangement which allows workers temporary breaks/leaves (Sweet, 2013).

Pay form: the way pay is provided: cash, deferred compensation, insurance, or paid time off.

Pay level: a comparison of average pay rates for an employer with market averages.

Pay structure: internal rates and ranges of pay assignments within an organization.

Pay system: organizational or contractual rules determining how workers' pay will change.

Pell grant: a federal program which provides tuition money to needs-based students for their first undergraduate degree.

Per capita income: the average or mean income of an individual.

Per capital gross national income: the sum of a country's population's income divided by the total population (Sweet, 2013).

Perlman, Selig: the founder of Syndicalism, a labor movement theory which favors trade unions' maintenance of the "business model of unionism" or servicing members' needs through the grievance and arbitration procedure.

Permanent umpire: an arbitrator who hears all cases in a specific geographic location.

Permissive bargaining issue: issues over which the parties are not required to bargain.

Perspective: a viewpoint based on some value and belief system.

Phillip Murray: a Scottish-born steelworker, first president of the United Steelworkers of America (USWA), and longest-serving president of the Congress of Industrial Organization (CIO).

Philosophy-laden: an employee relations program which emphasizes workers follow a value system commensurate with their personal belief system that renders unionization untenable.

Picketing: the act of parading at an employer's worksite for the purpose of making the public aware of a labor dispute and asking the firms' patrons not to cross the picket line.

Pinkerton guards: a private security agency formed by Allan Pinkerton in 1850 to perform duties such as military contract work and private law enforcement.

Planned obsolescence: in industrial design, the policy of deliberately planning or designing a product which becomes outdated or useless in some time period.

Plough back: the reinvestment of profit into a business instead of a distribution of the profit to shareholders.

Political action committee (PAC): a union organization which raises money for political candidates.

Polity: the exercise of power in a society.

Post-Fordism: a theory of manufacturing based on competitive strategies in which a firm varies its processes within shorter timeframes to control inputs, costs, and outputs.

Post-war accord: an unwritten agreement after WWII in which labor and management reduced militant antagonism to more subtle forms of aggression through the grievance and arbitration procedure.

Poverty: the state of being poor, having insufficient means of support necessary to maintain a reasonable standard of living.

Poverty line: an income below which the government determines a household/individual to be poor.

Poverty rate: the percentage of people or families below the poverty line.

Poverty threshold: the Census Bureau's measurement in dollars to determine a person's or family's poverty status.

Precarious work: part-time, contingent, or temporary work which is within the non-standard employment relationship.

Predatory unionism: "the situation in which the primary goal of the union is to gain the dues of employees and extract side payments from employers in return for beneficial contracts" (Fossum, 2002, p. 568).

Prejudice: a preconceived opinion not based on experience or reason.

Pricing Structure: a detailed pricing schedule or plan which allows a consumer to know a range of prices for goods or services.

Principled negotiations: prior knowledge of all information is revealed to both parties early in the negotiating process.

Private good: a good for which exclusion is possible and the cost of adding another use is positive (Rittenberg, 2011).

Procedurists: those who believe conflict can be settled peacefully thorough mediation and negotiation and not through violence.

Production committee: a unit-level committee plus their supervisor which acts on suggestions in the Scanlon plan.

Professional Air Traffic Controllers Organization (PATCO) strike: federal employees belonging to PATCO struck for increased pay, shorter hours, and better retirement. President Reagan refused to grant their requests and fired the union workers, saying their strike activity was an issue of national safety. Reagan effectively broke the union.

Professional association: an organization which pursues professional interests without the benefit of a bargaining representative.

Professional employee: an educated employee, as defined by the NLRA, who works without supervision in a professional job.

Profit sharing: compensation in the form of bonuses based on the firm's profitability.

Progressive tax system: a system of taxation in which higher-income households and individuals pay a larger share of their earnings in taxes.

Project labor agreements: a terminal agreement covering a construction job for which the unions agree not to strike and the firm agrees to hire only union labor.

Proletariat: a class of industrial wage earners who sell their labor because they possess no capital or means of production.

Property rights: rules which specify how an owner can use a resource (Rittenberg, 2011).

Protectionism: an economic policy designed to protect states or countries through the restriction or restraint of quotas, duties, and/or tariffs on imports.

Protestant work ethic: an outgrowth of mercantilism and the Protestant Reformation which promotes hard work, thrift, morality, self-discipline, and efficiency as the way to wealth, success, and salvation.

Protocol of Peace: a 1910 contract limiting work by gender which assured men of higher wages in certain positions.

Public choice theory: a body of economic thought based on the assumption that individuals make public sector choices in order to maximize their own utility (Rittenberg, 2011).

Public good: a good for which the exclusion is prohibitive (such as clean air, a sunset, etc.) and the marginal cost of an additional user is zero (Rittenberg, 2011).

Public interest theory: a theory assuming governments seek to allocate resources most efficiently.

Pullman Car Strike: a strike in 1894 lead by the American Railway workers again George Pullman's Railroad when wages were cut but required rents to live in the company town were not reduced. A national boycott and strike of Pullman railway cars ended in Debs being jailed. The strike cemented solidarity of national unions, and paved the way for federal troops to marshal forces with corporations against organized labor.

Puritan morality (puritanism): a doctrine of strict discipline and moral behavior in religious matters, polity, and worship which emerged during the 16th century within the Church of England (Anglicanism).

Quality circles: a group of workers who meet periodically to discuss work-related issues and apply statistical process control methods to improve the quality of production.

Quality of work life: a program to improve the working environment in order to increase worker safety and enjoyment.

Quickie strikes: short work stoppages which disrupt the flow of production.

Quintile: 20 percent of a population.

Race: a social classification system which categorizes a set of humans who share physical and genetic similarities than other humans.

Racism: belief, doctrine, prejudice, discrimination, behavior, attitudes, or conditions which foster inherent differences among human populations with physical and genetic similarities.

Racketeer Influenced and Corrupt Organization Act (RICO): a federal law which criminalizes racketeering cases and extends penalties and a civil cause of action performed as part of an ongoing investigation.

Raid elections: an election which determines whether a new union should succeed the present union.

Raiding: the practice of one union organizing members from an existing union.

Railway Labor Act: a 1926 federal labor law which recognizes the right of collective bargaining in the transportation industry.

Ratio of income to poverty: the percentage of income which is below an individual's or family's poverty threshold. For instance, a family who has income which is less than half of their poverty threshold is said to be 50 percent below poverty.

Rational choice theory: an economic principle that assumes individuals always maximize their own utility by making logical decisions which provide them with the greatest benefit or satisfaction.

Recession: two consecutive quarters of falling real gross national product resulting in a decline in business activity (See panic and depression).

Recognition picketing: informational picketing to make the public aware the firm's workers are not represented by a union.

Reduced work arrangement: a type of flexible work arrangement which temporarily schedules reduced working hours (Sweet, 2013).

Redundancy: a European notion in which surplus workers resulting from the introduction of technology into the firm are permanently terminated.

Regional director: NLRB official who has broad powers in representative elections and adjudicating unfair labor practices.

Religion: "a complex system, organized or unorganized, by which individuals relate to deity and to their own existence" (Day, 1989, p. 34).

Rent-seeking behavior: attempts to influence public choices to maximize one's own utility.

Representation: the union's role as the sole representative bargaining agent for a group of workers.

Representation "R" cases: certification election petitions.

Representative election: an election held by the NLRB in order to certify a union as the representative agent for a group of workers wishing to unionize.

Republican motherhood: the idealization of motherhood as the natural conduit through which values of piety and republicanism could be instilled in future generations.

Republicans: a U.S. political party which favors conservatism and values individual freedoms.

Resource allocation: the process which determines who gets what resource for what price.

Resource ownership: the owner of resources such as land, capital, and labor in an economic system.

Reuther, Walter: an American labor leader, president of the UAW from 1946-1970, president of the CIO from 1952-1955, and president of the AFL-CIO from 1955-1968.

Revolutionary union: an approach to unionism which moves the capitalist system to one of socialism.

Right-to-work laws: a state provision under Taft-Hartley which authorizes the prohibition of negotiation of union or agency shop clauses and effectively dismantles the mechanism by which union dues are collected.

Riis, Jacob: a Danish immigrant, photographer, and photo journalist, who chronicled the lives of indigent people in New York City. His autobiography is *The Making of an American* (1901).

Robber baron: a pejorative term given to wealthy, powerful nineteenth-century businessmen who engage in unscrupulous business practices in order to increase profits for their companies.

Roll up: the amount by which overtime payments and fringe benefits increase as base wage rates increase.

Rucker plan: a gainsharing program in which worker bonuses are tied to group productivity as gauged by the historical value added by direct labor and any improvement in value added.

Scanlon plan: a gainsharing bonus tied to group productivity.

Scarce good: a good for which the choice of one alternative requires giving up another alternative.

Scarcity: the condition of having to choose among alternatives.

Scientific Management: a management theory of workflow focused on efficiency. Also known as Taylorism and developed by Fredrick Winslow Taylor in 1911, scientific management dictated a high degree of specialization requiring the fewest movements in the shortest time necessary, thus avoiding the need for individual workers to make decisions or acquire skills. The only quality needed from the worker was obedience.

Screening committee: under the Scanlon plan, a committee charged with handling suggestions given it by lower-level production committees.

Scrip: a form of monetary exchange which represents payment for labor, goods, or services.

Secondary boycott: an action which encourages the public to refrain from doing business with an uninvolved party in a labor dispute; they are unlawful under federal labor law.

Selective incentive: a private benefit provided by a union such as jobs.

Self-fulfilling prophecy: an expectation or belief that will come to fruition.

Self-managed work teams (SMWT): work teams which self-direct themselves.

Seniority: a status attained by employees based on continuous service with one employer.

Serfs: peasants who worked for lords or barons during feudalism from the 9th-16th centuries.

Service for fee: the idea within union circles that members pay union dues and in return expect stewards and staff to represent their interests.

Service Model of unionism: a form of representation which focuses on maintaining members' rights via collective bargaining; also known as business unionism.

Sex: the biological and physiological characteristics defining men and women.

Sexism: belief, doctrine, prejudice, discrimination, behavior, attitude, or condition which fosters stereotypes of social roles based on biological and psychological differences in men and women.

Sharecropping: an employment relationship in which a landowner extracts from a tenant agricultural produce and labor in exchange for living on the land.

Sherman Antitrust Act: 1890 federal antitrust legislation prohibiting any contract, conspiracy, or combination of business interests in restraint of foreign or interstate trade. The act effectively prohibited firms from fixing prices or any single organization from becoming a monopoly. It was created to counter the rising power of Standard Oil and US Steel and was hailed as the working people's Magna Carta.

Shop steward: an elected or appointed shop-floor union representative who is responsible for servicing member needs such as grievance processing and contract interpretation.

Sick out: a concerted action to withhold labor within firms where strikes are prohibited.

Sinclair, Upton: author of *The Jungle* (1906), an early twentieth-century novel which exposed the horrible conditions of the meat-packing factories in Chicago.

Sit-down strike: an illegal strike in which the employees "sit down" in the workplace and refuse to leave, thus denying the employer the use of the facility.

Skill-base pay: a pay rate based on an employee's skills and abilities rather than on the job to which she or he is assigned.

Slave: an individual who is considered property and owned by another person.

Slave labor: forced labor in which the laborer has no right to his or her own labor.

Social capital: a resource bank of human contacts.

Social class: an individual's place in the social hierarchy.

Social closure: the maintenance of status by the collective through the use of power and the control of resources and work processes.

Social cognition theory: a learning theory which says individuals learn by observation, modeling, and motivation.

Social justice: the ability of all humans to achieve their potential in a responsible society which provides equitable treatment, opportunity, and resource allocation.

Social media: web-based interactions between users who generate their own content.

Social structure: the arrangement of institutions in which humans interact and live together.

Social welfare: "a social institution [which] enhance[s] the social and economic well-being of society's members, and/or ...ensure[s] their conformity to current societal norms, standards, and ideologies" (Day, 1989, p. 36).

Socialism: a variety of economic and political theories which advocate for the collective or governmental ownership and allocation of resources.

Socialist Party: one of any number of political parties which associates itself with some form of socialism, an economic system characterized by social, collective, or government ownership and administration or allocation of the means of production.

Solidarity: the unity or agreement among individuals who share a common interest.

Space of disloyalty: a vacuum in an organization in which dissident leaders move to fill the opening (space) left through conflict, dissatisfaction, or disbelief.

Specialization: producing the goods/services for which there exists comparative advantage.

Spillover: the implementation of an outcome from collective bargaining to an unrepresented group.

Spillover effect: the idea that wage gains from collective bargaining are mimicked in a nonunion firm.

Spray and pray approach: exposing workers to online soft skills content such as critical thinking or team development courses (spraying) and praying some of the substance of the course(s) translates into cultural capital for the worker.

Staff representative: national or international union official who represents the interests of the membership.

Standard employment relationship: a socially constructed relationship of full-time employment between employers who control compensation for employees based on hours worked, using the employer's capital, and under the employer's control.

Standard of living: a level of material comfort as gauged by the goods and services an individual can purchase.

Statistical discrimination: an economic theory based on aggregate group characteristics, such as averages or statistical data, which promotes inequality between demographic groups.

Statutory law: law developed by legislatures through initiatives or referendums.

Steelworkers' trilogy: three Supreme Court decisions which establish arbitration as the final decision-making step in the grievance process.

STEM: educational programs which promote studies in science, technology, engineering, and mathematics to help enhance the nation's global competitiveness; Acronym for science, technology, engineering, and math skills for which workers need increased training and education.

Stereotypes: an assumption or notion projecting an often erroneous or distorted image or viewpoint of a social group.

Stewards: elected/appointed union officials responsible for interpreting contractual language for union members and filing member grievances.

Strategic action: a plan to achieve some specific goal involving a series of tactics. For instance, workers, individually or collectively, lay out a series of actions/events which influence their position within an economic, social, cultural, or political environment.

Strike: withholding one's labor from the owner of production for the purpose of disrupting production.

Structural adjustment policy: an economic policy with a financing mechanism through which the International Monetary Fund and the World Bank make loans with strict payback requirements to underdeveloped countries.

Structure: the influence and/or power an existing institution has over an individual or collective.

Subcontracting: assigning part or all duties associated with the management or administration of a firm to a third party.

Subsidy: financial assistance given by a government to a person/group regarded in the public's best interest.

Superseniority: seniority granted without regard to age or length of service.

Supplementary unemployment benefits: employer-provided benefits plus government funded unemployment benefits to bring an unemployed workers' wages into line with earned wages.

Sympathy strike: a strike by an uninvolved union in support of another striking union.

Syndicalism: a labor movement theory which replaces capitalism with confederations of collectivized trade unions or industrial unions. This theory posits labor unions are the means to overthrow economic aristocracy and run society fairly in the interest of the majority of workers through union democracy. Industry is run then through a system of cooperative confederations and mutual aid.

Taft-Hartley Act: major labor law legislation passed in 1947 which gave to employers the right to file unfair labor practice suits against unions and gave to states the ability to pass right-to-work legislation.

Take-off: an economic period during the Industrial Revolution which required a stable agrarian economy, well executed and enforced production methods, risk-taking entrepreneurs with capital backing willing to pursue profits in commerce, and institutions for mobilizing capital such as banks or financial institutions.

Tariff: a tax, duty, or custom imposed on imports.

Task-oriented labor: an orientation to work relating to naturally occurring phenomena such as agricultural or nature cycles (seasons of the year, sunrise to sunset).

Taylorism: a management theory of workflow focused on efficiency. Also known as scientific management and developed by Fredrick Winslow Taylor in 1911, Taylorism dictated a high degree of specialization requiring the fewest movements in the shortest time necessary, thus avoiding the need for individual workers to make decisions or acquire skills. The only quality needed from the worker was obedience.

Team concept: a work organizational design in which all workers are autonomous and can perform all group tasks.

Tenant farming: an employment relationship in which a landowner provides land and capital to an individual who in turn provides labor and product from the land to the landowner.

Theory of Social Traditionalism: an ideology which holds that individuals are responsible for their own well-being based on the decisions they have made and no outside (governmental) help should flow to an individual.

Threat effect: the impact of union wages on non-union firms who raise workers' wages because unions threaten to unionize the firms' workers.

Time-oriented labor: an orientation to work relating to artificial constructs such as working days, hours, minutes, and so forth.

Totality of conduct: the aggregate conduct of labor and management in determination of unfair labor practices.

Traditional leadership: a theory of leadership which advocates a system of rewards and punishments to control followers.

Transfer payment: a government payment made to eligible individuals for social welfare.

Treaty of Detroit: a collective bargaining agreement between the United Auto Workers (UAW) and General Motors (GM) which recognized the UAW as the sole bargaining representing agent of the GM workers.

Triangle Waist Fire: an industrial tragedy in March, 1911, caused by a fire in the Ashe Building in Manhattan, New York, in which 146 immigrant workers, mostly young females, died because exit doors were locked, fire escapes were inadequate, and the fire department equipment was insufficient. The firm, the Triangle Waist Company, refused to take culpability for the fire which stirred public sentiment against worker abuses and was the catalyst for some fire safety procedures pushed by Francis Perkins, Roosevelt's Secretary of Labor.

Trusteeship: the oversight of a local union which has violated its constitution by a national union.

Twenty-four-hour rule: a NLRB policy prohibiting union and management campaigning in certification elections 24 hours prior to the election.

Two-tier pay plan: a pay structure in which groups of workers are paid differently for performing the same work. Generally, new hires are paid a lower wage during a probationary period.

Umpire: an arbitrator designated by name in a collective bargaining agreement who hears disputes for the duration of the contract.

Unearned income: income from investment, rents, stocks and bonds, and interest.

Unemployment rate: the percentage of the labor force that is unemployed (Rittenberg, 2011).

Unfair labor practice: a violation by union or management of Taft-Hartley, Section 8 which can be filed with the National Labor Relations Board against unions or employers.

Unfair labor practice strike: an employee strike protesting an unfair labor practice for which striking employees cannot be discharged or permanently replaced. Because economic strikers can be replaced, most unions couple an economic strike with an unfair labor practice strike because it protects employees' jobs for the duration of the strike.

Union: an organization representing the interests of nonsupervisory employees required to collectively bargain for those employees.

Union democracy: a body of union members who exert supreme power over themselves or through representatives of their choosing; union members governing themselves.

Unionism: the camaraderie or bond formed between workers and their families in order to collectively act to better their wages and working conditions.

Union security: a level of security negotiated into an agreement such as the closed shop.

Union shop: a contractual clause which requires all employees of a unionized firm to become union members as a condition of employment.

United Auto Workers (UAW): a labor union representing workers in the auto industry. It is also known as the International Union, United Automobile, Aerospace and Agricultural Implement Workers of American and represents workers in the United States, Canada, and Puerto Rico. www.uaw.org/.

United Mine Workers of America (UMWA): an international labor union representing mine workers in underground and surface coal mining, manufacturing, health care, and public services. Founded in 1890 in Columbus, Ohio, the UMWA was a driving force behind the formation of the Congress of Industrial Organization (CIO). www.umwa.org/.

United Steelworkers of America (USW): the USW grew out of the Steel Workers Organizing committee (SWOC) in 1942. Phillip Murray was elected first president. www.usw.org/.

Uplift unionism: the labor movement's approach to making gains for society as a whole.

Uprising of the 20,000: a 1909-1910 strike in New York City of garment workers protesting low wages and sweatshop working conditions.

US Department of Labor: established by Congress in 1913, the Department of Labor includes the Bureau of Labor Statistics, the Bureau of Immigration and Naturalization, and the Children's Bureau. The department promotes and develops the welfare of workers, retirees, job seekers, and improves working conditions and profitable employment. www.dol.gov/dol/aboutdol/#whoweare.

Used car industry: an industry created by Alfred Sloan as a way to change public opinion toward the idea that the longevity and usefulness of a product could equate with the disposability of a product.

Value-free economics: sometimes called positive economics, is a branch of economics which describes/explains some economic phenomena through the use of facts and cause/effect behavioral relationships and testing economic theories.

Vassal: an individual in feudal times who exchanged loyalty and service to the lord or baron in exchange for military protection and partial use of the land.

Vehelahn v. Gunter: 1896 Massachusetts Supreme Court ruling which found the union guilty of intentionally coercing and intimidating employers through pickets, strikes, and boycotts. The decision is known for the dissenting opinion from Justice Oliver Wendell Homes which argued the unions should be allowed to use collective force against employers in order for workers to compete with the strength of capital.

Vertical integration: the process by which steps in the production and distribution of goods are owned/run by a single owner/employer.

Voice power: the mechanism by which employees' concerns are heard by management.

Wage earner: individual who earns income by selling his or her labor.

Wage theft: the act of stealing from wage earners what they have rightfully earned.

Wagner Act: (also known as the National Labor Relations Act) a major piece of labor law legislation passed in 1935 in the Roosevelt Administration which gave workers the right to collectively bargain, choose a bargaining representative of their choice, join a union, or not to do any of the above.

Wagner-Peyser Act: this act provided for and established a national employment system and created the Employment Service in the Department of Labor. The act was amended in 1998 to include employment services as part of the One-stop services delivery system which provides universal access to an integrated array of labor exchange services. www.doleta.gov/programs/wagner_peyser.cfm.

Walsh-Healey Government Contracts Act: a federal law passed in 1936 which applies to government contracts exceeding $15,000 and requires overtime pay for hours in excess of 8 per day or 40 per week, sets minimum wage equal to prevailing wage, and prohibits the employment of youth under 16 and convicts.

War Labor Disputes Act: a congressional act in 1943 which gave to Roosevelt the power to seize and operate privately owned industrial war plants during WWII.

Wealth: assets minus liability.

Welfare capitalism: a firm's practice of providing benefits to its employees in an effort to prevent the employees from forming unions.

Whip-sawing: a negotiating tactic in which unions seek to settle consecutive agreements with better outcomes.

Wildcat strike: an unauthorized work stoppage if the contract has a no-strike clause.

Wobblies: nickname for the Industrial Workers of the World. See Industrial Workers of the World.

Wollstonecraft's Dilemma: a term denoting inequality in gendered work which refers to Mary Wollstonecraft, an eighteenth-century female writer who fought for equal rights for women.

Women in Industry Service: an agency created in 1918 within the Department of Labor charged with protecting women's wages, health, and ensuring efficiency within production. It became the Women's Bureau in 1920.

Women's Bureau: a federal agency in the Department of Labor charged with the duty to "formulate standards and policies which shall promote the welfare of wage-earning women, improve their working conditions, increase their efficiency, and advance their opportunities for profitable employment" (Bureau, Women's, 2012).

Work council: European standing bodies which act to improve working conditions and wages for employees.

Workforce Investment Act: a federal law passed in 1998 which provides monies to consolidate, coordinate, and improve employment, training, literacy, and vocational rehabilitation programs in the United States.

Working poor: workers who have full or part-time employment yet still fall below some measurement of poverty such as a ratio of income to poverty.

Working to rule: the practice of working to the strictest interpretation of the job rules.

World Bank: an international financial institution created after WWII to help reduce or alleviate poverty in developing countries.

Yellow dog contract: A pledge employers required from workers not to join/associate with a labor union during the term of their employment with the business.

References

2014 Poverty guidelines. (2014). Washington, DC: Office of the Assistant Secretary for Planning and Evaluation. Retrieved from aspe.hhs.gov/poverty/14poverty.cfm.

Adamic, L. (1945). *A nation of nations.* New York: Harper.

Adams, M., Bell, L., and Griffin, P. (Ed.). (2007). *Teaching for diversity and social justice.* New York: Routledge.

Akchurin, M. and Lee, C.S. (2013). Pathways to empowerment: Repertories of women's activism and gender earnings equality. *American Sociological Review, 78*(4), 679–703. doi: 10.1177/0003122413494759.

American community survey information guide (2013). Washington, DC: U.S. Census Bureau. Retrieved from www.census.gov/acs/www/about_the_survey/acs_information_guide/flip book/.

Aronowitz, S. (2005). On the future of American labor. *WorkingUSA: The Journal of Labor and Society, 8*, 271–291.

Asher, R. and Stephenson, C. (1990). American capitalism, labor organization, and the racial/ethnic factor: An exploration. In R. S. Asher, C. (Ed.), *Labor divided: Race and ethnicity in the US labor struggles 1835–1960.* Albany: State University of New York Press.

Association, American Anthropological. (1998). Statement on "race." Arlington, VA: American Antrhopological Association.

Autor, D., Levy, R., and Murnane, R. (2003). The skill content of recent technological change: An empirical exploration. *Quarterly Journal of Economics, 118*(5), 1279–1333.

Barnett, R. E. (2001). The original meaning of the commerce clause. *The University of Chicago Law Review*, 101–147.

Baron, J. H., Hannan, M. T., Hsu, G. and Kocak, O. (2007). In the company of women: Gender inequaltiy and the logic of bureaucracy in start-up firms. *Work and Occupations, 34*(35–66).

Bedwell, W. L., Fiore, S. M., and Salasi, E. (2011). *Developing the 21st century (and beyond) workforce: A review of interpersonal skills and measurement strategies.* Stellenbosch University. Retrieved from www7.nationalacademies.org/BOTA/21st_Century_Workshop_Salas_Fiore_Paper.pdf; scholar.sun.ac.za

Bernhardt, A., Milkman, R., Theodore, N., Heckathorn, D., Auer, M., DeFilippis, J., Spiller, M. (2009). Broken laws, unprotected workers: Violations of employment and labor laws in Ameria's cities. *National Employment Labor Project.* University of Illinois, Chicago: UCLA Institute for Research on Labor and Employment.

Bishaw, A. (2013). *Poverty: 2000–2012.* Washington, DC: U.S. Census Bureau. Retrieved from www.census.gov/prod/2013pubs/acsbr12–01.pdf.

Blau, R. D., and Kahn, L. M. (2013). Female labor supply: Why is the US falling behind? Cambridge: National Bureau of Economic Research.

Bobo, K. (2011). *Wage theft in America: Why millions of working Americans are not getting paid and what we can do about it* (2nd ed.). New York: The New Press.

Bolman, L. G. , and Deal, T. E. (2013). *Reframing organizations: Artistry, choice, and leadership*. San Francisco, CA: Wiley.

Borjas, G. J. (2006). Making it in America: Social mobility in the immigrant population. *The Future of Children, 16*(2), 55–71. doi: 10.3386/w12088

Boulding, K. E. (1941). *Economic analysis*. New York: Harper and Row.

Bourdieu, P. (1997). *Outline of a theory of practice*. Cambridge: Cambrideg University Press.

Bradford, W. (1856). *History of Plymouth plantation*. Boston: Little, Brown, and Company.

Brecher, J. (1997). *Strike!* Cambridge, MA: South End Press.

Brightbill, C. K. (1961). *Man and leisure*. Englewood Cliffs, N.J.: Prentice-Hall.

Bronfenbrenner, K. (2005). The nature and process of union-organizing efforts among U.S. women workers since the mid-1990s. *Work and Occupations, 32*(4), 441–463. doi: 10.1177/0730888405278989.

Bunker, J. (1995). *Heroes in dungarees: The story of the American merchant marine in World War II*. Annapolis, MD: Naval Institute Press.

Bureau, Census. (2012). Table H-2. Share of aggregate income received by each fifth and top 5 percent of households, all races: 1967 to 2012. Washington, DC: Census bureau.

Bureau, U.S. Census. (2014). *How the census bureau measures poverty*. Washington, DC: Social, Economic, and Housing Statistics Division: Poverty. Retrieved from www.census.gov/hhes/www/poverty/about/overview/measure.html.

Bureau, Women's. (2012). Our history: An overview 1920–2012. Retrieved 02.08.2013, 2013, from www.dol.gov/wb/info_about_wb/interwb.htm.

Burkhauser, R. V., Feng, S., and Jenkins, S. (2009). Using the P90/P10 ratio to measure US inequality trends with current population survey data: A view from insdie the census bureau vaults. *Review of Income and Wealth, 55*(1), 166–185.

Carter, Allan Murray. (1959). *Theory of wages and employment*: Richard D. Irwin Homewood, Ill.

Center, Khell. (2011). The 1911 Triangle Factory Fire. Retrieved April 19, 2014, from www.ilr.cornell.edu/trianglefire/index.html.

Characteristics of minimum wage workers, 2013. (2014). Washington, DC: Bureau of Labor Statistics.

Cici, S. , Williams, W., and Barnett, S. (2009). Women's underrepresentation in science: Sociocultural and biological considerations. *Psychological Bulletin, 135*, 218–261.

Citro, C. F., and Michael, R. T. (Ed.). (1995). *Measuring poverty: A new approach*. Washington, DC: National Academy Press.

Clawson, D. and Clawson, M. (1999). What has happened to the US Labor Movement? Union decline and renewal. *Annual Review of Sociology, 25*, 95–119.

Combating poverty: Understanding new challenges for families, Senate (2012). Commerce Clause (1992).

Commons, J. (1913). *Labor and administration*. New York: Macmillan.

Commons, J. (1905). *Trade unionism and labor problems* (1st ed.). New York: Augustus Kelley.

Commons, J. (1909). American shoemakers: 1648–1895. *Quarterly Journal of Economics, 24*(4), 39–83.

Commons, J. (1919). *Industrial goodwill*. New York: McGraw-Hill.

Commons, J. (1921). *Industrial government*. New York: Macmillan.

Commons, J. (1934). *Institutional economics: Its place in political economy*. New York: Macmillan.

Commons, J.R., Phillips, U.B., Gilmore, E.A. and Sumner, H.L. (Ed.). (1910). *A Documentary history of American industrial society*. Cleveland, Ohio: The Arthur H. Clark Company.

Cooper, D., and Essrow, D. (2013). Low-wage workers are older than you think. Washington, DC: Economic Policy Institute.

Cooper, D., and Hall, D. (2013). Raising the federal minimum wage to $10.10 would give working families, and the overall economy, a much-needed boost. Washington, DC: Economic Policy Institute.

Cott, N. F. (2002). Passionlessness: An interpretation of Victorian sexual ideology, 1790–1850. In H. Tierney (Ed.), *Women's Studies Encyclopedia*. New York: Greenwood Press.

Crowley, M., Tope, D., Chamberlain, L. J., and Hodson, R. (2010). New Taylorism at work: Occupational change in the post-Fordist era. *Social Problems, 57*(3), 421–447.

Danziger, S. and Wimer, C. (2014). The poverty and inequality report. Stanford, CA. The Standford Center on Poverty and Inequality.

Davies, J., Shorrocks, A., Sandstrom, S., and Wolff, E. (2006). The world distribution of household wealth. London: United Nations University, World Institute for Development Economics Research.

The Davis-Bacon Act, Public Law 71–798 C.F.R. (1931).

Davis, James R., and Welton, Ralph E. (1991). Professional ethics: Business students' perceptions. *Journal of Business Ethics, 10*(6), 451–463. doi: 10.1007/bf00382829.

Day, P. J. (1989). *A new history of social welfare*. Englewood, N.J.: Prentice-Hall.

DeNavas-Walt, B., Proctor, B. D., and Smith, J. C. (2011). *Income, poverty, and health insurance coverage in the United States: 2011*. Washington, DC: Economics and Statistics Administration: U.S. Census Bureau. Retrieved from www.census.gov/prod/2012pubs/p60–243.pdf.

Devinatz, V. G. (1999). *High tech betrayal: Working and organizing on the shop floor*. East Lancing, MI: Michigan University Press.

DiTomaso, N., Post, C. and Parks-Yancy, R. (2007). Workforce diversity and inequity: Power, status, and numbers. *Annual Review of Sociology, 33*, 473–501.

Domhoff, G. W. (2013). *Who rules America? The triumph of the corporate rich* (7th ed.). New York: McGraw-Hill.

Dubofsky, M., and Dulles, F. R. (2004). *Labor in America: A history*. Wheeling, IL: Harlan Davidson, Inc.

Dunlop, J. T. (1950). *Wage determination under trade unions*. Augustus M Kelley.

Dunlop, J. T. (1958). *Industrial relations systems*. New York: Holt.

Dwyer, R. (1977). Workers' education, labor education, labor studies: An historical delineation. *Review of Educational Research, 47*(1), 179–207. doi: 10.3102/00346543047001179.

Edginton, C. R. , Jordan, D. J., DeGraaf, D. G., and Edginton, S.R. (2002). *Leisure and life satisfaction: Foundational perspectives* (3rd ed.). New York: McGraw-Hill.

Edginton, C. R. and Chen, P. (2008). *Leisure as transformation*. Urbana, Illinois: Sagamore.

Educational attainment. (2013). Retrieved from: www.census.gov/hhes/socdemo/education/.

England, P., Budig, M., and Folbre, N. (2002). Wages of virtue: The relative pay of care work. *Social Problems, 49*, 455–473.

The Equal Pay Act of 1963 (1963).

Fair Labor Standards Act (1938).

Feagin, J. R. and McKinney, K. R. (2003). *The many costs of racism*. Lanham, MD: Rowman and Littlefield.

Federation, National Civic. National Civic Federation Records. In M. A. Division (Ed.). New York: New York Public Library.

Feldberg, R. L. (1984). Comparable worth: Toward theory and practice in the United States. *Signs, 10*(2), 312–328.

Fink, D. (1998). *Cutting into the meatpacking line: Workers and change in the rural midwest*. Chapel Hill: University of North Carolina Press.

Fisher, G. M. (2003). *Remembering Mollie Orshansky: The developer of the poverty thresholds*. Washington, DC: Office of Retirement and Disability Policy. Retrieved from www.ssa.gov/policy/docs/ssb/v68n3/v68n3p79.html.

Folbre, N., Howes, C., and Leana, C. (2012). A care policy and research agenda. In N. Folbre (Ed.), *For love and money: Care provision in the United States*. New York: Sage.

Foner, P. (1986). *May Day: A short history of the international workers' holiday, 1886–1986*. Canada: International Publishers Co. Inc.

Fossum, J. (2005). *Labor relatons: Development, structure, and process* (9th ed.). New York: McGraw-Hill.

Fossum, John. (2002). *Labor Relations: Development, Structure, and Process*. Boston: McGraw-Hill.

Foucault, M. (1967). *Madness and civilization*. London: Tavistock.

Fredrickson, G. M. (1988). *The arrogance of race: Historical perspective on slavery, racism, and social inequality*. Hanover, New Hampshire: Wesleyan University Press.

Freeman, J. (1971). On the origins of the women's liberation movement. *American Journal of Sociology, 78*(4), 792–811.

Freeman, J. (1999). On the origins of social movments. In J. J. Freeman, V. (Ed.), *Waves of protest: Social movements since the sixties*. Lanham, MD: Rowman and Littlefield.

Freeman, R. B. (2009). Globalization and inequality. In W. Salverda, Nolan, B., and Smeeding, T. M. (Ed.), *The Oxford handbook of economic inequality* (pp. 575–598). New York: Oxford University Press.

Fuller, S., and Vosko, L. F. (2008). Temporary employment and social inequality in Canada: Exploring intersections of gender, race and immigration status. *Social Indicators Research, 88*(1), 31–50.

Galbraith, J. K. (1956). *American capitalism: The concept of countervailing power*. Boston: Houghton Mifflin.

Gilman, C. P. (1900). *Women and economics: A study of the economic relation between men and women as a factor in social evolution* Retrieved from play.google.com/books/reader?id=zkYqAAAAYAAJ&printsec=frontcover&output=reader&authuser=0&hl=en.

Goldin, C. , and Katz, L. F. (2007). The race between education and technology: The evolution of U.S. educational wage differentials, 1890 to 2005. *Working Paper 12984*. Cambridge: National Bureau of Economic Research.

Gonos, G. (1997). The contest over "employer" status in the postwar United States: The case of temporary help firms. *Law and Society Review, 31*, 81–110.

Gonos, G. (1998). The interaction between market incentives and government actions. In K. C. Barker, K. (Ed.), *American employment relations in transition*. New York: Cornell University Press.

Gordon, M. M. (1964). *Assimilation in America*. New York: Oxford.

Gorz, A. (1989). *Critique of pure reason*. London: Verso.

Graham, L. (1995). *On the line at Subaru-Isuzu*. Ithaca, NY: ILR/Cornell.

Grenier, Guillermo. (1988). *Inhuman relations: Quality circles and anti-unionism in American industry* (Vol. Temple University Press): Philadelphia.

Guidelines for multinational enterprises: Responsible supply chain management—OCED—2002–Annual report on the OECD guildlines for multinational enterprises. (2002). Retrieved December 19, 2012, from www.oecd.org/corporate/guidelinesformultinationalenterprises/responsiblesupplychainmanagement-2002–annualreportontheoecdguidelinesformultinationalenterprises.htm.

Hall, R. E. and Leiberman, M. (2003). *Microeconomics: Principles and applications* (2nd ed.). Mason, Ohio: Thompson-Southwestern.

He, D. and McHenry, P. (2013). *Does labor force participation reduce informal caregiving?* Economics and the Thomas Jefferson Program in Public Policy. College of William and Mary. Williamsburg, VA.

Heimert, A. (1953). Puritanism, the wilderness, and the frontier. *The New England Quarterly, 26*(3), 361–382.

Hill, E. M. and Hill M. A. (1990). Gender differences in child care and work: An interdisciplinary perspective. *The Journal of Behavioral Economics, 19*(1), 81–101.

Hogan, J. F. (2014). *The 1937 Chicago steel strike: Blood on the prarie*. Charleston, SC: The History Press.

Hogler, R. (2004). *Employment relations in the United States: Law, policy and practice*. Thousand Oaks: Sage.

Huffman, M. L., and Cohen, P. N. (2004). Racial wage inequality: Job segregation and devaluation across U.S. labor markets. *American Journal of Sociology, 109*, 902–936.

Hunt, G. (2002). Organized labour, sexual diversity, and unionism in Canada. In F. L. Colgan, S. (Ed.), *Gender, Diversity and Trade Unions: International Perspective* (pp. 257–274). New York: Routledge.

Immigration Act of 1917 (1917).

Ironmonger, D. (2001). *Household production and the household economy*. Research paper. Economics. University of Melbourne.

Isajiw, W. W. (1992). *Challenges of Measuring an Ethnic World: Science, politics and reality: Proceedings of the Joint Canada-United States Conference on the Measurement of Ethnicity*. Paper presented at the Joint Canada-United States Conference on the Measurement of Ethnicity, Ottawa, Ontario, Canada.

Issac, L. and Christiansen, L. (2002). How the civil rights movement revitalized labor militancy. *American Sociological Review, 67*, 722–746.

Issuance of restraining orders and injunction; limitation; public policy § 101 (1932).

Jacoby, S. (1985). *Employing bureaucracy: Managers, unions, and the transforamtion of work in American industry*. New York: Columbia University Press.

Jacoby, S. (1997). *Modern manors: Welfare capitalism since the New Deal*. Princeton: Princeton University Press.

Kalleberg, A. L. (2009). Precarious work, insecure workers: Employment relations in transition. *American Sociological Association, 74*(1), 1–22. doi: 10.1177/000312240907400101.

Kalleberg, A. L., Reskin, B. F., and Hudson, K. (2000). Bad jobs in America: Standard and nonstandard employment relations and job quality in the United States. *American Sociological Association, 65*(2), 256–278.

Kaufman, B. E. (2001). Human resources and industrial relations: Commonalities and differences. *Human Resource Management Review, 11*(4), 339–374.

Kaufman, B. E. (2003). John R. Commons and the Wiconsin School on industrial relations strategy and policy. *Industrial and Labor Relations Review, 57*(1), 3–30.

Kaufman, B. E. (2012). An institutional economic analysis of labor unions. *Industrial Relations, 51*(1), 438–471.

Kelley, R. D. (1999). Building bridges: The challenge of organized labor in communities of color. *New Labor Forum, 5*(Fall/Winter), 42–58.

Kerr, C., Harbison, F., Dunlop, J., and Meyers, C. (1955). The labour problem in economic development: A framework for a reappraisal. *International Labour Review, 72*, 223–235.

Kim, C. and Sakamoto, A. (2008). The rise of intra-occupational wage inequality in the U.S. 1983–2002. *American Sociological Review, 73*(129–57).

King, M. L. Jr. . (1960). Facing the challenge of a new age. *Phylon, 49*(3/4), 283–292.

Kirschenman, J., and Neckerman, K. . (1991). We'd love to hire them, but: The meaning of race for employers. In C. P. Jenks, P. (Ed.), *The urban underclass* (pp. 26–61). Washington, DC: Brookings Institution.

Korpi, Walter. (2010). Class and gender inequalities in different types of welfare states: The Social Citizenship Indicator Program (SCIP). *International Journal of Social Welfare, 19*, S14–S24. doi: 10.1111/j.1468–2397.2010.00730.x.

Krieger, L. H. (1995). The content of our categories: A cognitive bias approach to discrimination and equal employment opportunity. *Stanford Law Review, 47*(6), 1161–1248.

Labor, US Department of. (2008). *Married parents' use of time, 2003–2006*. (USDL 08–0619). Washington, DC: US Bureau of Labor Statistics. Retrieved from www.bls.gov/news.release/atus2.nr0.htm.

Labor, US Department of. (2012a). *Access to and use of leave: 2011 data from the American time use survey summary*. (USDL-12–1948). Washington, DC: US Bureau of Labor Statistics. Retrieved from www.bls.gov/news.release/leave.nr0.htm.

Labor, US Department of. (2012b). *American time use survey: 2011 results*. (USDL-12–1246). Washington, DC: US Bureau of Labor Statistics. Retrieved from www.bls.gov/news.release/atus.nr0.htm.

Labor, US Department of. (2012c). Employment Law Guide. Retrieved 01/27, 2013, from www.dol.gov/compliance/guide/fmla.htm#who.

Larson, S. and Nissen, B. (Ed.). (1984). *Theories of the Labor Movement*. Detroit, MI: Wayne State University Press.

Larson, S. and Nissen, B. (Ed.). (1987). *Theories of the labor movement*. Detroit: Wayne State University.

Lavender, C. (1999). *The Cult of Domesticity and True Womanhood*. Department of History, College of Staten Island, City University of New York.

Lee, J. and Bean, F. D. (2004). America's changing color lines: Immigration, race/ethnicity, and multiracial identification. *Annual Review of Sociology, 30*, 224–242.

Leitner, M. J. and Leitner, S. F. (2012). Concepts of leisure. *Leisure enhancement*. Urbana, Illinois: Sagamore.

Levine, L. (2012). The U.S. income distribution and mobility: Trends and international comparisons (pp. 22). Washington, DC: Congressional Research Service.

Lily Ledbetter Fair Pay Act of 2009 (2009).

Longhi, S., Nijkamp, P., and Poot, J. (2010). Joint impacts of immigration on wages and employment: Review and meta-analysis. *Journal of Geographical Systems, 12*(4), 355–387. doi: 10.1007/s10109–010–0111–y.

Lynch, M. J. (2011). Wage theft in America (why millions of working Americans are not getting paid—and what we can do about it). *Contemporary Justice Review, 14* (2), 255–258. doi: 10.1080/10282580.2011.565988.

Macartney, S., Bishaw, A., and Fontenot, K. (2013). Poverty rates for selected detailed race and Hispanic groups by state and place: 2007–2011 (A. C. S. Briefs, Trans.). Washington, DC: U.S. Census Bureau.

Machlup, F. (1952). *Political economy of monopoly*. Baltimore: John Hopkins Univesity Press.

Magg, E., and Carasso, A. (2014). Taxation and the family: What is the Earned Income Tax Credit? Washington, DC: Tax Policy Center.

Marlowe, J.H. (1986). Social intelligence: Evidence for multidimensionality and construct independence. *Journal of Educational Psychology, 78*(1), 52–58.

Marx, K. (1859). *Contribution to the critique of political economy* (S. W. Ryazanskaya, Trans.). Moscow: Progress Publishers.

Marx, K. and Engels, F. (2012). *The Communist Manifesto*. New Haven, CT: Yale University Press.

Michaelsen, Robert S. (1953). Changes in the Puritan Concept of Calling or Vocation. *The New England Quarterly, 26*(3), 315–336. doi: 10.2307/362847.

Miles, R. (1987). *Capitalism and unfree labour: Anomaly or necessity*. London: Tavistock Publications.

Miles, R. and Brown, M. (2003). *Racism* (2 ed.). New York: Routledge.

Milkman, R. (1997). *Farewell to the factory: Auto workers in the late twentieth century*. Berkley, CA: University of California Press.

Mishel, L. (2013). Declining value of the federal minimum wage is a major factor driving inequality. Washington, DC: Economic Policy Institute.

Moss, P., and Tilley, C. (2001). *Stories employers tell: Race, skill and hiring in America*. New York: Sage.

National Labor Relations Act, Title 29, Chapter 7, Subchapter II, Pub. L. No. 74–198, 449 Stat. (1935 July 5, 1935).

Neulinger, J. (1981). *To leisure: An introduction*. Boston: Allyn and Bacon.

NLRB v. Jones and Laughlin Steel Corporation, 419 C.F.R. (1937).

Olson, M. (1971). *The logic of collective action: Public goods and the theory of groups*. Cambridge, MA: Harvard University Press.

Pager, D. (2003). The mark of a criminal record. *American Journal of Sociology, 108*, 937–975.

Parkin, F. (Ed.). (1974). *Strategies of social closure in class formation*. London: Tavistock.

Parkin, F. (Ed.). (1979). *Social closure and class formation*. Los Angeles: University of California Press.

Perlman, M. (1960). Labor movement theories: Past, present, and future. *Industrial and Labor Relations, 13*(3), 338–348.

Perlman, S. (1922). *A history of trade unionism in the United States*: The Macmillan Company.

Perlman, S. (1968). *A theory of the labor movement*. New York: Augustus M. Kelley.

Peterson, T., and Saporta, I. (2004). The opportunity structure for discrimination. *American Journal of Sociology, 109*, 852–901.

Pieper, J. (1952). *Leisure, the basis of culture*. New York: Pantheon.

Policy basics: The earned income tax credit. (2014). Washington, DC: Center on Budget and Policy Priorities.

A profile of the working poor, 2011. (2011) *Bureuau of Labor Statistics Reports.* Washington, DC U.S. Bureau of Labor Statistics.

The Railway Labor Act, ch. 347, 44 Stat. 577 C.F.R. § 24312 (1926).

Ramirez, S. A. (2004). What we teach when we teach about race: The problem of law and pseudo-economics. *Journal of Legal Education, 54*, 365–379.

Rawls, J. (1971). *A theory of justice.* Cambridge, MA: Belknap Press of Harvard University Press.

Ray, R., Cornick, J.C., and Schmitt, J. (2008). Parental leave policies in 21 countries: Assessing generosity and gender equality. Washington, DC: Center for Economic and Policy Research.

Reagan, R. (Writer) and G. Peters, and Woolley, J. T. (Director). (1986). Radio address to the nation on welfare reform [speech].

Research, UC Davis Center for Poverty. (2013). Official poverty statistics. UC Davis.

Reskin, B. F. (2003). Including mechanisms in our models of ascriptive inequality. *American Sociological review, 68*, 1–21.

Ridgeway, C. L., and Correll, S. J. (2004). Unpacking the gender system: A theoretical perspective on cultural beliefs in social relations. *Gender Sociology, 18*(4), 510–531.

Rifkin, J. (2014). *Zero marginal cost society.* New York City: Palgrave Macmillan.

Riis, J. A. (1890, 1997). *How the other half lives: Studies among the tenements of New York.* New York: Penguin.

Rittenberg, L. and Tregarthen, T. (2011). *Principles of economics.* Irvington, New York: Flatworld Knowledge.

Rodgers, D. T. (1978). *The work ethic in industrial America, 1850–1920.* Chicago: University of Chicago Press.

Rogers, B. (2010). Toward third-party liability for wage theft. *Berkeley Journal of Employment and Labor law, 31*(1), 1–64.

Roscigno, V. J., Garcia, L. M., and Bobbitt-Zeher, D. . (2007). Social closure and processes of race/sex employment discrimination. In G. Wilson (Ed.), *Race, ethnicity, and inequality in the U.S. labor market: Critical issues in the new millenium* (Vol. 609). Thousand Oaks: Sage.

Ross, I. M. (1998). The invention of the transistor. *Proceedings of the IEEE, 86*(1), 7–28. doi: 10.1109/5.658752.

Rostow, W. W. (1956). The take-off into sulf-sustained growth. *The Economic Journal, 66*(261), 25–48.

Russell, R. V. (2009). *Pastimes* (4th ed.). Urbana, Illinois: Sagamore.

Schofield, A. (1983). Rebel girls and union maids: The woman question in the journals of the AFL and IWW, 1905–1920. *Feminist Studies, 9*(2), 335–358.

Schumpeter, J. (1989). *Essays: On entrepreneurs, innovations, business cycles, and the evolution of capitalism.* New Brunswick, NJ: Transaction.

Seamen's Act. (2003). Encyclopedia.com.

Service, Women in Industry. (1919). Annual report of the director of the woman in industry service. Washington, DC: Department of Labor.

Short, K. S. (2011). *The supplemental poverty measure: Examining the incidence and depth of poverty in the U.S. taking account of taxes and transfers.* Paper presented at the 86th Annual Conference of the Western Economic Association International Session: A New Supplemental Poverty Measure for the U.S., Standford University.

Shreve, E. O. (1948). Objective: Industrial peace. *Industrial and Labor Relations Review, 1*(13), 431–442.

Sieh, E. W. (1987). Garmet workers: Perceptions of inequity and employee theft. *British Journal of Criminology, 27*, 174–190.

Slichter, S. (1931). Pharoah dreams again. *Atlantic Monthly, 148*(August), 248–252.

Sorensen, J. B. (2004). The racial demography of racial employment segregation. *American Journal of Sociology, 110*, 626–671.

Soul, G. (1957). The economics of leisure. *Annals of the American Academy of Political and Social Science, 313*, 16–17.

Spalter-Roth, R., Hartmann, H., and Collings, N. (1994). What do unions do for women? Washington, DC: Institute for Women's Policy Research.

Spickard, P. (2007). *Almost all aliens: Immigration, race, and colonialism in American history and identity*. New York: Routledge.

Stainback, K., Tomaskovic-Devey, D., and Skaggs, S. (2008). Social contacts and race/ethnic job matching. *Social Forces, 87*(2), 857–886.

Stainback, K., Tomaskovic-Devey, D., and Skaggs, S. (2010). Organizational approaches to inequality: Inertia, relative power, and environments. *Annual Review of Sociology, 36*, 225–247.

Loewe v. Lawlor, 389 C.F.R. (1908).

Gompers v. Bucks Stove and Range Company, 372 C.F.R. (1911).

Lawlor v. Loewe, 358 C.F.R. (1915).

Wilson v. New, 797 C.F.R. (1917).

Duplex Printing Press Co. v. Deering, 45 C.F.R. (1921).

Statistics, Bureau of Labor. (2012). Economic news release: Union members summary (Vol. 2012). Washington, DC: Department of Labor.

Statistics, Bureau of Labor. (2013). *Foreign-born workers: Labor force characteristics*. (USDL-13–0991). Washington, DC: Retrieved from www.bls.gov/news.release/pdf/forbrn. pdf.

Stockton, F. T. (1911). *The closed shop in American trade unions*. Baltimore: John Hopkins Press.

Surhone, L.M., Tennoe, M.T., and Henssonow, S. (2010). *Vegelahn V. Guntner*: Betascript Publishing.

Sweet, S. and Meiksins, P. (2013). *Changing contours of work: Jobs and opportunities in the new economy*. Los Angeles: Sage.

Table 1. Enrollment status of the population 3 years old and over, by sex, age, race, Hispanic origin, foreign born, and foreign-born parentage: October, 2012. (2012).

Taylor, F.W. (1947). *Scientific management*. New York and London: Harper and Row.

Tichi, C. (Ed.). (1998). *Rebecca Harding Davis: Life in the iron-mills*. Boston: St. Martin's Press.

Tilly, C. (2005). *Social movements: 1768–2004*. Boulder, CO: Paradigm.

Tilly, C. (1998). *Durable inequality*. Berkeley: University of California Press.

Title VII of the Civil Rights Act of 1964 (1964).

Tomaskovic-Devey, D. (1993). *Gender and racial inequality at work: The sources and consequences of job segregation*. Ithaca, New York: ILR Press.

Toner, J. (1942). *The closed shop*. Washington, DC: American Council on Public Affairs.

Twomey, D. P. (2010). *Labor and employment law: Texts and cases* (14th ed.). Mason, Ohio: Cengage.

Vallas, S. (2003). The adventures of managerial hegemony: Teamwork, ideology, and worker resistance. *Social Problems, 50*(2), 204–225. doi: 10.1525/sp.2003.50.2.204.

Voss, J. (1967). The definition of leisure. *Journal of Economic Issues, 1*(1/2), 91–106.

Wages: Minimum wage. (2012). Retrieved December 19, 2012.

Webb, S. and Webb. B. (1902). *Industrial democracy*. London: Longmans.

Weber, M. (1978). *Economy and society. An outline of interpretive sociology*. G. W. Roth, C. (Ed.)

Weiss, A. (1995). Human capital vs. signalling explanations of wages. *American Economic Association, 9*(4), 133–145.

Western, B. and Rosenfeld, J. (2011). Unions, norms, and the rise of U.S. wage inequality. *American Sociological Review, 76*. doi: 10.1177/0003122411414817.

Whyte, W. H. (1956). *The organization man*. New York: Simon and Schuster.

Williams, J. (2000). *Unbending gender: Why family and work conflict and what to do about it*. New York Oxford University Press.

Williamson, L. (2013). U.S. labor market continued to improve in 2012. *Monthly Labor Review*(March), 3–21.

Wittke, C. (1940). *We who built America: The saga of the immigrant*. New York Prentice-Hall.

Wolff, E. M. (2004). Changes in household wealth in the 1980s and 1990s in the U.S. *Working Paper No. 407*. Annandale-on-Hudson, New York: The Levy Economic Institute of Bard College.

Wolff, E. M. (2012). *The asset price meltdown and the wealth of the middle class*. New York: New York University.

Wollstonecraft, M. (1792). *A vindication of the rights of woman with strictures on political and moral subjects*. Boston: Peter Edes for Thomas and Andrews, Faust's statue, no. 45, Newbury-street.

Woody, T. (1957). Leisure in the light of history. *Annals of the American Academy of Political and Social Science, 313*, 5.

Wright, E. O. (2002). Foundations of class analysis in the Marxist tradition. In E. O. Wright (Ed.), *Alternative foundations of class analysis*.

Wright, E.O (1997). *Class counts: Comparative studies in class analysis*. Cambridge: Cambridge University Press.

Index

About the Author

Marquita R. Walker is associate professor in the Department of Labor Studies, School of Social Work, at Indiana University Purdue University Indianapolis (IUPUI), has taught in the fields of labor studies or labor education for the past ten years, and has been involved with organized labor and collective bargaining for more than thirty years. Her scholarly and career interests focus on the assessment of student learning outcomes in a distributed learning environment, workers' education, and the training of dislocated workers. In addition to publications in peer-reviewed journals, she has developed applications relating to labor and collective bargaining for mobile devices. She holds a doctorate in educational leadership and policy analysis and a master's degree in public affairs from the University of Missouri, Columbia, and a master's and bachelor's degree in English from Missouri State University and Drury University respectively.